MULTICULT

JAMES ~. ~~DANKS, Series Editor~~

(continued)

CRITICAL RACE THEORY
in Education

A Scholar's Journey

Gloria Ladson-Billings

TEACHERS COLLEGE PRESS

TEACHERS COLLEGE | COLUMBIA UNIVERSITY
NEW YORK AND LONDON

Published by Teachers College Press,® 1234 Amsterdam Avenue, New York, NY 10027

Cover image by kali9 / iStock by Getty Images.

Chapter 1 originally appeared as "Toward a Critical Race Theory of Education,"by G. Ladson-Billings, & W. F. Tate IV, 1995, *Teachers College Record*, 97(1), 47–68. Copyright 1995 by Teachers College, Columbia University. Reprinted with permission.

Chapter 2 originally appeared as "Critical Race Theory—What It Is Not!," by G. Ladson-Billings, in M. Lynn & A. D. Dixson (Eds.), *Handbook of Critical Race Theory in Education* (pp. 34–47), 2013, Routledge. Copyright © 2013 Taylor & Francis. Reprinted with permission of Taylor and Francis Group LLC.

Chapter 3 originally appeared as "From the Achievement Gap to the Education Debt: Understanding Achievement in U.S. Schools," by G. Ladson-Billings, 2006, *Educational Researcher*, 35(7), 3–12. Copyright © 2006 SAGE Publications. Reprinted with permission.

Chapter 4 originally appeared as "Through a Glass Darkly: The Persistence of Race in Education Research and Scholarship," by G. Ladson-Billings, 2012, *Educational Researcher*, 41(4), 115–120. Copyright © 2012 SAGE Publications. Reprinted with permission.

Chapter 5 originally appeared as "New Directions in Multicultural Education: Complexities, Boundaries, and Critical Race Theory," by G. Ladson-Billings, in J. A. Banks & C. A. M. Banks (Eds.), *Handbook of Research in Multicultural Education* (2nd ed., pp. 50–65), 2003, Jossey-Bass. Copyright © 2003 John Wiley and Sons. Reprinted with permission.

Chapter 6 originally appeared as "Landing on the Wrong Note: The Price We Paid for Brown," by G. Ladson-Billings, 2004, *Educational Researcher*, 33(7), 3–13. Copyright © 2004 SAGE Publications. Reprinted with permission.

Chapter 7 originally appeared as "Racialized Discourses and Ethnic Epistemologies," by G. Ladson-Billings, in N. Denzin & Y. Lincoln (Eds.), *Handbook of Qualitative Research* (2nd ed., pp. 257–277), 2000, Sage. Copyright © 2000 SAGE Publications. Reprinted with permission.

Chapter 8 originally appeared as "Critical Race Theory and the Postracial Imaginary," by J. K. Donnor & G. Ladson-Billings, in N. Denzin & Y. Lincoln (Eds.), *Handbook of Qualitative Research* (5th ed., pp. 195–213), 2017, Sage. Copyright © 2017 SAGE Publications. Reprinted with permission.

The Afterword originally appeared as "The Social Funding of Race: The Role of Schooling," by G. Ladson-Billings, 2018, *Peabody Journal of Education*, 93(1), 90–105. Reprinted with permission.

Library of Congress Cataloging-in-Publication Data is available at loc.gov

ISBN 978-0-8077-6583-8 (paper)
ISBN 978-0-8077-6584-5 (hardcover)
ISBN 978-0-8077-7981-1 (ebook)

Printed on acid-free paper
Manufactured in the United States of America

Contents

Series Foreword

Since the publication of her book *The Dreamkeepers: Successful Teachers of African American Children* in 1994 and her widely cited article on culturally relevant pedagogy in the *American Educational Research Journal* in 1995, Gloria Ladson-Billings has been one of the most eloquent, visionary, prolific, and influential voices calling for the transformation of the nation's schools and classrooms to make them more equitable for African Americans and other students of color. Ladson-Billings, along with scholars such as Geneva Gay (2018), Kathryn H. Au (2011), and Carol D. Lee (2007), is also a progenitor of culturally relevant or culturally responsive pedagogy—a teaching and learning intervention that has facilitated structural explanations for the underachievement of low-income students and students of color and given deficit explanations less credence.

In addition to her innovative, original, and visionary work on culturally relevant pedagogy, Ladson-Billings—and her coauthor William F. Tate IV—are pioneers who adapted the groundbreaking scholarship on critical race theory in law by scholars such as Derrick Bell (1987), Richard Delgado (1991), Mari Matsudo (1989), and Charles Lawrence (1987) to education. In the Introduction to this volume, Ladson-Billings chronicles the events that led to the publication of her pathbreaking article (with Tate) in *Teachers College Record* in 1995. She also details the problems and challenges that educators experience when they try to adapt the ideas that she and Tate describe for educational practice. This volume consists of a collection of Ladson-Billings's extensive writings on critical race theory and other topics that describe reforms required to reduce educational inequality. The first part of this book focuses on critical race theory and its educational implications. The second part deals with inequality and education. The final part centers on epistemology and research methodologies. As the author points out in her Introduction, all of the chapters in this book are interrelated because they describe how race is related in complex and intractable ways to educational inequality.

Chapter 3 of this volume, which is adapted from Ladson-Billings's 2006 American Educational Research (AERA) Presidential Address, explicates concepts and explanations related to constructing new paradigms for enhancing social justice and educational equality. This chapter focuses on epistemological issues and the need to expand theoretical and research concepts, explanations, and paradigms. The address expanded the epistemological terrain within AERA by deconstructing the "achievement gap" construct. Ladson-Billings states why educators need to expand this construct in ways that will enable them to focus on the structural causes of the differential achievement of students of color and mainstream White American students rather than on the perceived deficits of marginalized students as the major cause of their lower academic achievement. She writes, "We do not have an achievement gap; we have an education debt" (p. 63). Ladson-Billings argues that rather than focus on the *achievement gap*, educators should concentrate on the *education debt* in order to make progress in improving the academic achievement of students who are members of marginalized racial, ethnic, linguistic, and cultural groups. She explains why a focus on the achievement gap diverts attention from dealing with the deep *structural problems* that are the root cause of the differential achievement of low-income students of color and mainstream White students.

Ladson-Billings states that the education debt has been created in U.S. society by *historical, economic, sociopolitical,* and *moral* decisions. The historical debt results from the educational inequalities that students of color have experienced in the past in U.S. society and schools. Funding disparities between schools in low-income communities and those in wealthier communities is the major cause of the economic debt. The exclusion of people of color from the political process created the sociopolitical debt. The discrepancy between our values and our actions constitute the moral debt. Providing equal educational opportunities for students of color and low-income students will contribute to the reduction of this moral debt.

This book is an important addition to the Multicultural Education Series, whose major purpose is to provide preservice educators, practicing educators, graduate students, scholars, and policymakers with an interrelated and comprehensive set of books that summarizes and analyzes important research, theory, and practice related to the education of ethnic, racial, cultural, and linguistic groups in the United States and the education of mainstream students about diversity. The dimensions of multicultural education, developed by Banks (2004) and described in the *Handbook of Research on Multicultural Education* and in the *Encyclopedia of Diversity in Education* (Banks, 2012), provide the conceptual framework for the development of the publications in the Series. The dimensions are content integration, the knowledge construction process, prejudice reduction, equity pedagogy, and an empowering school culture and social structure. The books in the Multicultural Education Series provide research, theoretical, and practical knowledge about the behaviors and learning characteristics of students of color (Conchas & Vigil, 2012; Lee, 2007), language minority students (Gándara & Hopkins 2010; Valdés, 2001; Valdés, Capitelli, & Alvarez, 2011), low-income students (Cookson, 2013; Gorski, 2018), and other minoritized population groups, such as students who speak different varieties of English (Charity Hudley & Mallinson, 2011), and LGBTQ youth (Mayo, 2014).

Critical race theory is a major emphasis in this book. A number of other books in the Multicultural Education Series focus on *institutional and structural racism* and ways to reduce it in educational institutions, which is an especially relevant topic because of the national and international protests and dialogues about institutionalized racism that began after George Floyd, an African American man in Minneapolis, died when a White police officer pressed his knee to Floyd's neck for more than 8 minutes on May 25, 2020. Books in the Multicultural Education Series that focus on race include Özlem Sensoy and Robin DiAngelo (2017), *Is Everyone Really Equal? An Introduction to Key Concepts in Social Justice Education* (Second Edition); Gary Howard (2016), *We Can't Teach What We Don't Know: White Teachers, Multiracial Schools* (Third Edition); Zeus Leonardo (2013), *Race Frameworks: A Multidimensional Theory of Racism and Education*; and Daniel Solórzano and Lindsay Pérez Huber (2020), *Racial Microaggressions: Using Critical Race Theory in Education to Recognize and Respond to Everyday Racism.*

Gloria Ladson-Billings has previously enriched the Multicultural Education Series by contributing two books to it: *Beyond the Big House: African American Educators on Teacher Education* (2005); and *Education Research in the Public Interest: Social Justice, Action, and Policy* (2006, co-edited with William F. Tate). I am pleased to welcome her third book to the Series, which consists of incisive, visionary, and prescient articles that have inspired innovations and transformations to improve educational equality for all of the nation's students.

—James A. Banks

REFERENCES

Au, K. (2011). *Literacy achievement and diversity: Keys to success for students, teachers, and schools.* Teachers College Press.

Banks, J. A. (2004). Multicultural education: Historical development, dimensions, and practice. In J. A. Banks & C. A. M. Banks (Eds.), *Handbook of research on multicultural education* (2nd ed., pp. 3–29). Jossey-Bass.

Banks, J. A. (2012). Multicultural education: Dimensions of. In J. A. Banks (Ed). *Encyclopedia of diversity in education* (vol. 3, pp. 1538–1547). Sage Publications.

Bell, D. (1987). *And we are not yet saved: The elusive quest for racial justice.* Basic Books.

Charity Hudley, A. H., & Mallinson, C. (2011). *Understanding language variation in U.S. schools.* Teachers College Press.

Conchas, G. Q., & Vigil, J. D. (2012). *Streetsmart schoolsmart: Urban poverty and the education of adolescent boys.* Teachers College Press.

Cookson, P. W., Jr. (2013). *Class rules: Exposing inequality in American high schools.* Teachers College Press.

Delgado, R. (1991). Brewer's plea: Critical thoughts on common cause. *Vanderbilt Law Review, 44*(1), 1–14.

Gándara, P., & Hopkins, M. (Eds.). (2010). *Forbidden language: English language learners and restrictive language policies.* Teachers College Press.

Gay, G. (2018). *Culturally responsive teaching: Theory, research, and practice* (3rd ed.). Teachers College Press.

Gorski, P. C. (2018). *Reaching and teaching students in poverty: Strategies for erasing the opportunity gap* (2nd ed.). Teachers College Press.

Howard, G. (2016). *We can't teach what we don't know: White teachers, multiracial schools* (3rd ed.). Teachers College Press.

Ladson-Billings, G. (1994). *The dreamkeepers: Successful teachers of African American children.* Jossey-Bass.

Ladson-Billings, G. (1995). Toward a theory of culturally relevant pedagogy. *American Educational Research Journal, 32*(3), 465–491.

Ladson-Billings, G. (2005). *Beyond the big house: African American educators on teacher education.* Teachers College Press.

Ladson-Billings, G., & Tate, W. F. (1995). Toward a critical race theory of education. *Teachers College Record, 97*(1), 47–68.

Ladson-Billings, G., & Tate, W. F. (Eds.) (2006). *Education research in the public interest: Social justice, action, and policy.* Teachers College Press.

Lawrence, C. (1987). The id, the ego, and equal protection: Reckoning with unconscious racism. *Stanford Law Review, 39*, 317–388.

Lee, C. D. (2007). *Culture, literacy, and learning: Taking bloom in the midst of the whirlwind.* Teachers College Press.

Leonardo, Z. (2013). *Race frameworks: A multicultural theory of racism and education.* Teachers College Press.

Matsuda, M. (1989). Public response to racist speech: Considering the victim's story. *Michigan Law Review, 87*, 2320–2381.

Mayo, C. (2014). *LGBTQ youth and education: Policies and practices.* Teachers College Press.

Sensoy, Ö., & DiAngelo, R. (2017). *Is everyone really equal? An introduction to key concepts in social justice education* (2nd ed.). Teachers College Press.

Solórzano, D., & Huber, L. P. (2020). *Racial microaggressions: Using critical race theory in education to recognize and respond to everyday racism.* Teachers College Press.

Valdés, G. (2001). *Learning and not learning English: Latino Students in American schools.* Teachers College Press.

Valdés, G., Capitelli, S., & Alvarez, L. (2011). *Latino children learning English: Steps in the journey.* Teachers College Press.

Introduction

When I was in the midst of preparing this manuscript, the Trump administration's Office of Management and Budget declared that the federal government would not fund any racial sensitivity training or antiracist professional learning for federal agencies because this work was deemed racist (National Public Radio Staff, 2020). Singled out as particularly egregious was any mention of "White privilege" and "Critical Race Theory." A few days later these prohibitions were extended, and officials in the Department of Education indicated they would be reviewing similar activities within that unit. Instead of racial sensitivity training, the president claimed his administration would promote "patriotic education." He signed an executive order that required contracts to include a provision that said contractors with the federal government would not have "workplace training that inculcates in its employees any form of race or sex stereotyping or any form of race or sex scapegoating" or the contractors would face the cancellation of contracts.

This executive order prompted a flurry of responses from learned societies and other academics. The American Educational Research Association and the National Academy of Education offered a joint statement endorsed by 27 learned societies (see https://naeducation.org/naed-and-aera-joint-statement-in-support-of-anti-racist-education/) attesting to the value of research that addresses antiracist education and a focus on diversity and racial sensitivity. The deans of the five University of California law schools also published a statement defending "Critical Race Theory" as a legitimate and important line of legal scholarship (see https://law.ucla.edu/news/joint-statement-deans-university-california-law-schools-about-value-critical-race-theory-0) and offering support for their faculty who teach and publish in this scholarly tradition.

The timing and context of this executive order were set for near the end of the summer of 2020 when the nation was suffering from the effects of the COVID-19 pandemic and had witnessed a spate of killings of unarmed Black citizens, primarily by law enforcement—George Floyd, Ahmaud Arbery, Breonna Taylor, and Jacob Blake. Arbery was murdered by father and son vigilantes. Jacob Blake was shot in the back seven times by the Kenosha, WI, police. As a result of these killings, cities and towns across the nation (and in the case of George Floyd, the world) erupted into massive protests despite the COVID-19 prohibitions on large gatherings. In some cases, such as in Minneapolis, Seattle, and Philadelphia, portions of the protests disintegrated into uprisings and insurrections, and small groups of protestors began destroying property and hurling objects at the police. The Trump administration insisted that the remedy to these protests was to deploy the National Guard as a show of force to bring the cities "under control."

Despite the constitutional right to peaceful protest, the president seemed to believe that the only possible position for citizens to take was to support law enforcement. His attitude toward the protestors was on full display on Sunday, May 31, 2020, when he had law enforcement use tear gas to disperse protestors gathered in Washington, DC, so he could walk across the street from the White House to a nearby church, St. John's Episcopal, for a photo opportunity (Rogers, 2020). These kinds of public displays represent a denial of racism, such as Trump's previous equivocation concerning the racist and neo-Nazi demonstrations in Charlottesville, VA, and the refusal to denounce White supremacy in the first 2020 election-year presidential debate, and clearly exacerbated the racial divisions that have risen to the surface of our society since his election.

Critical race theory (CRT) predates the words and actions of Donald Trump. My own scholarly journey into issues of racial disparities in education goes back 3 decades. In the next section I describe how I came to CRT, its reception in education, and the subsequent growth of CRT in education. Like all origin stories, this one is selective. It reflects my experience and a timeline I recall. At the same time as I was trying to develop this work in the Midwest, education scholars on the West Coast also were grappling with it. My "advantage" is that my coauthor, William F. Tate, and I got our work to publication first, and as a result we are credited with introducing the theory to the field of education.

When I arrived at the University of Wisconsin–Madison in the fall of 1991, I had just completed my National Academy of Education Spencer post-doctoral fellowship. This project formed the basis of the work I would do on culturally relevant pedagogy. My primary goal during my first years at Wisconsin was to complete the manuscript on culturally relevant pedagogy to meet my book contract deadline. Mentors and colleagues alike assured me that the University of Wisconsin–Madison would provide the kind of environment that would support my research and writing goals. I had collected my data and was ready to write.

At my previous institution I had a heavy teaching load—seven courses over 3 quarters—with little time to write or reward for doing so. I was able to do my project only because the post-doctoral fellowship bought out my teaching time. Five other assistant professors arrived at UW–Madison concurrently with me. Among that group was William F. Tate, a newly minted PhD from the University of Maryland. Tate's research interests and doctoral preparation were in mathematics education. He was entering the nation's mathematics education powerhouse at Wisconsin. Names like Thomas Romberg, Elizabeth Fennema, Thomas Carpenter, Walter Secada, and John Harvey were on the lips of everyone who understood innovation and change in mathematics education.

A few months into my work at Wisconsin, William Tate, senior professor Carl Grant, and I started working on a paper that addressed the aftermath of the *Brown v. Board of Education* decision of 1954. During the course of our work together, Tate and I realized we were beginning to think along similar lines about the intractability of race and its implications for education. Tate's fiancé, Kimberly Cash, who was a recent law school graduate, shared an article with him that he later shared with me. The article was Kimberlé Crenshaw's "Race, Reform, and Retrenchment: Transformation and Legitimation in Antidiscrimination Law" (1988). I read the article and was intrigued by Crenshaw's argument. She asserted that neoconservatives and critical scholars failed to take into account the deeply rooted racism that defines and delimits life in the United States. While the neoconservatives contend that we have entered a period of "colorblindness," and the critical theorists minimize the power of race as a hegemonic force in the society, critical race theory exposes the seeming neutrality of societal norms that must be addressed if we are to reach the full equality promised by the Constitution.

William Tate and I began reading an entire body of work related to what Crenshaw identified as critical race theory. I recalled having read a book by legal scholar Derrick Bell, *And We Are Not Yet Saved: The Elusive Quest for Racial Justice* (1987), that had a similar theoretical bent. At that point Tate and I decided that we needed to read more deeply into the notion of critical race theory. In the University of Wisconsin law library, we found more work by Bell and Crenshaw. We also found law review articles by Richard Delgado, Mari Matsudo, Charles Lawrence, Cheryl Harris, Linda Green, Patricia Williams, and others. We also learned that Wisconsin had been an incubator for critical race theory and that professors who did work in critical race theory, such as Patricia Williams and Linda Green, were still teaching at Wisconsin. Both Kimberlé Crenshaw and Richard Delgado had done fellowships and faculty visits, respectively, at Wisconsin.

As we continued to read, we realized that critical race theory was a legal theory that took on a broad set of issues—employment, college admissions, housing, incarceration, contracts, education, and many other civil rights issues. However, we could find no work done by education researchers that employed CRT in its analysis of education inequality. This was the niche that Tate and I believed we could carve out to say something significant to explain ongoing educational disparities based on race.

A characteristic that attracted us to CRT was that it provided a robust theoretical understanding of race. We had read many theories on class and gender, but race seemed to be undertheorized. In general, the scholarship on race focused on genetic inferiority and limitations. On the other hand, more liberal scholarship seemed to see race only as a variable to be controlled or manipulated. We viewed CRT as the first scholarship to theorize race and connect it to notions of property rights.

After much reading, we began to discuss how we could craft a synthetic paper to discuss CRT in education. We knew we had to begin by introducing CRT to a new audience—education researchers—and make the case for why CRT helps to explain educational disparities based on race better than other theories do. We produced a draft of the paper and decided we wanted to give it a "test-drive" in our department. This occurred before we had the luxury of an Internet that could distribute a 40-page document conveniently and easily. Thus, we duplicated approximately 50 copies of the paper and left them in the main office of our department. We sent a mass email to our colleagues announcing our intent to hold a colloquium on a paper we were working on. We scheduled the gathering on a Friday afternoon, perhaps hoping that we would get a small turnout. After all, we were two assistant professors with limited time in a department filled with curriculum and instruction luminaries. We were not sure how they would receive these "brash" new untenured professors.

Much to my surprise, on the day of the colloquium the room was filled to capacity. Many of our colleagues, along with a large number of graduate students, showed up. We explained what we were trying to argue and were hit with all kinds of questions. Again, to my surprise, the questions were not hostile. They were insightful and seemed designed to push our thinking. At the end of the session, a number of colleagues handed us their copies of the paper with comments, questions, additional references, and perspectives. We worked on a second draft of the paper and decided to submit it as a proposal to the 1993 American Educational Research Association (AERA) annual meeting in Atlanta, GA.

Our paper, "Toward a Critical Race Theory of Education," was accepted in the AERA format entitled "Advanced Paper Sessions." The idea of this format was for annual meeting attendees to write to us for a copy of the paper to read in advance of the session so there could be a discussion of its substance. We received *no* requests for the paper! I was not optimistic about the session and told Tate not to be discouraged if no one showed up. I had been a regular attendee at AERA since graduate school and knew that a session could be feast or famine. Some sessions were full to overflowing and others had barely any attendees. Tate's primary disciplinary meeting was the National Council of Teachers of Mathematics, and AERA was a new experience for him.

We entered our assigned room and sat waiting. As the time for the session approached, people started filing in. When the session chair stood to convene the session, the room was filled to capacity. Tate and I presented the main ideas of the paper and started fielding questions. It appeared that there were two factions in attendance at our session. One group was excited about this new work and wanted to know as much as they could about it. Another group was clearly annoyed at what we were saying. They peppered us with questions about why we were privileging race. They asked, "What about gender? What about class?" We made our defense for a more robust theorizing of race and argued that we were not obligated to look at other forms of difference in this initial paper on CRT.

Later during the annual meeting, a woman approached me and asked what had happened in our session because her roommate, a well-known scholar in the area of diversity, came back to their hotel room furious after attending the session. At that point I suggested to Tate that we had to quickly get the paper into good enough shape to send it out for publication. I was concerned that forces were amassing against us and might take actions to subvert our ability to reach a broader audience. We spent the summer of 1993 editing and tightening the paper and by fall submitted it initially to one of the field's more prestigious journals. Initially, after 6 months, the journal expressed interest in the paper. We were so excited. Publication in this journal would be a "tenure maker"! However, another 6 months passed, and we heard from the editors that they were no longer interested in publishing it.

Crushed, we took the time to revise the paper yet another time and resubmitted it to what we saw as an equally prestigious journal, *Teachers College Record*. Although I was publishing in other areas and my book, *The Dreamkeepers: Successful Teachers of African American Children* (1994), had been greeted with critical acclaim, the tenure stakes remained high. The CRT paper, according to my tenure review chair, Thomas Popkewitz, could be my best insurance. It would demonstrate to the university's divisional committee my intellectual versatility. Although I was required to submit all of my published works, Wisconsin has a system that requires the departments to identify two "signature" pieces. One piece would be my book, and I initially thought the other would be a theoretical piece on culturally relevant pedagogy published in the *American Educational Research Journal* (Ladson-Billings, 1995). However, Popkewitz, a seasoned scholar, had a strategy for writing my tenure case that was designed to show two lines of inquiry. Unfortunately, the CRT paper was not yet published. Popkewitz called then-editor of *Teachers College Record*, Gary Natriello, to ask what decision he was making on the manuscript. Natriello quickly responded that they intended to publish the piece and agreed to send a letter attesting to that decision.

Since the publication of "Toward a Critical Race Theory in Education" the article has been cited over 7,000 times according to a May 2021 check of Google Scholar. The article has been republished in several outlets and has spurred articles in educational policy, leadership, administration, and special education, among other areas. It has generated myriad inquiries into how race functions in school and society. It has led to an important interrogation of race in our research and scholarship. Instead of merely a variable, race has become a site of contestation and inquiry, and for that reason I believe this work has some worth.

Critical race theory in education has emerged as an important subfield. I wrote a subsequent article, "Just What Is Critical Race Theory and What Is It Doing in a Nice Field Like Education?" (Ladson-Billings, 1998), in which I cautioned education scholars about writing in this theoretical vein. My concern was that far too many scholars would be derivative and, rather than doing the heavy lifting of reading legal scholarship as Tate and I had done back in the early 1990s, merely would use our *Teachers College Record* article as their only exposure to the theory. We were fearful that education scholars would produce superficial scholarship to pose an argument and call it CRT whether it was or not.

Tate (1997) wrote a comprehensive article on the history of the movement and its role in education. On the West Coast, Solorzano and Villalpando (1998) began writing about the role of CRT in higher education, and in the United Kingdom, Gillborn (1997), who had been writing about race and racism in British schools for some time, found CRT to be a useful tool for understanding the highly predictable and systemic racial inequalities that occurred in schools there. Interesting, in the United Kingdom CRT initially was not embraced because of the longstanding commitment to class as the social fault line. However, the data supported Gillborn's assertion. With increased immigration from former British colonies in Black Africa and the Caribbean, racial tensions were becoming more evident.

More recently, both Gillborn and I have engaged in conversations (via podcasts) with scholars and teachers in Scotland about how CRT explains the emerging educational inequalities in their schools between students who are European Scots and those from Pakistan and parts of Africa. My work also has been cited by French scholars (Bentouhami & Möschel, 2017). The spread of the theoretical perspective in education is both gratifying and frustrating. Like any theorist, I garner some satisfaction from others embracing, debating, and wrestling with my work. Those who engage it with integrity push my thinking and force me to be more careful as I pursue my work. Unlike other issues that I have written and researched about, CRT has been work I have had to defend from both conservative and liberal critiques.

The critiques from the Right were to be expected. Perspectives on this side argue that we are now a "colorblind" society where race is of declining significance. They pull on threads from Martin Luther King Jr.'s iconic "I Have a Dream" speech to assert that race does not matter, and we just need to focus on the "content of our character." For them, critical race theory is a divisive, White people–blaming polemic with no basis in academic scholarship. The society is colorblind, and the law is colorblind. The meritocracy determines achievement and reward. Race should not be considered in job placement, college admissions, or financial dealings such as banking, mortgages, or suitability for rental property. The 2008 election of President Barack Obama served as proof positive that racism was a thing of the past, they declared. There was no place for a CRT analysis of inequality.

The critiques from the Left were a bit more varied. The liberal scholars who focus on multicultural education believed that CRT was incorrect to privilege race. Instead, they felt that CRT minimized the import and impact of gender, class, sexuality, and other differences. My own analysis of the differences between multicultural education and critical race theory lies in what I see as foundational differences. Tate and I (Ladson-Billings & Tate, 1995) argued that multicultural education emerged out of the civil rights movement and rests on a foundation of human rights. It asserts that the dignity of each human being, regardless of their differences, must be honored and respected. There is nothing wrong with that perspective. However, it fails to acknowledge that the United States as a nation is not founded on human rights. Rather, it is founded on property rights. African Americans arrived on these shores as "property"! The first mortgage system emerged in the agricultural South by "mortgaging" the bodies of Black people so that planters could purchase more land (Da Costa, 2019; Martin, 2010). CRT insists on acknowledging the role that property plays in constituting the nation. A classic CRT law review article by Harris (1993) outlines the property rights that Whites carry in their own bodies and their value over every other group of people.

Over the past few years we have seen many instances of White women (in particular) using their White skin privilege to call the police on Black people performing normal, everyday tasks such as having a barbecue in the park, selling bottles of water in front of their own homes, bird watching, or attempting to swim in a pool in a neighborhood where they were residents. These types of behaviors underscore the notion that White people believe their White skin privilege should give them the right to circumscribe and delimit what Black people can do and where they can do it.

In addition, critiques from the Left include those from a critical perspective. Marxist scholars reject race as the primary fault line along which inequality exists (Cole, 2017). They insist that class differences must remain at the center of any discussions of inequality, not race. Centering race has caused tension among the "critical" scholarship community. However, when we consider that African Americans, regardless of their social class position, suffer systemic, institutional, interpersonal, and individual racism, we cannot distill their inequitable treatment down to class.

The challenge to CRT from all sides places it in a kind of epistemological nobody's land, and the constant scrutiny of the theory means that those who subscribe to this paradigm must guard it carefully. Thus, Tate and I become the "quality control" inspectors of CRT. Often when young scholars complain that they cannot get their articles that use CRT published, I tell them that it is probably because someone like me rejected them, not the White editor. I review these manuscripts with special scrutiny because I recognize how exposed and vulnerable we are. Sloppy or lazy scholarship will be held up as an example of what is wrong with CRT. Far too many scholars have not read deeply enough, or they lift up a tenet of CRT like counter-storytelling but fail to link it back to a legal principle. Instead their manuscripts read like a personal grievance without anything generative to contribute to the field to build the knowledge base or help the next group of scholars.

Now while half of the chapters in this volume are explicitly critical race theory in their theoretical grounding, the others are not. However, all of the chapters in this volume do address race and inequality in education. This is the bigger rubric under which I have always done my work. Everything we hope to accomplish as a society will be thwarted if we do not do everything within our power to minimize inequality, and the place where I, as a scholar, have decided to attack inequality is at the difficult notion of race.

Throughout this Introduction I have treated race like something real and something we all understand. Indeed, we operate in our lives as if this were so. We fill out forms—applications, medical forms, the census—where we identify ourselves racially. We congregate and socialize along what might be called racial lines. We talk about racial affinity groups. We worship, recreate, and sometimes live in communities based on what we know as race. But what do our behaviors mean if "race" is not a real thing? Omi and Winant (2014) challenged us to understand how race as a social construct does have material consequences. This can happen only when the society agrees upon what constitutes a concept.

Nobel Laureate Toni Morrison (1992) pointed out that race "has become metaphorical—a way of referring to and disguising forces, events, classes, and expressions of social decay and economic division far more threatening to the body politic than biological 'race' ever was" (p. 63). As a scholar deeply interested and invested in educational inequality, I am compelled to examine how race operates in our schools and educational systems. For much of its history in research, race has operated as a "background" variable. Researchers did not question its validity or authenticity. They just named it.

The United States has been identifying people by race for centuries (Strmic-Pawl et al., 2018). The categories in the first census, conducted in 1790, were White, Black, and other, with Whites constituting 80% of the U.S. population, Blacks 18%, and "other" 2%. Over time the categories expanded and contracted. At one point the choices for "Black" included "mulatto," "quadroon," and "octoroon." Today, because people self-identify, individuals completing the census can check any racial category they want, and the government cannot tell them their designation is incorrect. Here two examples are instructive.

I was working on a research project at an elementary school in the San Francisco Bay Area. When I interviewed the principal, I asked her to tell me about the school's demographics. She responded, "Do you want to know what it actually is or what it is on paper?" With raised eyebrows I said, "Why don't you tell me about both?" According to the principal, her school was targeted for desegregation because, sitting in an almost exclusively Black neighborhood, the population was better than 90% Black. The district began reassigning students based on race, and about 60% of the students were to be bused outside of the neighborhood. Simultaneously, as the school prepared to receive a large number of White students, the district began a massive physical plant renovation. The building was painted, the windows were repaired, new carpeting and tile were laid, and a large infusion of technology—computers, video cameras, monitors, and so on—occurred. When the Black families saw these improvements being made for the incoming White students, they reenrolled their children and produced what the principal described as "the largest 'Native American' population in the district"!

A second example comes from NBC sportscaster Mike Tirico (Macur, 2017). Tirico, by the phenotypical markers most commonly used to determine racial identity in the United States—skin color, hair texture, nose and lip size—would easily be identified as Black. However, in an interview, the sportscaster, who was raised by a single White woman of Italian descent, declared he was Italian, not Black. Of course, Tirico's declaration caused a backlash and reignited the conversation about who is Black. Conversations about racial identity arose in 2008 when Barack Obama first ran for president. There were many conversations about whether, having been raised by his White mother and grandparents, he was actually Black. More recently, Senator Kamala Harris in her bid for vice president of the United States had to defend her racial qualification as a Black and South Asian Indian woman.

The question of racial identification is at least a twofold one—internal and external. Individuals are who they say they are, as in the case of children at the San Francisco school or Mike Tirico, Barack Obama, and Kamala Harris. And, they are who the society constructs them to be. While professional golfer Tiger Woods actually created an identity category for himself—"Calabasian"—he is identified by the wider society as a "Black golfer."

In a recently published volume (Dixson et al., 2020), I stated in the Afterword that the question was not whether race was a condition or a process. Indeed, it is both. But more than those two options, race in the United

States is a "project." It is a project because it is "an ongoing, dynamic, evolutionary, never-ending concept of being" (Ladson-Billings, 2020, p. 225). The question we must ask ourselves is what is the work that race is doing in the society? As an education researcher, I am particularly interested in what work race is doing in education and schooling. From the available data it appears that race continues to function as a way to reinscribe hierarchy and inequality. When federal legislation (i.e., No Child Left Behind) required schools to disaggregate test data by race, we quickly saw that even those schools we previously held up as exemplary were woefully lacking in their ability to meet the educational needs of Black and Latinx students.

Today, the entire nation regularly is reminded of the little regard the nation seems to have for Black people. The names Trayvon Martin, Tamir Rice, Sandra Bland, Eric Garner, Rekia Boyd, Oscar Grant, Botham Jean, Armaud Arbery, George Floyd, and Breonna Taylor are all too familiar to the American public, and the reasons their lives were lost are attributable primarily to their race. They did not get the benefit of the doubt or the presumption of innocence their White peers receive. They did not enjoy the constitutional guarantee of the 14th Amendment—equal protection under the law. Indeed, Isabel Wilkerson (2020) cites abolitionist minister William Goodell, who observed in 1853, "He [the Black person] is accounted criminal for acts which are deemed innocent in others . . . punished with a severity from which all others are exempted. He is under the control of the law, though unprotected by the law, and can know law only as an enemy" (p. 146).

This structural racism has formed the basis for much of my research interests. I have wanted to know why race is such a predictable indicator of school achievement. I have wanted better and more powerful explanations for why something the nation put in place as far back as 1619 continues to plague us. We have conquered smallpox, polio, measles, mumps, and diphtheria. We have perfected high-speed transportation. We have electronic technologies that allow students to visit the Library of Congress without leaving the comfort of their homes. We have sophisticated gig economies that allow us to summon a car, rent a house, and have food delivered to our front door. However, we cannot seem to get past the fiction of race that tears at the very fabric of the nation.

In 2020 we saw a resurgence of hate crimes throughout the nation. White supremacist hate groups have marched proudly in our streets, brandishing weapons to intimidate anyone who would challenge their premise that their White skin gives them rights superior to those who are not categorized as White. According to the U.S. Department of Justice, almost 60% of reported hate crimes fall in the category of race, ethnicity, and/or ancestral origin (see https://www.justice.gov/hatecrimes/hate-crime-statistics). Thus, there is a need to confront race as a factor contributing to problems related to national division and animus between and among groups.

ORGANIZATION OF THE BOOK

In this volume I have assembled a group of my papers that deal with educational inequality based on race. The volume is divided into three parts: (1) Critical Race Theory, (2) Issues of Inequality, and (3) Epistemology and Methodologies. The first part examines critical race theory. I include the article that started it all, Ladson-Billings and Tate (1995). This article lays out the tenets of CRT and details how it applies to aspects of schooling—curriculum, discipline, funding, and other issues. It seemed appropriate to begin with the article that helped me begin this intellectual journey.

The second article (Ladson-Billings, 2013) in this part is a chapter I wrote to challenge the ways critical race theory in education seemed to spiral out of control and become distorted. Rather than create a sophisticated theoretical understanding of race, many of the articles that emerged in the almost 10 years between the first article by Tate and me and this chapter were thin complaints about some personal racial injustice. This chapter was designed to return the focus back to the power of CRT as a theory that carefully and systematically could examine race and racism. It called for education researchers to study the legal literature to at least recognize how legal precedents shaped the arguments and allowed the work to move beyond the boundaries of legal scholarship.

The second part deals with issues of inequality. Although I have always been interested in inequality, I have not always had an opportunity to build my intellectual understanding of how it operates in our society. As a teacher I could see that Black students were regularly at the bottom of academic performance and the top of discipline statistics—suspensions, expulsions, and assignment to special education without fair or objective criteria. The parts I could not see were the generational accumulation of wealth and advantage on the side of White, middle-class students and the simultaneous mounting education debt (Ladson-Billings, 2006) of Black and other students of color. I could not see clearly the systems of inequality that made it nearly impossible for students of color to combat the structures that worked against them—such as tracking, underfunded schools, inexperienced and less well-prepared teachers, and lack of access to enriched curriculum. I also could not fully recognize the symbol systems that made it seem like things were "fair" while in truth coded language and perceptions of students based on dress, speech and language, experiences, and family structures kept them in a place of inequality.

As a researcher I gained access to tons of data and scholars from a variety of disciplines, and could begin to piece together the way inequality was a complex system, not merely a random constellation of idiosyncratic personal qualities that kept individuals from succeeding. Nor was it a blanket set of "cultural flaws" like language or the so-called culture of poverty. I began to write on educational inequality by better understanding societal inequality. This part of the volume includes the article that formed the basis of my 2006 American Educational Research Association presidential address, "From the Achievement Gap to the Education Debt: Understanding Achievement in U.S. Schools." In this article I attempted to re-conceptualize what has become an almost universal term—"achievement gap." This article details the historical, economic, political, and moral debt that the nation has accumulated in its failed attempt at educating Black, Latinx, Indigenous, and some Asian-descent students.

In another article, based on my 2011 *Brown* lecture, I discussed how race was constitutive of all of the social sciences that flow into our understanding of the field of education (Ladson-Billings, 2012). In this article I argued that until education research recognized its race-based foundation, we were likely to keep repeating studies and analyses that failed to fully interrogate how race operates in our thinking and conceptualizations.

The third paper in this part, "New Directions in Multicultural Education" (2003), raises a question about where CRT fits in the multicultural education discourse. In the initial CRT article, Ladson-Billings and Tate asserted that the tension between multicultural education and CRT exists because the two are built upon very different paradigms. Multicultural education springs directly from the legacy of U.S. civil rights and the civil rights tradition, which emerged from a steadfast belief in the legitimacy of human rights. CRT, on the other hand, is linked to the notion that civil rights was an incomplete if not failed project and that in the United States the paramount rights are not human rights but rather property rights.

The final article in this part is "Landing on the Wrong Note: The Price We Paid for *Brown*" (2004). This article dispels the notion that *Brown* was designed to aid school desegregation and looks at it as a foreign policy strategy to thwart Soviet advances among non-aligned nations. CRT scholars read *Brown* as an "interest convergence" that never really fulfilled its promise.

The third and final part of the volume examines epistemology and methodologies regarding race. Discussions about race need better methodological tools. Those tools require a sophisticated approach to reading and parsing race. The first article in this part is titled "Racialized Discourses and Ethnic Epistemologies" (Ladson-Billings, 2000). It challenges traditional orthodoxy by calling into question the legitimacy of Enlightenment thinking and universalist presumptions.

In the second paper of the part, Donnor and Ladson-Billings (2017) collaborate to examine post-Obama America and the loss of hope throughout the United States and specifically throughout Black America. The paper, "Critical Race Theory and the Postracial Imaginary," challenges the notions of race being "over" and argues that race is even more re-inscribed following the 2016 election and the rise of the "alt-Right" and White supremacist sentiments.

The volume ends with a Postscript that looks back at this journey through critical race theory in education. More than a summary, it takes a bit of a prospective look into what is on the horizon and what other scholars are starting to explore. Indeed, it offers a bit of hope for the scholarship that explores race. It is a reprint of an article I wrote in 2004 but would not allow to be published until 2018. In this article I attempt to tell the story of how race is "fully funded" in our society to the degree that it seems impossible to "un-make" it and render it insignificant. The article is a challenge to teacher educators and others who believe a few semesters of coursework in equity, diversity, multicultural education, or ethnic studies will be enough to undo the years of social re-inscription of beliefs and values about race and its importance in how we order the society.

REFERENCES

Bell, D. (1987). *And we are not yet saved: The elusive quest for racial justice.* Basic Books.

Bentouhami, H., & Möschel, M. (Eds.). (2017). *Critical race theory: Une introduction aux grands textes fondateurs.* Dalloz.

Cole, M. (2017). *Critical race theory and education: A Marxist perspective* (2nd ed.). Palgrave.

Crenshaw, K. (1988). Race, reform, and retrenchment: Transformation and legitimation in antidiscrimination law. *Harvard Law Review, 101*(7), 1331–1387.

Da Costa, P. N. (2019, September 1). *America's first bond market was backed by enslaved human beings.* Forbes. https://www.forbes.com/sites/pedrodacosta/2019/09/01/americas-first-bond-market-was-backed-by-enslaved-human-beings/

Dixson, A., Ladson-Billings, G., Suarez, C., Trent, W., & Anderson, J. (Eds.). (2020). *Condition or process? Researching race in education.* American Educational Research Association.

Donnor, J. K., & Ladson-Billings, G. (2017). Critical race theory and the postracial imaginary. In N. Denzin & Y. Lincoln (Eds.), *Handbook of qualitative research* (5th ed., pp. 195–213). Sage.

Gillborn, D. (1997). Racism and reform: New ethnicities/old inequalities? *British Educational Research Journal, 23*(3), 345–360.

Harris, C. (1993). Whiteness as property. *Harvard Law Review, 106*(8), 1707–1791.

Ladson-Billings, G. (1994). *The dreamkeepers: Successful teachers of African American children.* Jossey Bass.

Ladson-Billings, G. (1995). Toward a theory of culturally relevant pedagogy. *American Educational Research Journal, 35*, 465–491.

Ladson-Billings, G. (1998). Just what is critical race theory and what's it doing in a nice field like education? *International Journal of Qualitative Studies in Education, 11*(1), 7–24.

Ladson-Billings, G. (2000). Racialized discourses and ethnic epistemologies. In N. Denzin & Y. Lincoln (Eds.), *Handbook of qualitative research* (2nd ed., pp. 257–277). Sage.

Ladson-Billings, G. (2004). Landing on the wrong note: The price we paid for *Brown*. *Educational Researcher, 33*(7), 3–13.

Ladson-Billings, G. (2006). From the achievement gap to the education debt: Understanding achievement in U.S. schools. *Educational Researcher, 35*(7), 3–12.

Ladson-Billings, G. (2012). Through a glass darkly: The persistence of race in education research. *Educational Researcher, 41*, 115–120.

Ladson-Billings, G. (2013). Critical race theory—What it is not! In M. Lynn & A. D. Dixson (Eds.), *Handbook of critical race theory in education* (pp. 34–47). New York: Routledge.

Ladson-Billings, G. (2020). Afterword. In A. Dixson, G. Ladson-Billings, C. Suarez, W. Trent, & J. Anderson (Eds.), *Condition or process? Researching race in education* (pp. 225–228). American Educational Research Association.

Ladson-Billings, G., & Tate, W. F. (1995). Toward a critical race theory of education. *Teachers College Record, 97*(1), 47–68.

Macur, J. (2017, July 15). Mike Tirico would like to talk about anything but Mike Tirico. *New York Times*, Sports Section, p. 4.

Martin, B. (2010). Slavery's invisible engine: Mortgaging human property. *The Journal of Southern History, 76*(4), 817–866.

Morrison, T. (1992). *Playing in the dark: Whiteness and the literary imagination.* Harvard University Press.

National Public Radio Staff. (2020). Trump expands ban on racial sensitivity training to federal contractors. https://www.npr.org/2020/09/22/915843471/trump-expands-ban-on-racial-sensitivity-training-to-federal-contractors

Omi, M., & Winant, H. (2014). *Racial formation in the United States* (3rd ed.). Routledge.

Rogers, K. (2020, June 1). Protestors dispersed with tear gas so Trump could pose at church. *New York Times*. https://www.nytimes.com/2020/06/01/us/politics/trump-st-johns-church-bible.html

Solorzano, D., & Villalpando, O. (1998). Critical race theory, marginality, and the experience of students of color in higher education. *Sociology of Education, 21*, 211–222.

Strmic-Pawl, H. V., Jackson, B. A., & Garner, S. (2018). Race counts: Racial and ethnic data on the U.S. census and the implications for tracking inequality. *Sociology of Race and Ethnicity, 4*(1), 1–13.

Tate, W. F. (1997). Critical race theory and education: History, theory, and implications. *Review of Research in Education, 22*(1), 195–247.

Wilkerson, I (2020). *Caste: The origins of our discontents*. Random House.

Part I

CRITICAL RACE THEORY

CHAPTER 1

Toward a Critical Race Theory of Education

With William F. Tate IV

The presentation of truth in new forms provokes resistance, confounding those committed to accepted measures for determining the quality and validity of statements made and conclusions reached, and making it difficult for them to respond and adjudge what is acceptable.

—Derrick Bell, *Faces at the Bottom of the Well*

I am not included within the pale of this glorious anniversary! Your high independence only reveals the immeasurable distance between us. The blessings in which you this day, rejoice, are not enjoyed in common. The rich inheritance of justice, liberty, prosperity and independence bequeathed by your fathers, not by me . . .

—Frederick Douglass, *My Bondage and My Freedom*

In 1991 social activist and education critic Jonathan Kozol delineated the great inequities that exist between the schooling experiences of white middle-class students and those of poor African-American and Latino students. And, while Kozol's graphic descriptions may prompt some to question how it is possible that we allow these "savage inequalities," this article suggests that these inequalities are a logical and predictable results of a racialized society in which discussions of race and racism continue to be muted and marginalized.[1]

In this article we attempt to theorize race and use it as an analytic tool for understanding school inequity.[2] We begin with a set of propositions about race and property and their intersections. We situate our discussion in an explication of critical race theory and attempt to move beyond the

boundaries of the educational research literature to include arguments and
new perspectives from law and the social sciences. In doing so, we acknowledge and are indebted to a number of scholars whose work crosses disciplinary boundaries.[3] We conclude by exploring the tensions between our
conceptualization of a critical race theory in education and the educational
reform movement identified as multicultural education.

UNDERSTANDING RACE AND PROPERTY

Our discussion of social inequity in general, and school inequity in particular, is based on three central propositions:[4]

1. Race continues to be a significant factor in determining inequity in
    the United States.
2. U.S. society is based on property rights.
3. The intersection of race and property creates an analytic tool
    through which we can understand social (and, consequently,
    school) inequity.

In this section we expand on these propositions and provide supporting
"meta-propositions" to make clear our line of reasoning and relevant application to educational or school settings.

Race as Factor in Inequity

The first proposition—that race continues to be a significant factor in determining inequity in the United States—is easily documented in the statistical and demographic data. Hacker's look at educational and life chances
such as high school dropout rates, suspension rates, and incarceration rates
echoes earlier statistics of the Children's Defense Fund.[5] However, in what
we now call the postmodern era, some scholars question the usefulness of
race as a category.

Omi and Winant argue that popular notions of race as either an
ideological construct or an objective condition have epistemological limitations.[6] Thinking of race strictly as an ideological construct denies the
reality of a racialized society and its impact on "raced" people in their
everyday lives. On the other hand, thinking of race solely as an objective
condition denies the problematic aspects of race—how do we decide who
fits into which racial classifications? How do we categorize racial mix-
tures? Indeed, the world of biology has found the concept of race virtually useless. Geneticist Cavalli-Sforza asserts that "human populations are
sometimes known as ethnic groups, or 'races.' . . . They are hard to define
in a way that is both rigorous and useful because human beings group

themselves in a bewildering array of sets, some of them overlapping, all of them in a state of flux."[7]

Nonetheless. even when the concept of race fails to "make sense," we continue to employ it. According to Nobel Laureate Toni Morrison:

> Race has become metaphorical—a way of referring to and disguising forces, events, classes, and expressions of social decay and economic division far more threatening to the body politic than biological "race" ever was.
>
> Expensively kept, economically unsound, a spurious and useless political asset in election campaigns, racism is as healthy today as it was during the Enlightenment. It seems that is has a utility far beyond economy, beyond the sequestering of classes from one another, and has assumed a metaphorical life so completely embedded in daily discourse that it is perhaps more necessary and more on display than ever before.[8]

Despite the problematic nature of race, we offer as a first meta-proposition that race, unlike gender and class, remains untheorized.[9] Over the past few decades theoretical and epistemological considerations of gender have proliferated.[10] Though the field continues to struggle for legitimacy in academe, interest in and publications about feminist theories abound. At the same time, Marxist and co-Marxist formulations about class continue to merit consideration as theoretical models for understanding social inequity.[11] We recognize the importance of both gender- and class-based analyses while at the same time pointing to their shortcomings vis-à-vis race. Roediger points out that "the main body of writing by White Marxists in the United States has both 'naturalized' whiteness and oversimplified race."[12]

Omi and Winant have done significant work in providing a sociological explanation of race in the United States. They argue that the paradigms of race have been conflated with notions of ethnicity, class, and nation because

> theories of race—of its meaning, its transformations, the significance of racial events—have never been a top priority in social science. In the U.S., although the "founding fathers" of American sociology . . . were explicitly concerned with the state of domestic race relations, racial theory remained one of the least developed fields of sociological inquiry.[13]

To mount a viable challenge to the dominant paradigm of ethnicity (i.e., we are all ethnic and, consequently, must assimilate and rise socially the same way European Americans have), Omi and Winant offer a racial formation theory that they define as "the sociohistorical process by which racial categories are created, inhabited, transformed and destroyed. . . . [It] is a process of historically situated *projects* in which human bodies and social structure are represented and organized." Further, they link "racial formation to the evolution of hegemony, the way in which society is organized and ruled." Their analysis suggests that "race is a matter of both social structure and cultural representation."[14]

By arguing that race remains untheorized, we are not suggesting that other scholars have not looked carefully at race as a powerful tool for explaining social inequity, but that the intellectual salience of this theorizing has not been systematically employed in the analysis of educational inequality. Thus, like Omi and Winant, we are attempting to uncover or decipher the social-structural and cultural significance of race in education. Our work owes an intellectual debt to both Carter G. Woodson and W. E. B. Du Bois, who, although marginalized by the mainstream academic community, used race as a theoretical lens for assessing social inequity.[15]

Both Woodson and Du Bois presented cogent arguments for considering race as *the* central construct for understanding inequality. In many ways our work is an attempt to build on the foundation laid by these scholars.[16] Briefly, Woodson, as far back as 1916, began to establish the legitimacy of race (and, in particular, African Americans) as a subject of scholarly inquiry.[17] As founder of the Association for the Study of Negro Life and History and editor of its *Journal of Negro History*, Woodson revolutionized the thinking about African Americans from that of pathology and inferiority to a multitextured analysis of the uniqueness of African Americans and their situation in the United States. His most notable publication, *The Mis-Education of the Negro*, identified the school's role in structuring inequality and demotivating African-American students:

> The same educational process which inspires and stimulates the oppressor with the thought that he is everything and has accomplished everything worthwhile, depresses and crushes at the same time the spark of genius in the Negro by making him feel that his race does not amount to much and never will measure up to the standards of other peoples.[18]

Du Bois, perhaps better known among mainstream scholars, profoundly impacted the thinking of many identified as "other" by naming a "double consciousness" felt by African Americans. According to Du Bois, the African American "ever feels his two-ness—an American, A Negro; two souls, two thoughts, two unreconciled strivings."[19] In a current biography of Du Bois, Lewis details the intellectual impact of this concept:

> It was a revolutionary concept. It was not just revolutionary; the concept of the divided self was profoundly mystical, for Du Bois invested this double consciousness with a capacity to see incomparably further and deeper. The African-American—seventh son after the Egyptian and Indian, the Greek and Roman, the Teuton and Mongolian—possessed the gift of "second sight in this American world," an intuitive faculty (prelogical, in a sense) enabling him/her to see and say things about American society that possessed a heightened moral

validity. Because he dwelt equally in the mind and heart of his oppressor as in his own beset psyche, the African American embraced a vision of the common-weal at its best.[20]

As a prophetic foreshadowing of the centrality of race in U.S. society, Du Bois reminded us that "the problem of the twentieth century is the problem of the color line."[21]

The second meta-proposition that we use to support the proposition that race continues to be significant in explaining inequity in the United States is that class- and gender-based explanations are not powerful enough to explain all of the difference (or variance) in school experience and performance. Although both class and gender can and do intersect race, as stand-alone variables they do not explain all of the educational achievement differences apparent between whites and students of color. Indeed, there is some evidence to suggest that even when we hold constant for class, middle-class African-American students do not achieve at the same level as their white counterparts.[22] Although Oakes reports that "in academic tracking, . . . poor and minority student are most likely to be placed at the lowest levels of the school's sorting system,"[23] we are less clear as to which factor—race or class—is causal. Perhaps the larger question of the impact of race on social class is the more relevant one. Space limitations do not permit us to examine that question.

Issues of gender bias also figure in inequitable schooling.[24] Females receive less attention from teachers, are counseled away from or out of advanced mathematics and science courses, and although they receive better grades than their male counterparts, their grades do not translate into advantage in college admission and/or the work place.[25]

But examination of class and gender, taken alone or together, do not account for the extraordinarily high rate of school dropout, suspension, expulsion, and failure among African-American and Latino males.[26] In the case of suspension, Majors and Billson argue that many African-American males are suspended or expelled from school for what they termed "non-contact violations"—wearing banned items of clothing such as hats and jackets, or wearing these items in an "unauthorized" manner, such as backwards or inside out.[27]

The point we strive to make with this meta-proposition is not that class and gender are insignificant, but rather, as West suggests, that "race matters," and, as Smith insists, "blackness matters in more detailed ways.[28]

The Property Issue

Our second proposition, that U.S. society is based on property rights, is best explicated by examining legal scholarship and interpretations of rights. To develop this proposition it is important to situate it in the context of critical race theory. Monaghan reports that "critical race legal scholarship developed in the 1970s, in part because minority scholars thought they were being overlooked in critical legal studies, a betterknown movement that examines the way law encodes cultural norms."[29] However, Delgado argues that despite the diversity contained within the critical race movement, there are some shared features:

> an assumption that racism is not a series of isolated acts, but is endemic in American life, deeply ingrained legally, culturally, and even psychologically;
> a call for a reinterpretation of civil-rights law "in light of its ineffectuality, showing that laws to remedy racial injustices are often undermined before they can fulfill their promise";
> a challenge to the "traditional claims of legal neutrality, objectivity, color-blindness, and meritocracy as camouflage for the self-interest of dominant groups in American society";
> an insistence on subjectivity and the reformulation of legal doctrine to reflect the perspectives of those who have experienced and been victimized by racism firsthand;
> the use of stories or first-person accounts.[30]

In our analysis we add another aspect to this critical paradigm that disentangles democracy and capitalism. Many discussions of democracy conflate it with capitalism despite the fact that it is possible to have a democratic government with an economic system other than capitalism. Discussing the two ideologies as if they were one masks the pernicious effects of capitalism on those who are relegated to its lowest ranks. Traditional civil rights approaches to solving inequality have depended on the "rightness" of democracy while ignoring the structural inequality of capitalism.[31] However, democracy in the U.S. context was built on capitalism.

In the early years of the republic *only* capitalists enjoyed the franchise. Two hundred years later when civil rights leaders of the 1950s and 1960s built their pleas for social justice on an appeal to the civil and human rights, they were ignoring the fact that the society was based on *property rights*.[32] An example from the 1600s underscores the centrality of property in the Americas from the beginning of European settlement:

> When the Pilgrims came to New England they too were coming not to vacant land but to territory inhabited by tribes of Indians. The governor of the Massachusetts Bay Colony, John Winthrop, created the excuse to take Indian land by declaring the area legally a "vacuum." The Indians, he said, had not "subdued" the land, and therefore had only a "natural" right to it, but not a "civil right." A "natural right" did not have legal standing.[33]

Bell examined the events leading up to the Constitution's development and concluded that there exists a tension between property rights and human rights.[34] This tension was greatly exacerbated by the presence of African peoples as slaves in America. The purpose of the government was to protect the main object of society—property. The slave status of most African Americans (as well as women and children) resulted in their being objectified as property. And, a government constructed to protect the rights of property owners lacked the incentive to secure human rights for the African American.[35]

According to Bell "the concept of individual rights, unconnected to property rights, was totally foreign to these men of property; and thus, despite two decades of civil rights gains, most Blacks remain disadvantaged and deprived because of their race."[36]

The grand narrative of U.S. history is replete with tensions and struggles over property—in its various forms. From the removal of Indians (and later Japanese Americans) from the land, to military conquest of the Mexicans,[37] to the construction of Africans as property,[38] the ability to define, possess, and own property has been a central feature of power in America. We do not suggest that other nations have not fought over and defined themselves by property and landownership.[39] However, the contradiction of a reified symbolic individual juxtaposed to the reality of "real estate" means that emphasis on the centrality of property can be disguised. Thus, we talk about the importance of the individual, individual rights, and civil rights while social benefits accrue largely to property owners.[40]

Property relates to education in explicit and implicit ways. Recurring discussions about property tax relief indicate that more affluent communities (which have higher property values, hence higher tax assessments) resent paying for a public school system whose clientele is largely nonwhite and poor.[41] In the simplest of equations, those with "better" property are entitled to "better" schools. Kozol illustrates the disparities: "Average expenditures per pupil in the city of New York in 1987 were some $5,500. In the highest spending suburbs of New York (Great Neck or Manhasset, for example, on Long Island) funding levels rose above $11,000, with the highest districts in the state at $15,000."[42]

But the property differences manifest themselves in other ways. For example, curriculum represents a form of "intellectual property."[43] The quality and quantity of the curriculum varies with the "property values" of the school. The use of a critical race story[44] appropriately represents this notion:

> The teenage son of one of the authors of this article was preparing to attend high school. A friend had a youngster of similar age who also was preparing to enter high school. The boys excitedly poured over course offerings in their respective schools' catalogues. One boy was planning on attending school in an

upper-middle-class white community. The other would be attending school in an urban, largely African-American district. The difference between the course offerings as specified in the catalogues was striking. The boy attending the white, middle-class school had his choice of many foreign languages—Spanish, French, German, Latin, Greek, Italian, Chinese, and Japanese. His mathematics offerings included algebra, geometry, trigonometry, calculus, statistics, general math, and business math. The science department at this school offered biology, chemistry, physics, geology, science in society, biochemistry, and general science. The other boy's curriculum choices were not nearly as broad. His foreign language choices were Spanish and French. His mathematics choices were general math, business math, and algebra (there were no geometry or trig classes offered). His science choices were general science, life science, biology, and physical science. The differences in electives were even more pronounced, with the affluent school offering courses such as Film as Literature, Asian Studies, computer programming, and journalism. Very few elective courses were offered at the African-American school, which had no band, orchestra, or school newspaper.

The availability of "rich" (or enriched) intellectual property delimits what is now called "opportunity to learn"[45]—the presumption that along with providing educational "standards"[46] that detail what students should know and be able to do, they must have the material resources that support their learning. Thus, intellectual property must be undergirded by "real" property, that is, science labs, computers and other state-of-the-art technologies, appropriately certified and prepared teachers. Of course, Kozol demonstrated that schools that serve poor students of color are unlikely to have access to these resources and, consequently, students will have little or no opportunity to learn despite the attempt to mandate educational standards.[47]

CRITICAL RACE THEORY AND EDUCATION

With this notion of property rights as a defining feature of the society, we proceed to describe the ways that the features of critical race theory mentioned in the previous section can be applied to our understanding of educational inequity.

Racism as Endemic and Deeply Ingrained in American Life

If racism were merely isolated, unrelated, individual acts, we would expect to see at least a few examples of educational excellence and equity together in the nation's public schools. Instead, those places where African Americans do experience educational success tend to be outside of the public schools.[48] While some might argue that poor children, regardless of race, do worse in school, and that the high proportion of African-American poor contributes to their dismal school performance, we argue that the cause of their poverty in conjunction with the condition of their schools and schooling is institutional and structural racism. Thus, when we speak of racism we refer to Wellman's definition of "culturally sanctioned beliefs which, regardless of the intentions involved, defend the advantages Whites have because of the subordinated positions of racial minorities." We must therefore contend with the "problem facing White people [of coming] to grips with the demands made by Blacks and Whites while at the same time *avoiding* the possibility of institutional change and reorganization that might affect them."[49]

A Reinterpretation of Ineffective Civil Rights Law

In the case of education, the civil rights decision that best exemplifies our position is the landmark *Brown v. Board of Education of Topeka, Kansas*. While having the utmost respect for the work of Thurgood Marshall and the National Association for the Advancement of Colored People (NAACP) legal defense team in arguing the *Brown* decision, with forty years of hindsight we recognize some serious shortcomings in that strategy. Today, students of color are more segregated than ever before.[50] Although African Americans represent 12 percent of the national population, they are the majority in twenty-one of the twenty-two largest (urban) school districts.[51] Instead of providing more and better educational opportunities, school desegregation has meant increased white flight along with a loss of African-American teaching and administrative positions.[52] In explaining the double-edged sword of civil rights legislation, Crenshaw argued that

> the civil rights community . . . must come to terms with the fact that anti-discrimination discourse is fundamentally ambiguous and can accommodate conservative as well as liberal views of race and equality. This dilemma suggests that the civil rights constituency cannot afford to view antidiscrimination doctrine as a permanent pronouncement of society's commitment to ending racial subordination. Rather, antidiscrimination law represents an ongoing ideological struggle in which occasional winners harness the moral, coercive, consensual power of law. Nonetheless, the victories it offers can be ephemeral and the risks of engagement substantial.[53]

An example of Crenshaw's point about the ambiguity of civil rights legislation was demonstrated in a high school district in Northern California.[54] Of the five high schools in the district, one was located in a predominantly African-American community. To entice white students to attend that school, the district funded a number of inducements including free camping and skiing trips. While the trips were available to all of the students, they were attended largely by the white students, who already owned the expensive camping and skiing equipment. However, these inducements were not enough to continuously attract white students. As enrollment began to fall, the district decided to close a school. Not surprisingly, the school in the African-American community was closed and all of its students had to be (and continue to be) bused to the four white schools in the district.

Lomotey and Staley's examination of Buffalo's "model" desegregation program revealed that African-American and Latino students continued to be poorly served by the school system. The academic achievement of African-American and Latino students failed to improve while their suspension, expulsion, and dropout rates continued to rise. On the other hand, the desegregation plan provided special magnet programs and extended day care of which whites were able to take advantage. What, then, made Buffalo a model school desegregation program? In short, the benefits that whites derived from school desegregation and their seeming support of the district's desegregation program.[55] Thus, a model desegregation program becomes defined as one that ensures that whites are happy (and do not leave the system altogether) regardless of whether African-American and other students of color achieve or remain.

Challenging Claims of Neutrality, Objectivity, Color-Blindness, and Meritocracy

A theme of "naming one's own reality" or "voice" is entrenched in the work of critical race theorists. Many critical race theorists argue that the form and substance of scholarship are closely connected.[56] These scholars use parables, chronicles, stories, counterstories, poetry, fiction, and revisionist histories to illustrate the false necessity and irony of much of current civil rights doctrine. Delgado suggests that there are at least three reasons for naming one's own reality in legal discourse:

1. Much of reality is socially constructed.
2. Stories provide members of outgroups a vehicle for psychic self-preservation.
3. The exchange of stories from teller to listener can help overcome ethnocentrism and the dysconscious conviction of viewing the world in one way.[57]

The first reason for naming one's own reality is to demonstrate how political and moral analysis is conducted in legal scholarship. Many mainstream legal scholars embrace universalism over particularity.[58] According to Williams, "theoretical legal understanding" is characterized, in Anglo-American jurisprudence, by the acceptance of transcendent, acontextual, universal legal truths or procedures.[59] For instance, some legal scholars might contend that the tort of fraud has always existed and that it is a component belonging to the universal system of right and wrong. This view tends to discount anything that is nontranscendent (historical), or contextual (socially constructed), or nonuniversal (specific) with the unscholarly labels of "emotional," "literary," "personal," or "false."

In contrast, critical race theorists argue that political and moral analysis is situational—"truths only exist for this person in this predicament at this time in history."[60] For the critical race theorist, social reality is constructed by the formulation and the exchange of stories about individual situations."[61] These stories serve as interpretive structures by which we impose order on experience and it on us.[62]

A second reason for the naming-one's-own-reality theme of critical race theory is the psychic preservation of marginalized groups. A factor contributing to the demoralization of marginalized groups is self-condemnation.[63] Members of minority groups internalize the stereotypic images that certain elements of society have constructed in order to maintain their power.[64] Historically, storytelling has been a kind of medicine to heal the wounds of pain caused by racial oppression.[65] The story of one's condition leads to the realization of how one came to be oppressed and subjugated and allows one to stop inflicting mental violence on oneself.

Finally, naming one's own reality with stories can affect the oppressor. Most oppression does not seem like oppression to the perpetrator.[66] Delgado argues that the dominant group justifies its power with stories—stock explanations—that construct reality in ways to maintain their privilege.[67] Thus, oppression is rationalized, causing little self-examination by the oppressor. Stories by people of color can catalyze the necessary cognitive conflict to jar dysconscious racism.

The "voice" component of critical race theory provides a way to communicate the experience and realities of the oppressed, a first step on the road to justice. As we attempt to make linkages between critical race theory and education, we contend that the voice of people of color is required for a complete analysis of the educational system. Delpit argues that one of the tragedies of education is the way in which the dialogue of people of color has been silenced. An example from her conversation with an African-American graduate student illustrates this point:

> There comes a moment in every class when we have to discuss "The Black Issue" and what's appropriate education for Black children. I tell you, I'm tired of arguing with those White people, because they won't listen. Well, I don't know if they really don't listen or if they just don't believe you. It seems like if you can't quote Vygotsky or something, then you don't have any validity to speak about your own kids. Anyway, I'm not bothering with it anymore, now I'm just in it for a grade.[68]

A growing number of education scholars of color are raising critical questions about the way that research is being conducted in communities of color.[69] Thus, without authentic voices of people of color (as teachers, parents, administrators, students, and community members) it is doubtful that we can say or know anything useful about education in their communities.

THE INTERSECTION OF RACE AND PROPERTY

In the previous section of this article we argued that race is still a significant factor in determining inequity in the United States and that the society is based on property rights rather than on human rights. In this section we discuss the intersection of race and property as a central construct in understanding a critical race theoretical approach to education.

Harris argues that "slavery linked the privilege of Whites to the subordination of Blacks through a legal regime that attempted the conversion of Blacks into objects of property. Similarly, the settlement and seizure of Native American land supported White privilege through a system of property rights in land in which the 'race' of the Native Americans rendered their first possession right invisible and justified conquest." But, more pernicious and long lasting than the victimization of people of color is the construction of whiteness as the ultimate property. "Possession—the act necessary to lay the basis for rights in property—was defined to include only the cultural practice of Whites. This definition laid the foundation for the idea that whiteness—that which Whites alone possess—is valuable and is property."[70]

Because of space constraints, it is not possible to fully explicate Harris's thorough analysis of whiteness as property. However, it is important to delineate what she terms the "property functions of whiteness," which include: (1) rights of disposition; (2) rights to use and enjoyment; (3) reputation and status property; and (4) the absolute right to exclude. How these rights apply to education is germane to our discussion.

Rights of Disposition. Because property rights are described as fully alienable, that is, transferable, it is difficult to see how whiteness can be construed as property.[71] However, alienability of certain property is limited (e.g., entitlements, government licenses, professional degrees or licenses held by one party and financed by the labor of the other in the context of divorce). Thus, whiteness when conferred on certain student performances is alienable.[72] When students are rewarded only for conformity to perceived "white norms" or sanctioned for cultural practices (e.g., dress, speech patterns, unauthorized conceptions of knowledge), white property is being rendered alienable.

Rights to Use and Enjoyment. Legally, whites can use and enjoy the privileges of whiteness. As McIntosh has explicitly demonstrated, whiteness allows for specific social, cultural, and economic privileges.[73] Fuller further asserts that whiteness is both performative and pleasurable.[74] In the school setting, whiteness allows for extensive use of school property. Kozol's description of the material differences in two New York City schools can be interpreted as the difference between those who possess the right to use and enjoy what schools can offer and those who do not:

> The [white] school serves 825 children in the kindergarten through sixth grade. This is approximately half the student population crowded into [black] P.S. 79, where 1,550 children fill a space intended for 1,000, and a great deal smaller than the 1,300 children packed into the former skating rink.[75]

This right of use and enjoyment is also reflected in the structure of the curriculum, also described by Kozol:

> The curriculum [the white school] follows "emphasizes critical thinking, reasoning and logic." The planetarium, for instance, is employed not simply for the study of the universe as it exists. "Children also are designing their own galaxies," the teacher says. . . .
>
> In my [Kozol's] notes: "Six girls, four boys. Nine White, one Chinese. I am glad they have this class. But what about the others? Aren't there ten Black children in the school who could enjoy this also?"[76]

Reputation and Status Property. The concept of reputation as property is regularly demonstrated in legal cases of libel and slander. Thus, to damage someone's reputation is to damage some aspect of his or her personal property. In the case of race, to call a white person "black" is to defame him or her.[77] In the case of schooling, to identify a school or program as nonwhite in any way is to diminish its reputation or status. For example, despite the prestige of foreign language learning, bilingual education as practiced in the United States as a nonwhite form of second language learning has lower status.[78] The term *urban*, the root word of *urbane*, has come to mean black. Thus, urban schools (located in the urbane, sophisticated cities) lack the status and reputation of suburban (white) schools and when urban students move to or are bused to suburban schools, these schools lose their reputation.[79]

The Absolute Right to Exclude. Whiteness is constructed in this society as the absence of the "contaminating" influence of blackness. Thus, "one drop of black blood" constructs one as black, regardless of phenotypic markers.[80] In schooling, the absolute right to exclude was demonstrated initially by denying blacks access to schooling altogether. Later, it was demonstrated by the creation and maintenance of separate schools. More recently it has been demonstrated by white flight and the growing insistence on vouchers, public funding of private schools, and schools of choice.[81] Within schools, absolute right to exclude is demonstrated by resegregation via tracking,[82] the institution of "gifted" programs, honors programs, and advanced placement classes. So complete is this exclusion that black students often come to the university in the role of intruders—who have been granted special permission to be there.

In this section we have attempted to draw parallels between the critical race legal theory notion of whiteness as property and educational inequity. In the final section we relate some of the intellectual/theoretical tensions that exist between critical race theory and multicultural education.

The Limits of the Multicultural Paradigm

Throughout this article we have argued the need for a critical race theoretical perspective to cast a new gaze on the persistent problems of racism in schooling. We have argued the need for this perspective because of the failure of scholars to theorize race. We have drawn parallels between the way critical race legal scholars understand their position vis-à-vis traditional legal scholarship and the ways critical race theory applied to education offers a way to rethink traditional educational scholarship. We also have referred to the tensions that exist between traditional civil rights legislation and critical race legal theory. In this section we identify a necessary tension between critical race theory in education and what we term the multicultural paradigm.

Multicultural education has been conceptualized as a reform movement designed to effect change in the "school and other educational institutions so that students from diverse racial, ethnic, and other social-class groups will experience educational equality."[83] In more recent years, multicultural education has expanded to include issues of gender, ability, and sexual orientation. Although one could argue for an early history of the "multicultural education movement" as far back as the 1880s when George Washington Williams wrote his history of African Americans, much of the current multicultural education practice seems more appropriately rooted in the intergroup education movement of the 1950s, which was designed to help African Americans and other "unmeltable" ethnics become a part of America's melting pot.[84] Their goals were primarily assimilationist through the reduction of prejudice. However, after the civil rights unrest and growing self-awareness of African Americans in the 1960s, the desire to assimilate was supplanted by the reclamation of an "authentic black personality" that did not rely on the acceptance by or standards of white America. This new vision was evidenced in the academy in the form of first, black studies and later, when other groups made similar liberating moves, ethnic studies.[85]

Current practical demonstrations of multicultural education in schools often reduce it to trivial examples and artifacts of cultures such as eating ethnic or cultural foods, singing songs or dancing, reading folktales, and other less than scholarly pursuits of the fundamentally different conceptions of knowledge or quests for social justice.[86] At the university level, much of the concern over multicultural education has been over curriculum inclusion.[87] However, another level of debate emerged over what became known as "multiculturalism."

Somewhat different from multicultural education in that it does not represent a particular educational reform or scholarly tradition, multiculturalism came to be viewed as a political philosophy of "many cultures" existing together in an atmosphere of respect and tolerance.[88] Thus, outside of the classroom multiculturalism represented the attempt to bring both students and faculty from a variety of cultures into the school (or academy) environment. Today, the term is used interchangeably with the ever-expanding "diversity," a term used to explain all types of "difference"—racial, ethnic, cultural, linguistic, ability, gender, sexual orientation. Thus, popular music, clothes, media, books, and so forth, reflect a growing awareness of diversity and/or multiculturalism. Less often discussed are the growing tensions that exist between and among various groups that gather under the umbrella of multiculturalism—that is, the interests of groups can be competing or their perspectives can be at odds.[89] We assert that the ever-expanding multicultural paradigm follows the traditions of liberalism—allowing a proliferation of difference. Unfortunately, the tensions between and among these differences are rarely interrogated, presuming a "unity of difference"—that is, that all difference is both analogous and equivalent.[90]

To make parallel the analogy between critical race legal theory and traditional civil rights law with that of critical race theory in education and multicultural education we need to restate the point that critical race legal theorists have "doubts about the foundation of moderate/incremental civil rights law."[91] The foundation of civil rights law has been in human rights rather than in property rights. Thus, without disrespect to the pioneers of civil rights law, critical race legal scholars document the ways in which civil rights law is regularly subverted to benefit whites.[92]

We argue that the current multicultural paradigm functions in a manner similar to civil rights law. Instead of creating radically new paradigms that ensure justice, multicultural reforms are routinely "sucked back into the system," and just as traditional civil rights law is based on a foundation of human rights, the current multicultural paradigm is mired in liberal ideology that offers no radical change in the current order.[93] Thus, critical race theory in education, like its antecedent in legal scholarship, is a radical critique of both the status quo and the purported reforms.

We make this observation of the limits of the current multicultural paradigm not to disparage the scholarly efforts and sacrifices of many of its proponents, but to underscore the difficulty (indeed, impossibility) of maintaining the spirit and intent of justice for the oppressed while simultaneously permitting the hegemonic rule of the oppressor.[94] Thus, as critical race theory scholars we unabashedly reject a paradigm that attempts to be everything to everyone and consequently becomes nothing for anyone, allowing the status quo to prevail. Instead, we align our scholarship and activism with the philosophy of Marcus Garvey, who believed that the black man was universally oppressed on racial grounds, and that any program of emancipation would have to be built around the question of race first.[95] In his own words, Garvey speaks to us clearly and unequivocally:

> In a world of wolves one should go armed, and one of the most powerful defensive weapons within the reach of Negroes is the practice of race first in all parts of the world.[96]

NOTES

1. Jonathan Kozol, *Savage Inequalities* (New York: Crown Publishers, 1991). For further discussion of our inability to articulate issues of race and racism see Toni Morrison, *Playing in the Dark: Whiteness and the Literary Imagination* (Cambridge: Harvard University Press, 1992); Cornel West, "Learning to Talk of Race," *New York Times Magazine*, August 2, 1992, pp. 24, 26; and Beverly Daniel Tatum, "Talking about Race, Learning about Racism: The Application of Racial Identity Development Theory in the Classroom," *Harvard Educational Review* 62 (1992): 1–24.

2. Throughout this article the term *race* is used to define the polar opposites of "conceptual whiteness" and "conceptual blackness" (Joyce King, "Perceiving Reality in a New Way: Rethinking the Black/white Duality of our Time [Paper presented at the annual meeting of the American Educational Research Association, New Orleans, April 1994]). We do not mean to reserve the sense of "otherness" for African Americans; rather, our discussion attempts to illuminate how discussions of race in the United States positions *everyone* as either "white" or "nonwhite." Thus, despite the use of African-American legal and educational exemplars, we include other groups who have been constructed at various times in their history as nonwhite or black. Readers should note that some of the leading legal scholars in the critical race legal theory movement are of Latino and Asian-American as well as African-American heritage.

3. See, for example, Patricia Hill Collins, *Black Feminist Thought* (New York: Routledge, 1991); Joyce King and Carolyn Mitchell, *Black Mothers to Sons: Juxtaposing African American Literature and Social Practice* (New York: Peter Lang, 1990); and Patricia Williams, *The Alchemy of Race and Rights: Diary of a Law Professor* (Cambridge: Harvard University Press, 1991).

4. These propositions are not hierarchical. Rather, they can be envisioned as sides of an equilateral triangle, each equal and each central to the construction of the overall theory.

5. Andrew Hacker, *Two Nations: Black and White, Separate, Hostile, Unequal* (New York: Ballantine Books, 1992); and Marian Wright Edelman, *Families in Peril: An Agenda for Social Change* (Cambridge: Harvard University Press, 1987).

6. Michael Omi and Howard Winant, "On the Theoretical Concept of Race," in *Race, Identity and Representation in Education*, ed. C. McCarthy and W. Crichlow (New York: Routledge, 1993), pp. 3–10.

7. Luigi Luca Cavalli-Sforza, "Genes, People and Languages," *Scientific American*, November 1991, p. 104.

8. Morrison, *Playing in the Dark*, p. 63.

9. This assertion was made forcefully by the participants of the Institute NHI (No Humans Involved) at a symposium entitled "The Two Reservations: Western Thought, the Color Line, and the Crisis of the Negro Intellectual Revisited," sponsored by the Department of African and Afro-American Studies at Stanford University, Stanford, Calif., March 3–5, 1994.

10. See, for example, Nancy Chodorow, *The Reproduction of Mothering* (Berkeley: University of California Press, 1978); Simone DeBeauvoir, *The Second Sex* (New York: Bantam Books, 1961); Vivian Gornick, "Women as Outsiders," in *Women in Sexist Society*, ed. V. Gornick and B. Moran (New York: Basic Books, 1971), pp. 70–84; Nancy Hartsock, "Feminist Theory and the Development of Revolutionary Strategy," *Capitalist Patriarch and the Case for Socialist Feminism*, ed. Z. Eisenstein (London and New York: Monthly Review Press, 1979); and Alison Jagger, *Feminist Theory and Human Nature* (Sussex, England: Harvester Press, 1983).

11. See, for example, Samuel Bowles and Herbert Gintis, *Schooling in Capitalist America* (New York: Basic Books, 1976); Martin Carnoy, *Education and Cultural Imperialism* (New York: McKay, 1974); Michael W. Apple, "Redefining Inequality: Authoritarian Populism and the Conservative Restoration," *Teachers College Record* 90 (1988): 167–84; and Philip Wexler, *Social Analysis and Education: After the New Sociology* (New York: Routledge & Kegan Paul, 1987).

12. David Roediger, *The Wages of Whiteness* (London: Verso, 1991), p. 6.

13. Michael Omi and Howard Winant, *Racial Formation in the United States from the 1960s to the 1990s*, 2nd ed. (New York: Routledge, 1994), p. 9.

14. Ibid., p. 56.

15. Carter G. Woodson, *The Mis-education of the Negro* (Washington, D.C.: Association Press, 1933); and W. E. B. Du Bois, *The Souls of Black Folk* (New York: Penguin Books, 1989; first published 1903).

16. Our decision to focus on Woodson and Du Bois in not intended to diminish the import of the scores of African-American scholars who also emerged during their time such as George E. Haynes, Charles S. Johnson, E. Franklin Frazier, Abram Harris, Sadie T. Alexander, Robert C. Weaver, Rayford Logan, Allison Davis, Dorothy Parker, and Benjamin Quarles. We highlight Woodson and Du Bois as early seminal thinkers about issues of race and racism.

17. See John Hope Franklin, *From Slavery to Freedom*, 6th ed. (New York: Alfred A. Knopf, 1988).

18. Woodson, *The Miseducation of the Negro*, p. xiii.

19. Du Bois, *The Souls of Black Folk*, p. 5. Other people of color, feminists, and gay and lesbian theorists all have appropriated Du Bois's notion of double consciousness to explain their estrangement from mainstream patriarchal, masculinist U.S. culture.

20. David Levering Lewis, *W. E. B. Du Bois: Biography of a Race, 1868–1919* (New York: Henry Holt, 1993), p. 281.

21. Du Bois, *The Souls of Black Folk*, p. 1.

22. See, for example, Lorene Cary, *Black Ice* (New York: Alfred A. Knopf); and Jeannie Oakes, *Keeping Track: How Schools Structure Inequality* (New Haven: Yale University Press, 1985).

23. Oakes, *Keeping Track*, p. 67.

24. American Association of University Women, *How Schools Shortchange Girls: A Study of Major Findings on Gender and Education* (Washington, D.C.: Author and National Education Association, 1992).

25. Myra Sadker, David Sadker, and Susan Klein, "The Issue of Gender in Elementary and Secondary Education," in *Review of Educational Research in Education*, vol. *19*, ed. G. Cerant (Washington, D.C.: American Educational Research Association, 1991), pp. 269–334.

26. Hacker, *Two Nations*, puts the dropout rate for African-American males in some large cities at close to 50 percent.

27. Robert Majors and Janet Billson, *Cool Pose: The Dilemmas of Black Manhood in America* (New York: Lexington Books, 1992).

28. Cornel West, *Race Matters* (Boston: Beacon Press, 1993); and David Lionel Smith, "Let Our People Go," *Black Scholar* 23 (1993): 75–76.

29. Peter Monaghan, "'Critical Race Theory' Questions the Role of Legal Doctrine in Racial Inequality," *Chronicle of Higher Education*, June 23, 1993, pp. A7, A9.

30. Delgado, cited in Monaghan, "Critical Race Theory." Quotations are from p. A7. For a more detailed explication of the first item in list, see Bell, *Faces at the Bottom of the Well*.

31. Manning Marable, *How Capitalism Underdeveloped Black America* (Boston: South End Press, 1983).

32. Derrick Bell, *And We Are Not Saved: The Elusive Quest for Racial Justice* (New York: Basic Books, 1987).

33. Howard Zinn, *A Peoples History of the United States* (New York: Harper & Row, 1980), p. 13.

34. Bell, *And We Are Not Saved*.

35. William Tate, Gloria Ladson-Billings, and Carl Grant, "The *Brown* Decision Revisited: Mathematizing Social Problems," *Educational Policy* 7 (1993): 255–75.

36. Bell, *And We Are Not Saved*, p. 239.

37. Ronald Takaki, *A Different Mirror: A History of Multicultural America* (Boston: Little Brown, 1993).

38. Franklin, *From Slavery to Freedom*.

39. Clearly, an analysis of worldwide tensions reinforces the importance of land to a people—Israel and the Palestinians, Iraq and Kuwait, the former Soviet bloc, Hitler and the Third Reich, all represent some of the struggles over land.

40. Even at a time when there is increased public sentiment for reducing the federal deficit, the one source of tax relief that no president or member of Congress would ever consider is that of denying home (property) owners their tax benefits.

41. See, for example, Howard Wainer, "Does Spending Money on Education Help?" *Educational Researcher* 22 (1993): 22–24; or Paul Houston, "School Vouchers: The Latest California Joke," *Phi Delta Kappan* 75 (1993): 61–66.

42. Kozol, *Savage Inequalities*, pp. 83–84.

43. This notion of "intellectual property" came into popular use when television talk show host David Letterman moved from NBC to CBS. NBC claimed that certain routines and jokes used by Letterman were the intellectual property of the network and, as such, could not be used by Letterman without permission.

44. Richard Delgado, "When a Story Is Just a Story: Does Voice Really Matter?" *Virginia Law Review* 76 (1990): 95–111.

45. See, for example, Floraline Stevens, *Opportunity to Learn: Issues of Equity for Poor and Minority Students* (Washington, D.C.: National Center for Education Statistics, 1993); idem, "Applying an Opportunity-to-learn Conceptual Framework to the Investigation of the Effects of Teaching Practices via Secondary Analyses of Multiple-case-study Summary Data," *The Journal of Negro Education* 62 (1993): 232–48; and Linda Winfield and Michael D. Woodard, "Assessment, Equity, Diversity in Reforming America's Schools," *Educational Policy* 8 (1994): 3–27.

46. The standards debate is too long and detailed to be discussed here. For a more detailed discussion of standards, see, for example, Michael W. Apple, "Do the Standards Go Far Enough? Power, Policy, and Practices in Mathematics Education," *Journal for Research in Mathematics Education* 23 (1992): 412–31; and National Council of Education Standards and Testing, *Raising Standards for American Education: A Report to Congress, the Secretary of Education, the National Goals Panel, and the American People* (Washington, D.C.: Government Printing Office, 1992).

47. Kozol, *Savage Inequalities*.

48. Some urban Catholic schools, black independent schools, and historically black colleges and universities have demonstrated the educability of African-American students. As of this writing we have no data on the success of urban districts such as Detroit or Milwaukee that are attempting what is termed "African Centered" or Africentric education. See also Mwalimu J. Shujaa, Ed., *Too Much Schooling, Too Little Education: A Paradox of Black Life in White Societies* (Trenton, N.J.: Africa World Press, 1994).

49. David Wellman, *Portraits of White Racism* (Cambridge, England: Cambridge University Press, 1977). Quotations are from pp. xviii and 42.

50. See, for example, Gary Orfield, "School Desegregation in the 1980s," *Equity and Choice*, February 1988, p. 25; Derrick Bell, "Learning from Our Losses: Is School Desegregation Still Feasible in the 1980s?," *Phi Delta Kappan* 64 (April 1983): 575; Willis D. Hawley, "Why It Is Hard to Believe in Desegregation," *Equity and Choice*, February 1988, pp. 9–15; and Janet Ward Schofield, *Black and White in School: Trust, Tension, or Tolerance?* (New York: Teachers College Press, 1989).

51. James Banks, "Teaching Multicultural Literacy to Teachers," *Teaching Education* 4 (1991): 135–44.

52. See Karl Taeuber, "Desegregation of Public School Districts: Persistence and Change," *Phi Delta Kappan* 72 (1990): 18–24; and H. G. Bissinger, "When Whites Flee," *New York Times Magazine*, May 29, 1994, pp. 26–33, 43, 50, 53–54, 56. On loss of professional positions, see Sabrina King, "The Limited Presence of African American Teachers," *Review of Educational Research* 63 (1993): 115–49; and Jacqueline Irvine, "An Analysis of the Problem of Disappearing Black Educators," *Elementary School Journal* 88 (1988): 503–13.

53. Kimberlé Williams Crenshaw, "Race, Reform, and Retrenchment: Transformation and Legitimation in Antidiscrimination Law," *Harvard Law Review* 101 (1988): 1331–87.

54. Ibid., p. 1335.

55. Kofi Lomotey and John Staley, "The Education of African Americans in Buffalo Public Schools" (Paper presented at the annual meeting of the American Educational Research Association, Boston, 1990).

56. Richard Delgado, "Storytelling for Opportunists and Others: A Plea for Narrative," *Michigan Law Review* 87 (1989): 2411–41.

57. See Richard Delgado et al., "Symposium: Legal Storytelling," *Michigan Law Review* 87 (1989): 2073. On dysconsciousness, see Joyce E. King, "Dysconscious Racism: Ideology, Identity and the Miseducation of Teachers," *Journal of Negro Education* 60 (1991): 135. King defines dysconsciousness as "an uncritical habit of mind (including perceptions, attitudes, assumptions, and beliefs) that justifies inequity and exploitation by accepting the existing order of things as given. . . . Dysconscious racism is a form of racism that tacitly accepts dominant White norms and privileges. It is not the *absence* of consciousness (that is, not unconsciousness) but an *impaired* consciousness or distorted way of thinking about race as compared to, for example, critical consciousness."

58. These notions of universalism prevail in much of social science research, including educational research.

59. Williams, *Alchemy of Race and Rights*.

60. Richard Delgado, "Brewer's Plea: Critical Thoughts on Common Cause," *Vanderbilt Law Review* 44 (1991): 11.

61. For example, see Williams, *Alchemy of Race and Rights*; Bell, *Faces at the Bottom of the Well*; and Mari Matsuda, "Public Response to Racist Speech: Considering the Victim's Story," *Michigan Law Review* 87 (1989): 2320–81.

62. Delgado, "Storytelling."

63. Ibid.

64. For example, see Crenshaw, "Race, Reform, and Retrenchment."

65. Delgado, "Storytelling."

66. Charles Lawrence, "The Id, the Ego, and Equal Protection: Reckoning with Unconscious Racism," *Stanford Law Review* 39 (1987): 317–88.

67. Delgado et al., "Symposium."

68. Lisa Delpit, "The Silenced Dialogue: Power and Pedagogy in Educating Other People's Children," *Harvard Educational Review* 58 (1988): 280.

69. At the 1994 annual meeting of the American Educational Research Association in New Orleans, two sessions entitled "Private Lives, Public Voices: Ethics of Research in Communities of Color" were convened to discuss the continued exploitation of people of color. According to one scholar of color, our communities have become "data plantations."

70. Cheryl I. Harris, "Whiteness as Property," *Harvard Law Review* 106 (1993): 1721.

71. See Margaret Radin, "Market-Inalienability," *Harvard Law Review* 100 (1987): 1849–906.

72. See Signithia Fordham and John Ogbu, "Black Student School Success: Coping with the Burden of 'Acting White,'" *The Urban Review* 18 (1986): 1–31.

73. Peggy McIntosh, "White Privilege: Unpacking the Invisible Knapsack." *Independent School*, Winter, 1990, pp. 31–36.

74. Laurie Fuller, "Whiteness as Performance" (Unpublished preliminary examination paper, University of Wisconsin–Madison, 1994).

75. Kozol, *Savage Inequalities*, p. 93.

76. Ibid., p. 96; emphasis added.

77. Harris, "Whiteness as Property," p. 1735.

78. David Spener, "Transitional Bilingual Education and the Socialization of Immigrants," *Harvard Educational Review* 58 (1988): 133–53.

79. H. G. Bissinger, "When Whites Flee," *New York Times Magazine*, May 29, 1994, pp. 26–33, 43, 50, 53–54, 56.

80. Derrick Bell, *Race, Racism, and American Law* (Boston: Little, Brown, 1980).

81. We assert that the current movement toward African-centered (or Africentric) schools is not equivalent to the racial exclusion of vouchers, or choice programs. Indeed, African-centeredness has become a logical response of a community to schools that have been abandoned by whites, have been stripped of material resources, and have demonstrated a lack of commitment to African-American academic achievement.

82. Oakes, *Keeping Track*.

83. James A. Banks, "Multicultural Education: Historical Development, Dimensions, and Practice," in *Review of Research in Education*, vol. 19, ed. L. Darling-Hammond (Washington, D.C.: American Educational Research Association, 1993). p. 3.

84. George Washington Williams, *History of the Negro Race in America from 1619–1880: Negroes as Slaves, as Soldiers, and as Citizens* (2 vols.) (New York: G. P. Putnam & Sons, 1882–1883). On the intergroup education movement, see, for example, L. A. Cook and E. Cook, *Intergroup Education* (New York: McGraw-Hill, 1954); and H. G. Traeger and M. R. Yarrow, *They Learn What They Live: Prejudice in Young Children* (New York: Harper and Brothers, 1952).

85. See, for example, Vincent Harding, *Beyond Chaos: Black History and the Search for a New Land* (Black Paper No. 2) (Atlanta: Institute of the Black World, August 1970); J. Blassingame, ed., *New Perspectives in Black Studies* (Urbana: University of Illinois Press, 1971); James A. Banks, ed., *Teaching Ethnic Studies* (Washington, D.C.: National Council for the Social Studies, 1973); and Geneva Gay, "Ethnic Minority Studies: How Widespread? How Successful?" *Educational Leadership* 29 (1971): 108–12.

86. Banks, "Multicultural Education."

87. In 1988 at Stanford University the inclusion of literature from women and people of color in the Western Civilization core course resulted in a heated debate. The university's faculty senate approved this inclusion in a course called Cultures, Ideas, and Values. The controversy was further heightened when then Secretary of Education William Bennett came to the campus to denounce this decision.

88. In the "Book Notes" section of the *Harvard Educational Review* 64 (1994): 345–47, Jane Davagian Tchaicha reviews Donaldo Macedo's *Literacies of Power* (Boulder: Westview Press, 1994) and includes two quotes, one from noted conservative Patrick Buchanan and another from Macedo on multiculturalism. According to Buchanan, "Our Judeo-Christian values are going to be preserved, and our Western heritage is going to be handed down to future generations, not dumped into some landfill called multiculturalism" (quoted in Tchaicha, p. 345). Macedo asserts that "the real issue isn't Western culture versus multiculturalism, the fundamental issue is the recognition of humanity in us and in others" (quoted in Tchaicha, p. 347).

89. In New York City, controversy over the inclusion of gay and lesbian is-sues in the curriculum caused vitriolic debate among racial and ethnic groups who opposed their issues being linked to or compared with homosexuals. Some ethnic group members asserted that homosexuals were not a "culture" while gay and lesbi-an spokespeople argued that these group members were homophobic.

90. Shirley Torres-Medina, "Issues of Power: Constructing the Meaning of Lin-guistic Difference in First Grade Classrooms" (Ph.D. diss. University of Wisconsin–Madison, 1994).

91. Richard Delgado, "Enormous Anomaly? Left-Right Parallels in Recent Writing about Race," *Columbia Law Review* 91 (1991): 1547–60.

92. See Bell, *And We Are Not Saved.*

93. See Cameron McCarthy, "After the Canon: Knowledge and Ideological Representation in the Multicultural Discourse on Curriculum Reform," in *Race, Identity and Representation*, ed. C. McCarthy and W. Crichlow (New York: Rout-ledge, 1994), p. 290; and Michael Olneck, "Terms of Inclusion: Has Multicultur-alism Redefined Equality in American Education?" *American Journal of Education* 101 (1993): 234–60.

94. We are particularly cognizant of the hard-fought battles in the academy waged and won by scholars such as James Banks, Carlos Cortez, Geneva Gay, Carl Gram, and others.

95. Tony Marlin, *Race First: The Ideological and Organizational Struggles of Marcus Garvey and the Universal Negro Improvement Association* (Dover, Mass.: The Majority Press, 1976).

96. Marcus Garvey, cited in ibid., p. 22.

CHAPTER 2

Critical Race Theory—
What It Is Not!

THE BEGINNING OF CRT IN EDUCATION

In the summer of 1993, William F. Tate and I submitted a proposal for the 1994 annual meeting of the American Educational Research Association (AERA). AERA was soliciting new forms of presentation so we selected a different format—the advanced paper session. This format called for prospective attendees to write authors in advance for their papers so that these sessions would be in-depth discussions of papers all the session attendees had previously read. Unfortunately, no one wrote for a copy of our paper, and Tate and I believed no one would show up to our session. It turned out that we were wrong. The session, bearing the title of the paper, "Toward a Critical Race Theory of Education" (TCRTE), was standing room only, and we had to discuss its substance with a group who were unfamiliar with the paper.

During the question and answer section of the presentation it was clear that some of the attendees were hostile to this new theoretical perspective. Surprisingly, the hostility came from some scholars who were typically allies—scholars whose work focused on multiculturalism and diversity. Apparently, our focus on race as a primary tenet of inequality violated the sacred rule of maintaining the race, class, and gender triumvirate. The "friendly fire" we received as a result of making race the axis of understanding inequity and injustice in the US spurred us to write what became the first article on CRT in education (Ladson-Billings & Tate, 1995).

While I have described the "public" introduction of CRT in education, it is important to include the less public foundational moves that made that first publication possible. Sometime in early 1992 William Tate shared a *Harvard Law Review* article by Professor Kimberlé Crenshaw (1988), "Race, Reform and Retrenchment: Transformation and Legitimation in Antidiscrimination Law." That article transformed how I thought about civil rights and race. Rather than accept the slow and incremental progress of traditional civil rights legislative and judicial processes or the notion that race was "just another variable," Crenshaw's article challenged my thinking and pushed me intellectually in new and important ways. To be sure, I had previously read Derrick Bell's *And We Are Not Saved: The Elusive Quest for Racial Justice* (1989), but I did not connect Bell's use of literary imagination with what was becoming an important movement in legal studies.

Reading the Crenshaw article forced Tate and me into the law library, where we found an entire group of scholars working in this tradition. Of course it was a wonderful irony that we were working at the University of Wisconsin-Madison, the place where the movement started. Both Professors Patricia Williams and Linda Greene were on our law school faculty, which gave us a bit of an advantage despite our outsider status as nonlegal scholars. Williams's book *The Alchemy of Race and Rights: Diary of a Law Professor* (1991) was another entry way into this new legal genre. Professor Greene pointed us to a variety of other scholars— Richard Delgado, Mari Matsuda, Charles Lawrence III, Neil Gotanda, Gary Peller, and Cheryl Harris, to name a few. The first thing we learned as we began this quest was just how much we did not know. Our challenge was not merely the density of legal writing but our ignorance about the precedents upon which many of the arguments rested. Thus, our work was not merely reading these scholars; it was reading them in relation to the legal cases they were citing.

After extensive reading Tate and I wrote a draft of a paper that tried to both explain CRT and describe its relevance and application to education. Tate and I had worked together on an earlier paper, "The Brown Decision Revisited: Mathematizing Social Problems" (Tate et al., 1993), where we tried to examine the way the *Brown* decision proposed a mathematical solution to a problem that was much more complex than mere numbers. In the midst of writing this paper Tate and I realized our perspectives about race were converging and moving away from that of other "diversity" scholars.[1] Because we knew we were undertaking what would be a radical departure from traditional work on inequity we thought it best to "test out" our work in our own department. Fortunately, we worked at a place where colleagues were eager to hear each other's ideas, and we distributed the paper widely throughout the department to colleagues and graduate students alike. We then convened a colloquium on a Friday afternoon.[2] We presented our main argument and then opened it up for questions. Those questions came fast and furious. What was surprising was that they were not hostile. People were genuinely trying to understand what our analysis meant for the future of educational disparities. Were we saying that the inequities were intractable? Yes, we were. Were we saying that the civil rights movement was a failed project? To some extent it was. Were we saying that racism would endure? Indeed we were.

Given the pessimism of our argument our colleagues pushed us to provide more evidence and to at least present people with a way to reconcile the belief in progress towards greater equality and the racial realism that we were promoting. No one said we had a flawed argument. Instead, people were worried that our argument might be so jolting that others would reject it out of hand. Over the next few weeks colleagues gave us scribbled notes on their copies of the manuscript to consider so that we might offer a tighter thesis—whether they agreed with us or not. I found that support some of the most helpful I have ever received in the academy. Even though people did not wholeheartedly agree, they were at least willing to provide good questions that forced us to bolster our position.

So, by the time we arrived at the AERA session, we felt as though we had already been through a rigorous vetting. The questions raised at that session were no tougher than what we had already endured. What was different about the AERA session was the hostility that we felt from supposed friends and allies. I suggested to Tate at the end of the session that we get the paper out for publication as soon as possible—before the detractors began to publish pieces against ours. We wanted a journal outlet that had a wide readership and good standing in the field. We decided on *Teachers College Record* and were pleased that the editor saw it as a promising article. With some minor edits the editor accepted the article for publication. To date that article has had over 1,000 citations and has been reprinted in several other volumes. Within a few years of publication of TCRTE a number of other CRT in education articles and book chapters began to appear. Tate (1997) published a comprehensive overview of the field and its major proponents that became an important baseline document for understanding the terrain of CRT in education. The following year I (Ladson-Billings, 1998) published an article that attempted to dissuade education researchers from delving into CRT without adequate grounding in the field. During this time Derrick Bell, Kimberlé Crenshaw, and Richard Delgado made visits to the University of Wisconsin-Madison and we had opportunities to sit and talk with them about our project. Bell also urged caution. Crenshaw encouraged us to keep reading in the field and keep spreading the word. Delgado was especially excited to hear about the work and was interested in possible collaborations. He was fearful that CRT might not go any farther in law and saw education as a logical extension of the work. In fact, Delgado developed an interest in publishing a CRT volume that would be accessible to high school students.

At about this same time Solorzano (1997) began publishing on CRT and building the project at UCLA. Since Kimberlé Crenshaw had two positions—one at Columbia Law School in the fall and another at UCLA Law School in the spring—the CRT project naturally spread from the early summer workshops at the University of Wisconsin-Madison to both coasts. Also, Solorzano had access to Neil Gotanda and Gary Peller at UCLA. Later Parker et al. (1999) began engaging the methodologies that CRT recruited to illuminate and illustrate its case. Afterwards, Lynn (1999), Taylor (1999), Solorzano and Yosso (2001), and Delgado Bernal (2002) were among the scholars who contributed to this literature.

The previously cited works laid the foundation for critical race theory in education. The field was in its infancy and like any new movement it was attracting many young scholars who were looking for new ways to think about their work and new methodologies for race scholarship. However, we must be clear that just because a scholar looks at race in her work it does not make her a critical race theorist. In "Through a Glass Darkly: The Persistence of Race in Education Research and Scholarship" (Ladson-Billings, 2012), I argued that all of the social sciences were infused with conceptions of race and racist notions, and since education draws heavily from the social sciences those views of race find their way into education scholarship and research. For example, most scholars of gifted and talented education do not focus on the fact that much of the field is built on the eugenicist perspectives of Lewis Terman (1925–59). Clearly, these scholars do not consider themselves race scholars, let alone critical race scholars.

Many scholars study disproportionality in special education designations, expulsion, and suspension but they would not call themselves critical race scholars. Scholars such as Skiba and Rausch (2006) carefully document issues of unequal disciplinary procedures and school exclusion. Although they document differential treatment based on race, these scholars would not call themselves critical race theorists. They use quantitative data to demonstrate the adverse impact of school rules and policies on African American and Latina/o students. The point is that writing about race and racial issues does not necessarily make one a critical race theorist. Those who are CRT scholars subscribe to a number of tenets that Delgado and Stefancic (2001) identify as hallmarks of CRT:

- belief that racism is normal or ordinary, not aberrant, in US society;
- interest convergence or material determinism;
- race as a social construction;
- intersectionality and anti-essentialism;
- voice or counter-narrative.

RACISM AS NORMAL

What do critical race theorists believe? . . . First, that racism is ordinary, not aberrational—"normal science," the usual way society does business, the common, everyday experience of most people of color in this country.

(Delgado & Stefancic, 2001, pp. 6–7)

The first tenet of CRT is the notion that racism is not some random, isolated act of individuals behaving badly. Rather, to a CRT scholar racism is the normal order of things in US society. This is the thing that distinguishes

CRT scholars from others who investigate race. Some focus on specific instances of racism or might admit to institutional racism. However, few outside of CRT would declare that racism is normal. Most argue that racism resides in individual (and sometimes corporate) beliefs and behaviors regarding the inferiority of people of another race. According to Delgado and Stefancic (2001), CRT scholars believe that racism "is the usual way society does business, the common, everyday experience of most people of color in this country" (p. 7).

In 1944 Swedish Nobel prize-winning social scientist Gunnar Myrdal concluded that racism was simply the failure of liberal democratic practices to align with liberal democratic theory. This concept was what Hochschild (1984) termed an "anomaly thesis," i.e., "race discrimination is a terrible and inexplicable anomaly stuck in the middle of our liberal democratic ethos" (p. 3). For more than two generations civil rights advocates and social scientists subscribed to this notion. Hochschild further opines that racism's ongoing presence long beyond slavery, Reconstruction, two world wars, and the landmark *Brown v. Board of Education* case (1954) "is not simply an excrescence on a fundamentally healthy liberal democratic body but is a part of what shapes and energizes the body" (p. 5). Further, Hochschild argues, "liberal democracy and racism in the United States are historically, even inherently, reinforcing; American society as we know it exists only because of its foundation in racially based slavery, and it thrives only because racial discrimination continues" (p. 5). Instead of Myrdal's "anomaly thesis" Hochschild says that this is a "symbiosis thesis." In a nutshell, this difference between anomaly and symbiosis forms the basis of the difference between most race theory and critical race theory.

INTEREST CONVERGENCE

Most racial remedies, however, when measured by their actual potential, will prove of more symbolic than substantive value to blacks.

(Bell, 1992, p. 646)

The late Professor Derrick A. Bell is considered the "Father of Critical Race Theory," perhaps because of his prolific writing on the topic, his instrumental role in educating many cohorts of law scholars who fostered the movement, and the principles by which he lived his life and his career.[3] One of Bell's theoretical propositions that accompany CRT is interest convergence. According to Bell (1980), White people will seek racial justice only to the extent that there is something in it for them. In other words, interest convergence is about alignment, not altruism. We cannot expect those who control the society to make altruistic or benevolent moves toward racial justice. Instead, civil rights activists must look for ways to align the interests of the dominant group with those of racially oppressed and marginalized groups.

A policy example of interest convergence came about when President John F. Kennedy issued Executive Order 10925 in March 1961 that included a provision that government contractors "take affirmative action to ensure that applicants are employed, and employees are treated during employment, without regard to their race, creed, color, or national origin." The intent of the order was to affirm the government's commitment to equal opportunity. Four years later, President Lyndon Johnson issued Executive Order 11246 prohibiting discrimination based on race, color, religion, and national origin by those organizations receiving federal contracts and subcontracts. However, in 1967 Johnson amended the order to include sex. That one move changed affirmative action from a racial justice policy to an interest convergence whose major beneficiaries are White women (and by extension other Whites—men, women, and children).

A second example of interest convergence occurred when former Arizona Governor Evan Meacham cancelled the state's Martin Luther King, Jr. Holiday. According to Meacham, the state could not afford another paid holiday and Dr. King was undeserving of a holiday. This move caused the cancellation of 45 conventions, with an estimated loss of $25 million. The most high-profile cancellation was the National Basketball Association's All Star Game. The reversal of the MLK Holiday decision was not a result of a change of heart on the part of Governor Meacham but rather a need to align the state's economic interests with the hope and symbolism the holiday represented for African Americans (Gross, 1993).

RACE AS A SOCIAL CONSTRUCTION

Race has been a constitutive element, an organizational principle, a "praxis" and structure that has constructed and reconstructed world society since the emergence of modernity, the enormous historical shift represented by the rise of Europe, the founding of modern nation-states and empires, the "conquista," the onset of African slavery, and the subjugation of much of Asia.

(Winant, 2001, p. 19)

Biologists, geneticists, anthropologists, and sociologists all agree that race is not a scientific reality. Despite what we perceive as phenotypic differences, the scrutiny of a microscope or the sequencing of genes reveals no perceptible differences between what we call races. As members of the same species, human beings are biologically quite similar. Just as a tabby cat and a calico cat are the same species with the ability to reproduce within their species so it is with humans. However, humans have constructed social categories and organization that rely heavily on arbitrary genetic differences like skin color, hair texture, eye shape, and lip size. They have used these differences as a mechanism for creating hierarchy and an ideology of White supremacy.

Smedley (1993) points out that there is a deep paradox between the scientific notion of "no-race" and the "social parameters of race by which we conduct our lives and structure our institutions" (p. 19). Thus, while critical race theorists accept the scientific understanding of no-race or no genetic difference, we also accept the power of a social reality that allows for significant disparities in the life chances of people based on the categorical understanding of race.

One of the most interesting instances of race as a social construction is that of President Barack Obama. During the 2008 presidential campaign, candidate Obama was regularly confronted by the notion that he was not "Black enough." Born of a "White" mother and a "Black" Kenyan father, many considered the circumstances of Barak Obama's upbringing so far outside of the experiences of most African Americans that he could not possibly be "really" Black. Some questioned his legitimacy to be president, presumably based on Article II Section I of the United States Constitution that states the office can only be held by a natural born citizen of at least 35 years of age who has lived in the country at least 14 years prior to election. There was no question about Barak Obama's age or length of residence but he was constantly dogged by the allegation that he was not born in the US. Interestingly, his opponent, Senator John McCain, was born in the Panama Canal Zone, yet no one ever questioned his legitimacy to be president. While we insist that race no longer matters in our society, President Obama's entire presidency has been suffused in race—even when he has worked hard to steer clear of race and race related issues in policy making and governing.

INTERSECTIONALITY AND ANTI-ESSENTIALISM

As CRT developed, scholars began to see "race" itself as the product of other social forces—for example as the product of heteropatriarchy in a post-industrial, post-colonial, capitalist society—or as in the United States, in a Euro-American heteropatriarchy.

(Valdes et al., 2002, p. 2)

According to Delgado & Stefancic, "Intersectionality means the examination of race, sex, class, national origin, and sexual orientation and how their combinations play out in various settings" (2001, p. 51). Because our society is organized along binaries, intersectionality is a difficult concept to research. We see things as black or white, east or west, rich or poor, right or left. When we move into the complexities of real life we recognize that we each represent multiple identities—race, class, gender, sexuality, ability, religion, and many more. We perform our identities in myriad ways and can never be certain to which of those identities others react. However, since race has been such a flashpoint in this society we almost always believe that our challenges stem solely from racial injustice. Imagine the following scenario:

> A Black woman walks into a luxury car dealer. She has just come from a stren-uous workout and is sweating in an old pair of sweat pants and a ratty T-shirt. She is not wearing makeup and her hair is pulled back in a ponytail. She does not look like a "typical" luxury car buyer.
>
> During her time in the showroom she notices that the salespeople introduce themselves to everyone but her. She has stood by a high-end model for at least 10 minutes but no salesperson has asked the customary "Can I answer any questions about this car for you?" Instead she is starting to feel invisible. Car salespeople are talking to everyone else in the showroom, including those who have arrived after she did. What seems to be the problem?

Because of the way race structures our everyday life experiences it is reasonable for most people to believe that the reason the woman is not re-ceiving any attention is her race. However, one might also argue that her less than professional appearance might make class the reason the salespeople are ignoring her. Perhaps the obvious class markers—dress, hair, and overall appearance—make her an unlikely candidate for a sale. Thus, class not race may be operating here. Or, since our society continues to maintain sexual asymmetry, perhaps the woman's gender has closed her off from receiving serious consideration as a luxury car buyer. However, CRT scholars are urged to look at the way all three identity/status categories may be operating simultaneously.

That same showroom might have been more welcoming had the wom-an arrived in high-end clothing and a nicely coiffed hairdo. It might have been more welcoming if the person in those same workout clothes were a man. We do not know which individual or combination of identity catego-ries is at work here. Rather than attempting to simplify and strip down to a single explanation, CRT scholarship is willing to engage in the "messiness" of real life.

Because of increasing globalization we should expect to see even more complexities. We see people we categorize as Black who speak what we perceive as European languages (e.g. French, Spanish, Portuguese, etc.). Or we try to neatly categorize who is Muslim or Jewish or Christian only to learn that people cross many traditional boundaries and align themselves in different groups and categories. CRT scholars recognize that the neatness was always artificial and arbitrary. If someone is gay or lesbian, is his or her racial identity thrown into question? Is race or sex privileged? Are these identities ever in conflict? These questions are a part of the work of CRT scholarship.

> Do all oppressed people have the same thing in common?
>
> (Delgado & Stefancic, 2001, p. 56)

The other side of intersectionality is essentialism. Critical race theory scholarship decries essentialism. Essentialism is a belief that all people perceived to be in a single group think, act, and believe the same things in the same ways. Such thinking leads to considerable misunderstanding and stereotyping. On the one hand there is the need for people to participate in group solidarity for social, cultural, and political purposes (Guinier & Torres, 2003). Thus, to identify as African American or a woman or an immigrant can be useful as a way to organize and garner political clout and social benefits. However, on the other hand, people do not relinquish their individual rights, perspectives, and lifestyles because they share group identities.

Recently, a well-known historically Black college/university declared that male students entering its business school would not be permitted to wear their hair in dreadlocks (Davis, 2012). This declaration sparked a lively debate among African Americans on social networking sites like Facebook and Twitter. Some agreed with the business school dean. Others vehemently opposed the decision. Still others offered mixed opinions that suggested the school was trying to protect its students from the harsh realities of a mainstream, corporate workplace and what it takes to "get ahead." There was not a "Black" position on this issue.

During the days after the O.J. Simpson trial verdict, when the former football star, sports commentator, and actor was acquitted of murdering his ex-wife and her male friend, tensions were high in many communities. The talk show hosts on both television and radio were discussing O.J. non-stop. The day the verdict was announced I was teaching a class of pre-service teachers. Our room did not have a television monitor so I took a portable radio to class, plugged in my earphone, and when the verdict was announced repeated it verbatim to the class. No sooner had I shared the verdict than a young White student sitting in the front row of the class began to cry. What about this murder—given the thousands of murders that occur in the US every year—made it personal to my student?

At the same moment one of our graduates (who happens to be White) was collecting data for her dissertation at a historically Black college/university. When the verdict was announced the students gathered around the student union big screen television jumped up in a triumphant shout when the announcement came. What was it about this verdict—given the thousands of court trials in the US—that had the Black students assembled in solidarity to receive it?

After a few days when it seemed that all people could talk about was the O.J. Simpson verdict, a White colleague stopped me in the corridor and asked, "So, Gloria, what *do* Black people think about the O.J. Simpson verdict?" For once I had what I think was the correct response. I smiled slowly and replied, "I don't know. What do *White* people think about it?" At that moment my colleague realized just how ridiculous the question was. There was no uniform "White" response to the verdict, and there certainly was no uniform "Black" response. The amount of within-group differences for any racial or ethnic group are greater that the between-group differences. CRT scholars guard against essentializing the perspectives and experiences of racial groups.

VOICE OR COUNTER-NARRATIVE

In the mid-sixties, Archie Shepp took his "fundamentally critical" tenor saxophone and stepped outside of the commercially laden mainstream's musical community of assumption and voiced his dissent beyond the ways it would be tolerated within the constraints of conventional jazz. Twenty-five years or so later, some legal scholars of color . . . are voicing . . . dissent from many of the law's underlying assumptions.

(Calmore, 1995)

Storytelling is one of the oldest human art forms. Ancient cultures maintained their histories and cultural sense of self through the stories they told and retold. Stories or narratives have been shared in every culture as a means of entertainment, education, and cultural preservation and to instill moral values. The very discipline we call history is about the cultural narrative that cultures, nations, and societies tell, particularly about themselves. The African proverb says, "Until lions have their historians, tales of the hunt shall always glorify the hunter." It captures the ethnocentric and hegemonic way stories can and do operate. Stories reflect a perspective or point of view and underscore what the teller, audience, society, and/or those in power believe to be important, significant, and many times valorizing and ethnocentric.

For example, many German school students went through school learning nothing about the Third Reich and Adolf Hitler's "final solution" to rid Germany (and indeed Europe) of Jews and others he deemed undesirable.

The story Germans hoped to tell about themselves focused more on their post-war achievements in arts, culture, innovation, and economic prosperity. Similarly, some West African nations tell an official story in their school textbooks that omits any acknowledgement of the transatlantic slave trade and its devastating impact on the development of the continent. The issue of embellishing or valorizing one's history and/or culture is common. However, the acceptance of that presentation as "truth" and "universal" can be deeply problematic (Ladson-Billings, 2000). When one group describes its worldview or story as "real history," "truth," or "objective science" and others' worldviews as myth, legend, and lore we validate one narrative while simultaneously invalidating the other.

In American jurisprudence opposing lawyers allegedly have the same evidence from which to construct a narrative—a story to tell a judge and/or jury. Both sides claim to be telling the "truth." Despite what story is presented to the public, the "counter-story" is a contrasting story that describes the story from a different vantage point. The ability to tell that story is important not just as a defense strategy but also as a way to unmoor people from received truths so that they might consider alternatives.

At the end of apartheid in South Africa it became important to construct "Truth and Reconciliation" panels for those who had been harmed by a brutal system of separation and oppression (Theissen, 1999). The painful experience had to be articulated by victims and acknowledged by perpetrators. The storytelling of the victims represented a series of counter-stories to the narrative the country had told itself and others for years. Telling the stories was both therapeutic and cathartic. It became one of the ways the new nation could reconstitute itself and move ahead. Unfortunately, the US tends to devalue the role of storytelling in social science. A story represents an instance and does not include enough "empirical" data points or a large enough sample to conform to Western science notions of "truth."

Critical race theorists use storytelling as a way to illustrate and underscore broad legal principles regarding race and racial/social justice. The point of storytelling is not to vent or rant or be an exhibitionist regarding one's own racial struggle. Unfortunately, far too many would-be critical race theorists in education use the narrative or counter-story in just that way. There is little or no principled argument to be made. The writer is mad because of an affront and the pen becomes a retaliatory weapon. The story does not advance larger concerns or help us understand how law or policy is operating.

Derrick Bell's "The Chronicle of the DeVine Gift" (1999) is an example of how a counter-story can be written that has personal reference but broader social justice meaning. In this chronicle Bell's alter ego, Geneva Crenshaw, is frustrated about the amount of work she has as the only African American law professor in a prestigious law school. This is exactly the situation in which Bell found himself at Harvard. But rather than rant about being overburdened he constructs a story or chronicle about what life might be like if a mysterious donor continued to steer high-quality candidates of color to the law school. Bell's chronicle suggests that a high-profile predominately White law school would reach a "tipping point" if "too many" candidates of color were hired.

Bell's story starts with his experience but quickly branches off into a speculative tale that points out the disingenuous way predominately White institutions that claim to be seeking to "diversify" their faculty and staff actually have no real intention of achieving true diversity, even when candidates of color are meritorious.

In another chronicle Bell (1989) describes what he calls "The Black crime cure," where a group of young Black men discover a magic pill that changes them from petty street criminals to outstanding citizens. They no longer do drugs, rob and steal, cut school, or participate in gang activity. They become model citizens as long as they keep taking the pills. Unfortunately law enforcement has less work to do—the gang task force is no longer needed, the drug enforcement task force has no purpose, and the nightly patrols in Black communities yield no suspects. At first, the larger community is delighted, but soon people begin to realize how lucrative crime is for the rest of the society. Now they must lay off police officers and prison guards. The security firms sell fewer security devices and need to cut back their work forces. The alternative schools and juvenile detention centers are without youth. The town's entire economy was based on the by-products of crime. To return things to their previous state, the police follow the Black youth to a cave outside of town and discover the source of the magic pills. After the youth leave, the police raid the cave, confiscate all the remaining pills, and blow up the site.

Again, Bell is not telling a story about himself. Instead he is exposing the ways that Black crime serves the interests of Whites. First, Black crime is rarely perpetuated on Whites, i.e., the victims of most Black crime are Black. Second, Black crime creates work opportunities for Whites—police officers, probation officers, prison construction firms, prison guards, lawyers, judges, and court workers all benefit from high rates of crime. The point of the chronicle is to get readers to consider Black crime from a very different perspective beyond the notion of pathological Black people to the economic benefits the "so-called pathology" provides for the White middle class.

In an attempt to develop chronicles and counter-stories that were more expansive and linked to broader educational policy issues I tried to write a chronicle that explained the way current education reform efforts were designed to subvert real reform in urban communities (Ladson-Billings, 2007). In this chronicle, which I titled "The Case of the Sacrificed Black Children—Part 2," I used Bell's (1989) earlier story about school desegregation ("The Case of the Sacrificed Black Children") to discuss how modern attempts at urban renewal made schools their centerpiece. Here draconian testing regimes and severe promotion and retention policies that everyone knew were designed to fail were a proxy for displacing urban families in order to provide corporate interests greater access to prime land and tax deductions in the form of TIFs (tax incremental financing). I tell this story not as a personal story but rather as a broader motif for explaining what citizens in urban areas across the nation were experiencing in the neighborhoods and schools, especially Black and Brown citizens.

Similarly, in a chapter in the book William Tate and I edited (Ladson-Billings, 2006) I wrote a story that predicted how the rebuilding in post-Katrina New Orleans would occur. When I shared the story in one audience one person said I was a "prophet." I was quick to correct him. There was nothing prophetic about what I was saying. I was merely articulating what was predictable, since it had happened so many times before. The chronicle did come to pass. Redevelopment in New Orleans emphasized middle and upper income residents, and poor people have been left to fend for themselves. The primary point here is that the chronicle or counter-story is about racial justice principles, not personal affront.

CODA

This chapter attempts to address central tenets of CRT that education scholars who want to work in this area must adhere to if they want to be true to the concepts developed by CRT innovators. I set out to write this chapter not merely to chastise scholars who have grabbed hold of CRT as a "sexy," "trendy," "new" thing that absolves them of the responsibility to do quality work. The point is not to have a rant or to claim that racial "navel gazing" is any more substantive than Eurocentric, positivist, functionalist navel gazing is. CRT scholars cannot rail against the failure of positivist research to be objective or neutral when our own scholarship is so specific to our personal concerns that it fails to help us grasp important principles of racial justice. To illustrate my concern, I end this chapter with what might be called a CRT "anti-chronicle."

A Game of Spades . . . or, "Are You Really Going to Play that Card?"

Khalia Winston sat in her office and placed her feet comfortably on her desk. She could hardly believe it. She had landed a tenure track position at a research-intensive university. She would teach one course each of the first two semesters, and receive two months of summer support, a graduate assistant, and a $25,000 research grant as a part of her start-up package. Her salary was about $5,500 higher than the other two new hires in her department. Her research focused on race and its impact on teacher education.

In her first few months Khalia learned her way around the
university. She taught her graduate course and received good
feedback from the graduate students who were looking for faculty
members whose primary focus was on race. Her faculty mentor told
her that, although she'd done excellent work on her dissertation,
at this university she would have to develop a new data set with
which to pursue her line of inquiry. When the internal research funds
competition came around Khalia did not get her proposal completed
in time and could not receive campus research funds. Undaunted,
Khalia continued working on her proposal and submitted it for an
external grant. Unfortunately, it was not selected for funding.

As the years passed Khalia continued to have success with
her graduate courses. She was popular among graduate students,
particularly graduate students of color. Her undergraduate courses
were a different story. The undergrads thought she was too strident
and left them guilt-ridden about their privilege and lack of exposure
to other cultures. Every semester her teaching evaluations were
bifurcated: high graduate course evals and low undergrad evals.
Swinging back and forth between these two poles, Khalia became
stressed out and struggled to focus on her writing.

Because she was one of two Black faculty members in her school,
Khalia was regularly called on to serve as a speaker or facilitator
for professional development throughout the community. Although
she enjoyed this attention she felt the need to get away from campus
and started going to conferences in big cities that dealt specifically
with race, diversity, and Black issues. A few times she had a paper
to present, but rarely did she turn the papers into manuscripts for
publication. When the time for her third-year review rolled around
Khalia had published only one book review and a short opinion piece
for an obscure newspaper. Her review chair informed her that things
were not looking good and he could not guarantee a vote for renewal.

At this point Khalia grew quite angry and started working on
a "manuscript" about her experience as a "Black" scholar in a
"White" institution. Throughout the manuscript Khalia castigated
her undergraduate students, colleagues who didn't "help" her, the
"unreasonable" demands on her time, and the failure of her chair to
provide her with accurate information about what she needed to do
to earn tenure. She submitted her manuscript without sharing it with
any senior scholars for feedback. When she received a "reject" letter
from the editors that included detailed reviews of the limitations of
her work she declared that all of academe was "racist" and it was
"impossible" for Black scholars to get their work published.

In a tearful conversation with the only senior Black colleague in
her department Khalia grew angrier as he asked her some pointed

questions—"How many original manuscripts did you write and get out the door?" "What did you do about the poor teaching evaluations?" "What did you do to protect your time for writing and research?" "How many of your conference papers are in good enough shape to be turned into manuscripts?"

Khalia's eyes burned with anger and the corners of her mouth turned into a snarl. "Oh, you too, huh?" she snapped.

"Me too, what?" her senior colleague asked.

"You're just as whitewashed as the rest of them. You ain't nothin' but a sell-out!" she barked as she rose to leave.

"Now you just wait a minute, young lady," her colleague's baritone voice reverberated throughout the office. Khalia stopped in her tracks. "One of the reasons you got this job is that I put my credibility on the line. It's not that you didn't have solid credentials, but they had a White candidate with an equally stellar resume. When she gave her job talk she knocked it out of the park. Your talk was mediocre at best, but I reminded my colleagues that few people give good 'job talks.' I convinced them to look carefully at your whole body of work and the 'promise' it offered. I lobbied to get you a higher salary because indeed you had 'rare bird status'—an African American woman graduate of a prestigious graduate program. But from the moment you arrived you dismissed any advice I gave you. You insisted that you knew what you were doing. When I cautioned you about going to too many conferences you insisted that you needed to get away from all of this "Whiteness." When I said you should at least turn your conference papers into publishable manuscripts you said you'd do it but you did not. When I advised you to try to work with your undergraduates and meet them where they were you dismissed me. Now I understand you're writing what amounts to a rant—and, yes, I know a lot of editors who share things with me—and you want to suggest that I'm the sell-out? No, honey, you don't get to use that card with me!"

This brief "chronicle" is a composite of instances I have heard throughout the country. The work of the critical race scholar must be as rigorous as that of any other scholarship (or perhaps more so). We have an obligation to point out the endemic racism that is extant in our schools, colleges, and other public spaces. We must deconstruct laws, ordinances, and policies that work to re-inscribe racism and deny people their full rights. And we must be careful to guard this movement that is entering its "academic adolescence." We must be willing to say what critical race theory is not.

NOTES

1. I am using the term "diversity scholars" to describe a number of scholars whose research takes a more inclusive approach (i.e. class, gender, race, ability, linguistic, etc. differences). This is not a critique of such scholarship, but I do distinguish it from the more race-focused approach Tate and I began undertaking in this work.

2. I must confess we called it on a Friday afternoon presuming few people would come. To our surprise the room was packed.

3. See Bell (2003).

REFERENCES

Bell, D. (1980). Brown v. Board of Education and the interest-convergence dilemma. *Harvard Law Review, 93*, 513.

Bell, D. (1989). *And we are not saved: The elusive quest for racial justice.* New York: Basic Books.

Bell, D. (1992). *Race and racism in American law.* New York: Aspen Law and Business.

Bell, D. (1999). The civil rights chronicles: The chronicle of the DeVine Gift. In R. Delgado & J. Stefancic (Eds.), *Critical race theory: The cutting edge* (2nd ed., pp. 468–478). Philadelphia, PA: Temple University Press.

Bell, D. (2003). *Ethical Ambition: Living a Life of Meaning and Worth.* New York: Bloomsbury Press.

Brown v. Board of Education, 347 U.S. 483, 492 (1954).

Calmore, J. (1995). Critical race theory, Archie Shepp, and fire music: Securing an authentic intellectual life in a multicultural world. In K. Crenshaw, N. Gotanda, G. Peller, & K. Thomas (Eds.), *Critical race theory: The key writings that formed the movement* (pp. 315–329). New York: New Press.

Crenshaw, K. (1988). Race, reform, and retrenchment: Transformation and legitimation in antidiscrimination law. *Harvard Law Review, 101*(7), 1331–1387.

Davis, K. (2012). Hampton Univ. students question continued ban on dreadlocks, cornrows in MBA program. *Afro American,* August 25 (retrieved August 26, 2012 from http://www.afro.com/sections/news/afro_briefs/story.htm?storyid=75974).

Delgado, R., & Stefancic, J. (2001). *Critical race theory: An introduction.* New York: NYU Press.

Delgado Bernal, D. (2002). Critical race theory, LatCrit theory and critical race gendered epistemologies: Recognizing students of color as holders and creators of knowledge. *Qualitative Inquiry, 8*(1), 105–126.

Gross, J. (1993). Arizona hopes holiday for King will mend its image. *New York Times,* January 17, p. 16.

Guinier, L., & Torres, G. (2003). *The miner's canary: Enlisting race, resisting power, transforming democracy.* Cambridge, MA: Harvard University Press.

Hochschild, I. J. (1984). *The New American dilemma: Liberal democracy and school desegregation.* New Haven, CT: Yale University Press.

Ladson-Billings, G. (1998). Just what is critical race theory and what's it doing in a *nice* field like education? *International Journal of Qualitative Studies in Education, 11*(1), 7–24.

Ladson-Billings, G. (2000). Racialized discourses and ethnic epistemologies. In N. Denzin & Y. Lincoln (Eds.), *Handbook of qualitative research* (2nd ed., pp. 257–277). Thousand Oaks, CA: Sage.

Ladson-Billings, G. (2006). Introduction. In G. Ladson-Billings & W. F. Tate (Eds.), *Education research in the public interest: Social justice, action, and policy* (pp. 1–13). New York: Teachers College Press.

Ladson-Billings, G. (2007). Can we at least have Plessy? The struggle for quality education. *North Carolina Law Review, 85,* 1279–1292.

Ladson-Billings, G. (2012). Through a glass darkly: The persistence of race in education research and scholarship. *Educational Researcher, 41*(4), 115–120.

Ladson-Billings, G., & Tate, W. F. (1995). Toward a critical race theory of education. *Teachers College Record, 97*(1), 47–68.

Lynn, M. (1999). Toward a critical race pedagogy: A research note. *Urban Education, 33*(5), 606–627.

Myrdal, G. (1944). *The American dilemma: The Negro problem and American democracy.* New York: Harper & Bros.

Parker, L., Deyhle, D., & Villenas, S. (1999) *Race is . . . race isn't: Critical race theory and qualitative studies in education.* Boulder, CO: Westview.

Skiba, R., & Rausch, M. K. (2006). Zero tolerance, suspension, and expulsion: Questions of equity and effectiveness. In C. Evertson & C. Weinstein (Eds.), *Handbook of classroom management: Research, practice and contemporary issues* (pp. 1063–1089). Mahwah, NJ: Lawrence Erlbaum.

Smedley, A. (1993). *Race in North America: Origin and evolution of a worldview.* Boulder, CO: Westview Press.

Solorzano, D. (1997). Images and words that wound: Critical race theory, racial stereotyping and teacher education. *Teacher Education Quarterly,* Summer, 5–19.

Solorzano, D., & Yosso, T. (2001). From racial stereotyping and deficit discourse toward a critical race theory of teacher education. *Multicultural Education, 9,* 2–8.

Tate, W. F. (1997). Critical race theory in education: History, theory, and implications. *Review of Research in Education, 22,* 195–247.

Tate, W. F., Ladson-Billings, G., & Grant, C. A. (1993). The Brown decision revisited: Mathematizing social problems. *Educational Policy, 7,* 255–275.

Taylor, E. (1999). Critical race theory: A primer. *Journal of Blacks in Higher Education, 19,* 122–124.

Terman, L. M. (1925–59). *Genetic studies of genius* (Vols. I–V). Stanford, CA: Stanford University Press.

Theissen, G. (1999). Common past, divided truth: The Truth and Reconciliation Commission in South African public opinion. Paper presented at International Institute for the Sociology of Law, Oñati, Spain, September.

Valdes, F., Culp, J. M., & Harris, A. (2002). Battles waged, won, and lost: Critical race theory at the turn of the millennium. In F. Valdes, J. M. Culp, & A. Harris (Eds.), *Crossroads, directions, and a new critical race theory* (pp. 1–6). Philadelphia, PA: Temple University Press.

Williams, P. (1991). *The alchemy of race and rights: Diary of a law professor.* Cambridge, MA: Harvard University Press.

Winant, H. (2001). *The world is a ghetto: Race and democracy since World War II.* New York: Basic Books.

Part II

ISSUES OF INEQUALITY

CHAPTER 3

From the Achievement Gap to the Education Debt

Understanding Achievement in U.S. Schools

I have spent a better part of this year reading the presidential addresses of a number of former AERA presidents. Most take the wise course of giving addresses about something they know well—their own research. Of course, I was not fully persuaded by their wisdom. Instead, I attempted to learn something new, and, unfortunately, the readers will have to determine whether I learned it well enough to share it with my professional colleagues.

The questions that plague me about education research are not new ones. I am concerned about the meaning of our work for the larger public—for real students, teachers, administrators, parents, policymakers, and communities in real school settings. I know these are not new concerns; they have been raised by others, people like the late Kenneth B. Clark, who, in the 1950s, was one of the first social scientists to bring research to the public in a meaningful way. His work with his wife and colleague Mamie formed the basis for the landmark *Brown v. Board of Education* (1954) case that reversed legal segregation in public schools and other public accommodations. However, in his classic volume *Dark Ghetto: Dilemmas of Social Power,* first published in 1965, Clark took social scientists to task for their failure to fully engage and understand the plight of the poor:

> To my knowledge, there is at present nothing in the vast literature of social science treatises and textbooks and nothing in the practical and field training of graduate students in social science to prepare them for the realities and complexities of this type of involvement in a real, dynamic, turbulent, and at times seemingly chaotic community. And what is more, nothing anywhere in the training of social scientists, teachers, or social workers now prepares them to understand, to cope with, or to change the normal chaos of ghetto communities. These are grave lacks which must be remedied soon if these disciplines are to become *relevant* [emphasis added] to the stability and survival of our society. (p. xxix)

Clark's concern remains some 40 years later. However, the paradox is that education research has devoted a significant amount of its enterprise toward the investigation of poor, African American, Latina/o, American Indian, and Asian immigrant students, who represent an increasing number of the students in major metropolitan school districts. We seem to study them but rarely provide the kind of remedies that help them to solve their problems.

To be fair, education researchers must have the freedom to pursue basic research, just as their colleagues in other social sciences do. They must be able to ask questions and pursue inquiries "just because." However, because education is an applied field, a field that local states manage and declare must be available to the entire public, *most* of the questions that education researchers ask need to address the significant questions that challenge and confound the public: Why don't children learn to read? What accounts for the high levels of school dropout among urban students? How can we explain the declining performance in mathematics and science at the same time that science and mathematics knowledge is exploding? Why do factors like race and class continue to be strong predictors of achievement when gender disparities have shrunk?

THE PREVALENCE OF THE ACHIEVEMENT GAP

One of the most common phrases in today's education literature is "the achievement gap." The term produces more than 11 million citations on Google. "Achievement gap," much like certain popular culture music stars, has become a crossover hit. It has made its way into common parlance and everyday usage. The term is invoked by people on both ends of the political spectrum, and few argue over its meaning or its import. According to the National Governors' Association, the achievement gap is "a matter of race and class. Across the U.S., a gap in academic achievement persists between minority and disadvantaged students and their white counterparts." It further states: "This is one of the most pressing education-policy challenges that states currently face" (2005). The story of the achievement gap is a familiar one. The numbers speak for themselves. In the 2005 National Assessment of Educational Progress results, the gap between Black and Latina/o fourth graders and their White counterparts in reading scaled scores was more than 26 points. In fourth-grade mathematics the gap was more than 20 points (Education Commission of the States, 2005). In eighth-grade reading, the gap was more than 23 points, and in eighth-grade mathematics the gap was more than 26 points. We can also see that these gaps persist over time (Education Commission of the States).

Even when we compare African Americans and Latina/os with incomes comparable to those of Whites, there is still an achievement gap as measured by standardized testing (National Center for Education Statistics, 2001). While I have focused primarily on showing this gap by means of standardized test scores, it also exists when we compare dropout rates and relative numbers of students who take advanced placement examinations; enroll in honors, advanced placement, and "gifted" classes; and are admitted to colleges and graduate and professional programs.

Scholars have offered a variety of explanations for the existence of the gap. In the 1960s, scholars identified cultural deficit theories to suggest that children of color were victims of pathological lifestyles that hindered their ability to benefit from schooling (Hess & Shipman, 1965; Bereiter & Engleman, 1966; Deutsch, 1963). The 1966 Coleman Report, *Equality of Educational Opportunity* (Coleman et al.), touted the importance of placing students in racially integrated classrooms. Some scholars took that report to further endorse the cultural deficit theories and to suggest that there was not much that could be done by schools to improve the achievement of African American children. But Coleman et al. were subtler than that. They argued that, more than material resources alone, a combination of factors was heavily correlated with academic achievement. Their work indicated that the composition of a school (who attends it), the students' sense of control of the environments and their futures, the teachers' verbal skills, and their students' family background all contribute to student achievement. Unfortunately, it was the last factor—family background—that became the primary point of interest for many school and social policies.

Social psychologist Claude Steele (1999) argues that a "stereotype threat" contributes to the gap. Sociolinguists such as Kathryn Au (1980), Lisa Delpit (1995), Michele Foster (1996), and Shirley Brice Heath (1983), and education researchers such as Jacqueline Jordan Irvine (2003) and Carol Lee (2004), have focused on the culture mismatch that contributes to the gap. Multicultural education researchers such as James Banks (2004), Geneva Gay (2004), and Carl Grant (2003), and curriculum theorists such as Michael Apple (1990), Catherine Cornbleth (and Dexter Waugh; 1995), and Thomas Popkewitz (1998) have focused on the nature of the curriculum and the school as sources of the gap. And teacher educators such as Christine Sleeter (2001), Marilyn Cochran-Smith (2004), Kenneth Zeichner (2002), and I (1994) have focused on the pedagogical practices of teachers as contributing to either the exacerbation or the narrowing of the gap.

But I want to use this opportunity to call into question the wisdom of focusing on the achievement gap as a way of explaining and understanding the persistent inequality that exists (and has always existed) in our nation's schools. I want to argue that this all-out focus on the "Achievement Gap" moves us toward short-term solutions that are unlikely to address the long-term underlying problem.

DOWN THE RABBIT-HOLE

Let me begin the next section of this discussion with a strange transition from a familiar piece of children's literature:

> Alice started to her feet, for it flashed across her mind that she had never before seen a rabbit with either a waistcoat-pocket, or a watch to take out of it, and burning with curiosity, she ran across the field after it, and fortunately was just in time to see it pop down a large rabbit-hole under the hedge. In another moment down went Alice after it, never once considering how in the world she was to get out again.
>
> —Lewis Carroll, *Alice's Adventures in Wonderland*

The relevance of this passage is that I, like Alice, saw a rabbit with a watch and waistcoat-pocket when I came across a book by economist Robert Margo entitled *Race and Schooling in the American South, 1880–1950* (1990). And, like Alice, I chased the rabbit called "economics" down a rabbit-hole, where the world looked very different to me. Fortunately, I traveled with my trusty copy of Lakoff and Johnson's (1980) *Metaphors We Live By* as a way to make sense of my sojourn there. So, before making my way back to the challenge of school inequality, I must beg your indulgence as I give you a brief tour of my time down there.

NATIONAL DEBT VERSUS NATIONAL DEFICIT

Most people hear or read news of the economy every day and rarely give it a second thought. We hear that the Federal Reserve Bank is raising interest rates, or that the unemployment numbers look good. Our ears may perk up when we hear the latest gasoline prices or that we can get a good rate on a mortgage refinance loan. But busy professionals rarely have time to delve deeply into all things economic. Two economic terms—"national deficit" and "national debt"—seem to befuddle us. A deficit is the amount by which a government's, company's, or individual's spending exceeds income over a particular period of time. Thus, for each budget cycle, the government must determine whether it has a balanced budget, a budget surplus, or a deficit. The debt, however is the sum of all previously incurred annual federal deficits. Since the deficits are financed by government borrowing, national debt is equal to all government debt.

Most fiscal conservatives warn against deficit budgets and urge the government to decrease spending to balance the budget. Fiscal liberals do not necessarily embrace deficits but would rather see the budget balanced by increasing tax revenues from those most able to pay. The debt is a sum that has been accumulating since 1791, when the U.S. Treasury recorded it as

$75,463,476.52 (Gordon, 1998). Thomas Jefferson (1816) said, "I . . . place economy among the first and most important virtues, and public debt as the greatest of dangers to be feared. To preserve our independence, we must not let our rulers load us with perpetual debt."

But the debt has not merely been going up. Between 1823 and 1835 the debt steadily decreased, from a high of almost $91 million to a low of $33,733.05. The nation's debt hit the $1 billion mark in 1863 and the $1 trillion mark in 1981. Today, the national debt sits at more than $8 trillion. This level of debt means that the United States pays about $132,844,701,219.88 in interest each year. This makes our debt interest the third-largest expenditure in the federal budget after defense and combined entitlement programs such as Social Security and Medicare (Christensen, 2004).

Even in those years when the United States has had a balanced budget, that is, no deficits, the national debt continued to grow. It may have grown at a slower rate, but it did continue to grow. President Clinton bragged about presenting a balanced budget—one without deficits—and not growing the debt (King, J., 2000). However, the debt was already at a frighteningly high level, and his budget policies failed to make a dent in the debt.

THE DEBT AND EDUCATION DISPARITY

By now, readers might assume that I have made myself firmly at home at the Mad Hatter's Tea Party. What does a discussion about national deficits and national debt have to do with education, education research, and continued education disparities? It is here where I began to see some metaphorical concurrences between our national fiscal situation and our education situation. I am arguing that our focus on the achievement gap is akin to a focus on the budget deficit, but what is actually happening to African American and Latina/o students is really more like the national debt. We do not have an achievement gap; we have an education debt.

Now, to be perfectly candid, I must admit that when I consulted with a strict economist, Professor Emeritus Robert Haveman of the University of Wisconsin's Department of Economics, La Follette Institute of Public Affairs, and Institute for Research on Poverty, he stated:

> The education debt is the foregone schooling resources that we could have (should have) been investing in (primarily) low income kids, which deficit leads to a variety of social problems (e.g. crime, low productivity, low wages, low labor force participation) that require on-going public investment. This required investment sucks away resources that could go to reducing the achievement gap. Without the education debt we could narrow the achievement debt.
>
>   . . . The message would be that you need to reduce one (the education debt, defined above) in order to close the other (the achievement gap). A parallel is

trying to gain a growing and robust economy with a large national debt over-hang. (February 6, 2006, e-mail)

In addition to this informal discussion with Haveman, I read a work by Wolfe and Haveman (2001) entitled *Accounting for the Social and Non-Market Benefits of Education,* which catalogues a series of what they term "non-market effects of schooling." The authors contend that "the literature on the intergenerational effects of education is generally neglected in assessing the full impact of education." Among the nonmarket effects that they include are the following:

- A positive link between one's own schooling and the schooling received by one's children
- A positive association between the schooling and health status of one's family members
- A positive relationship between one's own education and one's own health status
- A positive relationship between one's own education and the efficiency of choices made, such as consumer choices (which efficiency has positive effects on well-being similar to those of money income)
- A relationship between one's own schooling and fertility choices (in particular, decisions of one's female teenage children regarding nonmarital childbearing)
- A relationship between the schooling/social capital of one's neighborhood and decisions by young people regarding their level of schooling, nonmarital childbearing, and participation in criminal activities. (pp. 2–3)

While these economists have informed my thinking, I have taken a somewhat different tack on this notion of the education debt. The yearly fluctuations in the achievement gap give us a short-range picture of how students perform on a particular set of achievement measures. Looking at the gap from year to year is a misleading exercise. Lee's (2002) look at the trend lines shows us that there was a narrowing of the gap in the 1980s both between Black and White students and between the Latina/o and White students, and a subsequent expansion of those gaps in the 1990s. The expansion of the disparities occurred even though the income differences narrowed during the 1990s. We do not have good answers as to why the gap narrows or widens. Some research suggests that even the combination of socioeconomic and family conditions, youth culture and student behaviors, and schooling conditions and practices do not fully explain changes in the achievement gap (Lee).

However, when we begin looking at the construction and compilation of what I have termed the education debt, we can better understand why an achievement gap is a logical outcome. I am arguing that the historical, economic, sociopolitical, and moral decisions and policies that characterize our society have created an education debt. So, at this point, I want to briefly describe each of those aspects of the debt.

THE HISTORICAL DEBT

Scholars in the history of education, such as James Anderson (1989), Michael Fultz (1995), and David Tyack (2004), have documented the legacy of educational inequities in the United States. Those inequities initially were formed around race, class, and gender. Gradually, some of the inequities began to recede, but clearly they persist in the realm of race. In the case of African Americans, education was initially forbidden during the period of enslavement. After emancipation we saw the development of freedmen's schools whose purpose was the maintenance of a servant class. During the long period of legal apartheid, African Americans attended schools where they received cast-off textbooks and materials from White schools. In the South, the need for farm labor meant that the typical school year for rural Black students was about 4 months long. Indeed, Black students in the South did not experience universal secondary schooling until 1968 (Anderson, 2002). Why, then, would we not expect there to be an achievement gap?

The history of American Indian education is equally egregious. It began with mission schools to convert and use Indian labor to further the cause of the church. Later, boarding schools were developed as General George Pratt asserted the need "to kill the Indian in order to save the man." This strategy of deliberate and forced assimilation created a group of people, according to Pulitzer Prize writer N. Scott Momaday, who belonged nowhere (Lesiak, 1991). The assimilated Indian could not fit comfortably into reservation life or the stratified mainstream. No predominately White colleges welcomed the few Indians who successfully completed the early boarding schools. Only historically Black colleges, such as Hampton Institute, opened their doors to them. There, the Indians studied vocational and trade curricula.

Latina/o students also experienced huge disparities in their education. In Ferg-Cadima's report *Black, White, and Brown: Latino School Desegregation Efforts in the Pre– and Post–*Brown v. Board of Education *Era* (2004), we discover the longstanding practice of denial experienced by Latina/os dating back to 1848. Historic desegregation cases such as *Mendez v. Westminster* (1946) and the Lemon Grove Incident detail the ways that Brown children were (and continue to be) excluded from equitable and high-quality education.

It is important to point out that the historical debt was not merely imposed by ignorant masses that were xenophobic and virulently racist. The major leaders of the nation endorsed ideas about the inferiority of Black, Latina/o, and Native peoples. Thomas Jefferson (1816), who advocated for the education of the American citizen, simultaneously decried the notion that Blacks were capable of education. George Washington, while deeply conflicted about slavery, maintained a substantial number of slaves on his Mount Vernon Plantation and gave no thought to educating enslaved children.

A brief perusal of some of the history of public schooling in the United States documents the way that we have accumulated an education debt over time. In 1827 Massachusetts passed a law making all grades of public school open to all pupils free of charge. At about the same time, most Southern states already had laws forbidding the teaching of enslaved Africans to read. By 1837, when Horace Mann had become head of the newly formed Massachusetts State Board of Education, Edmund Dwight, a wealthy Boston industrialist, felt that the state board was crucial to factory owners and offered to supplement the state salary with his own money. What is omitted from this history is that the major raw material of those textile factories, which drove the economy of the East, was cotton—the crop that depended primarily on the labor of enslaved Africans (Farrow, Lang, & Frank, 2005). Thus one of the ironies of the historical debt is that while African Americans were enslaved and prohibited from schooling, the product of their labor was used to profit Northern industrialists who already had the benefits of education. Consider the real source of New England's wealth (from Farrow, Lang, & Frank, p. 6):

- By 1860, New England was home to 472 cotton mills, built on rivers and streams throughout the region.
- Just between 1830 and 1840, Northern mills consumed more than 100 million pounds of Southern cotton. With shipping and manufacturing included, the economy of much of New England was connected to textiles.
- By the 1850s, the enormous profits of Massachusetts industrialists had been poured into a complex network of banks, insurance companies, and railroads. But their wealth remained anchored to dozens of mammoth textile mills in Massachusetts, southern Maine, and New Hampshire.

This pattern of debt affected other groups as well. In 1864 the U.S. Congress made it illegal for Native Americans to be taught in their native languages. After the Civil War, African Americans worked with Republicans to rewrite state constitutions to guarantee free public education for all students. Unfortunately, their efforts benefited White children more than Black children. The landmark *Plessy v. Ferguson* (1896) decision meant that the segregation that the South had been practicing was officially recognized as legal by the federal government.

Although the historical debt is a heavy one, it is important not to over-look the ways that communities of color always have worked to educate themselves. Between 1865 and 1877, African Americans mobilized to bring public education to the South for the first time. Carter G. Woodson (1933/1972) was a primary critic of the kind of education that African Americans received, and he challenged African Americans to develop schools and curricula that met the unique needs of a population only a few generations out of chattel slavery.

THE ECONOMIC DEBT

As is often true in social research, the numbers present a startling picture of reality. The economics of the education debt are sobering. The fund-ing disparities that currently exist between schools serving White students and those serving students of color are not recent phenomena. Separate schooling always allows for differential funding. In present-day dollars, the funding disparities between urban schools and their suburban counterparts present a telling story about the value we place on the education of different groups of students.

The Chicago public schools spend about $8,482 annually per pupil, while nearby Highland Park spends $17,291 per pupil. The Chicago public schools have an 87% Black and Latina/o population, while Highland Park has a 90% White population. Per pupil expenditures in Philadelphia are $9,299 per pupil for the city's 79% Black and Latina/o population, while across City Line Avenue in Lower Merion, the per pupil expenditure is $17,261 for a 91% White population. The New York City public schools spend $11,627 per pupil for a student population that is 72% Black and Latina/o, while suburban Manhasset spends $22,311 for a student popula-tion that is 91% White (figures from Kozol, 2005).

One of the earliest things one learns in statistics is that correlation does not prove causation, but we must ask ourselves why the funding inequities map so neatly and regularly onto the racial and ethnic realities of our schools. Even if we cannot prove that schools are poorly funded *because* Black and Latina/o students attend them, we can demonstrate that the amount of fund-ing rises with the rise in White students. This pattern of inequitable funding has occurred over centuries. For many of these populations, schooling was nonexistent during the early history of the nation; and, clearly, Whites were not prepared to invest their fiscal resources in these strange "others."

Another important part of the economic component of the education debt is the earning ratios related to years of schooling. The empirical data suggest that more schooling is associated with higher earnings; that is, high school graduates earn more money than high school dropouts, and college graduates earn more than high school graduates. Margo (1990) pointed out that in 1940 the average annual earnings of Black men were about 48% of those of White men, but by 1980 the earning ratio had risen to 61%. By 1993, the median Black male earned 74% as much as the median White male.

While earnings ratios show us how people are (or were) doing at particular points in time, they do not address the cumulative effect of such income disparities. According to economists Joseph Altonji and Ulrech Doraszelski (2005),

> The wealth gap between whites and blacks in the United States is much larger than the gap in earnings. The gap in wealth has implications for the social position of African Americans that go far beyond its obvious implications for consumption levels that households can sustain. This is because wealth is a source of political and social power, influences access to capital for new businesses, and provides insurance against fluctuations in labor market income. It affects the quality of housing, neighborhoods, and schools a family has access to as well as the ability to finance higher education. The fact that friendships and family ties tend to be within racial groups amplifies the effect of the wealth gap on the financial, social, and political resources available to blacks relative to whites. (p. 1)

This economic analysis maps well onto the notion of education debt— as opposed to achievement gap—that I am trying to advance. So, while the income gap more closely resembles the achievement gap, the wealth disparity better reflects the education debt that I am attempting to describe.

THE SOCIOPOLITICAL DEBT

The sociopolitical debt reflects the degree to which communities of color are excluded from the civic process. Black, Latina/o, and Native communities had little or no access to the franchise, so they had no true legislative representation. According to the Civil Rights Division of the U.S. Department of Justice, African Americans and other persons of color were substantially disenfranchised in many Southern states despite the enactment of the Fifteenth Amendment in 1870 (U.S. Department of Justice, Civil Rights Division, 2006).

The Voting Rights Act of 1965 is touted as the most successful piece of civil rights legislation ever adopted by the U.S. Congress (Grofman,

Handley, & Niemi, 1992). This act represents a proactive attempt to eradicate the sociopolitical debt that had been accumulating since the founding of the nation.

Table 3.1 shows the sharp contrasts between voter registration rates before the Voting Rights Act of 1965 and after it. The dramatic changes in voter registration are a result of Congress's bold action. In upholding the constitutionality of the act, the Supreme Court ruled as follows:

> Congress has found that case-by-case litigation was inadequate to combat wide-spread and persistent discrimination in voting, because of the inordinate amount of time and energy required to overcome the obstructionist tactics invariably encountered in these lawsuits. After enduring nearly a century of systematic resistance to the Fifteenth Amendment, Congress might well decide to shift the advantage of time and inertia from the perpetrators of the evil to its victims. (*South Carolina v. Katzenbach*, 1966; U.S. Department of Justice, Civil Rights Division, 2006)

It is hard to imagine such a similarly drastic action on behalf of African American, Latina/o, and Native American children in schools. For example, imagine that an examination of the achievement performance of children of color provoked an immediate reassignment of the nation's best teachers to the schools serving the most needy students. Imagine that those same students were guaranteed places in state and regional colleges and universities. Imagine that within one generation we lift those students out of poverty.

Table 3.1. Black and White Voter Registration Rates (%) in Selected U.S. States, 1965 and 1988

State	MARCH 1965			NOVEMBER 1988		
	Black	White	Gap	Black	White	Gap
Alabama	19.3	69.2	49.9	68.4	75.0	6.6
Georgia	27.4	62.6	35.2	56.8	63.9	7.1
Louisiana	31.6	80.5	48.9	77.1	75.1	–2.0
Mississippi	6.7	69.9	63.2	74.2	80.5	6.3
North Carolina	46.8	96.8	50.0	58.2	65.6	7.4
South Carolina	37.3	75.7	38.4	56.7	61.8	5.1
Virginia	38.3	61.1	22.8	63.8	68.5	4.7

Note. From the website of the U.S. Department of Justice, Civil Rights Division, Voting Rights Section *(http://www.usdoj.gov/crt/votinglintro/ intro_c.htm)*, "Introduction to Federal Voting Rights Laws."

The closest example that we have of such a dramatic policy move is that of affirmative action. Rather than wait for students of color to meet predetermined standards, the society decided to recognize that historically denied groups should be given a preference in admission to schools and colleges. Ultimately, the major beneficiaries of this policy were White women. However, Bowen and Bok (1999) found that in the case of African Americans this proactive policy helped create what we now know as the Black middle class. As a result of the sociopolitical component of the education debt, families of color have regularly been excluded from the decision-making mechanisms that should ensure that their children receive quality education. The parent–teacher organizations, school site councils, and other possibilities for democratic participation have not been available for many of these families. However, for a brief moment in 1968, Black parents in the Ocean Hill–Brownsville section of New York exercised community control over the public schools (Podair, 2003). African American, Latina/o, Native American, and Asian American parents have often advocated for improvements in schooling, but their advocacy often has been muted and marginalized. This quest for control of schools was powerfully captured in the voice of an African American mother during the fight for school desegregation in Boston. She declared: "When we fight about schools, we're fighting for our lives" (Hampton, 1986).

Indeed, a major aspect of the modern civil rights movement was the quest for quality schooling. From the activism of Benjamin Rushing in 1849 to the struggles of parents in rural South Carolina in 1999, families of color have been fighting for quality education for their children (Ladson-Billings, 2004). Their more limited access to lawyers and legislators has kept them from accumulating the kinds of political capital that their White, middle-class counterparts have.

THE MORAL DEBT

A final component of the education debt is what I term the "moral debt." I find this concept difficult to explain because social science rarely talks in these terms. What I did find in the literature was the concept of "moral panics" (Cohen, 1972; Goode & Ben-Yehuda, 1994a, 1994b; Hall, Critcher, Jefferson, Clarke, & Roberts, 1978) that was popularized in British sociology. People in moral panics attempt to describe other people, groups of individuals, or events that become defined as threats throughout a society. However, in such a panic the magnitude of the supposed threat overshadows the real threat posed. Stanley Cohen (1972), author of the classic sociological treatment of the subject, entitled *Folk Devils and Moral Panics,* defines such a moral panic as a kind of reaction to

> A condition, episode, person or group of persons [that] emerges to become defined as a threat to societal values and interests; its nature is presented in a stylized and stereotypical fashion by the mass media; the moral barricades are manned by editors, bishops, politicians and other right-thinking people; socially accredited experts pronounce their diagnoses and solutions; ways of coping are evolved or . . . resorted to; the condition then disappears, submerges or deteriorates and becomes more visible. Sometimes the subject of the panic passes over and is forgotten, except in folklore and collective memory; at other times it has more serious and long-lasting repercussions and might produce such changes as those in legal and social policy or even in the way society conceives itself. (p. 9)

In contrast, a moral debt reflects the disparity between what we know is right and what we actually do. Saint Thomas Aquinas saw the moral debt as what human beings owe to each other in the giving of, or failure to give, honor to another when honor is due. This honor comes as a result of people's excellence or because of what they have done for another. We have no trouble recognizing that we have a moral debt to Rosa Parks, Martin Luther King, Cesar Chavez, Elie Wiesel, or Mahatma Gandhi. But how do we recognize the moral debt that we owe to entire groups of people? How do we calculate such a debt?

Typically, we think of moral debt as relational between nationstates. For example, at the end of World War II, Israel charged Germany not only with a fiscal or monetary debt but also with a moral debt. On the individual level, Fred Korematsu battled the U.S. government for 40 years to prove that Japanese Americans were owed a moral debt. In another 40-year span, the U.S. government ran a study of syphilis patients—withholding treatment after a known cure was discovered—and was forced to acknowledge its ethical breaches. In his 1997 apology to the survivors and their families, President Bill Clinton said, "The United States government did something that was wrong—deeply, profoundly, morally wrong. It was an outrage to our commitment to integrity and equality for all our citizens . . . clearly racist" (Hunter-Gault, 1997). Today, all human subject protocols reflect the moral debt we owe to the victims of that study.

David Gill (2000) asserts, in his book *Being Good,* that "we are living today in an ethical wilderness—a wild, untamed, unpredictable landscape" (p. 11). We bemoan the loss of civil discourse and rational debate, but the real danger of our discussions about morality is that they reside solely in the realm of the individual. We want people to take *personal* responsibility for their behavior, *personal* responsibility for their health care, *personal* responsibility for their welfare, and *personal* responsibility for their education. However, in democratic nations, that personal responsibility must be coupled with social responsibility.

What is it that we might owe to citizens who historically have been excluded from social benefits and opportunities? Randall Robinson (2000) states:

> No nation can enslave a race of people for hundreds of years, set them free bedraggled and penniless, pit them, without assistance in a hostile environment, against privileged victimizers, and then reasonably expect the gap between the heirs of the two groups to narrow. Lines, begun parallel and left alone, can never touch. (p. 74)

Robinson's sentiments were not unlike those of President Lyndon B. Johnson, who stated in a 1965 address at Howard University: "You cannot take a man who has been in chains for 300 years, remove the chains, take him to the starting line and tell him to run the race, and think that you are being fair" (Miller, 2005).

Despite those parallel lines of which Robinson speaks, in the midst of the Civil War Abraham Lincoln noted that without the 200,000 Black men who enlisted in the Union Army, "we would be compelled to abandon the war in 3 weeks" (cited in Takaki, 1998). Thus, according to historian Ron Takaki (1998), "Black men in blue made the difference in determining that this 'government of the people, by the people, for the people' did 'not perish from the earth'" (p. 21). What moral debt do we owe their heirs?

Think of another example of the ways that the labor and efforts of people of color have sustained the nation. When we hear the word "plantation," our minds almost automatically reflect back to the antebellum South. However, the same word evokes the Palolo Valley on the Hawaiian island of Oahu, where there were camps named "Young Hee," "Ah Fong," "Spanish A," "Spanish B," and "Alabama" (Takaki, 1998). This last camp—"Alabama"—was a Hawaiian plantation worked by Black laborers. Each of the groups that labored in the Hawaiian plantations—the Native Hawaiians, the Chinese, the Japanese, the Filipinos, the Koreans, the Portuguese, the Puerto Ricans, and the Blacks—drove a sugar economy that sated a worldwide sweet tooth (Wilcox, 1998). What do we owe their descendants?

And perhaps our largest moral debt is to the indigenous peoples whose presence was all but eradicated from the nation. In its 2004–2005 Report Card, the Bureau of Indian Affairs indicates that its high school graduation rate is 57%, with only 3.14% of its students performing at the advanced level in reading and 3.96% performing at the advanced level in mathematics. One hundred and twenty-two of the 185 elementary and secondary schools under the jurisdiction of the Bureau of Indian Affairs failed to meet Average Yearly Progress requirements in the 2004–2005 school year (Bureau of Indian Affairs, Office of Indian Education Programs, 2006).

The National Center for Education Statistics report *Status and Trends in the Education of American Indians and Alaska Natives* (Freeman & Fox,

2005) indicates that the dropout rate among this population is about 15%, which is higher than that of Whites, Blacks, or Asian/Pacific Islanders. Only 26% of American Indians and Alaska Natives completed a core academic track in 2000, while 57% of Asian/Pacific Islanders, 38% of Latina/os, 44% of African Americans, and 48% of Whites completed core academic tracks during the same year (Freeman & Fox).

Taken together, the historic, economic, sociopolitical, and moral debt that we have amassed toward Black, Brown, Yellow, and Red children seems insurmountable, and attempts at addressing it seem futile. Indeed, it appears like a task for Sisyphus. But as legal scholar Derrick Bell (1994) indicated, just because something is impossible does not mean it is not worth doing.

WHY WE MUST ADDRESS THE DEBT

In the final section of this discussion I want to attend to why we must address the education debt. On the face of it, we must address it because it is the equitable and just thing to do. As Americans we pride ourselves on maintaining those ideal qualities as hallmarks of our democracy. That represents the highest motivation for paying this debt. But we do not always work from our highest motivations.

Most of us live in the world of the pragmatic and practical. So we must address the education debt because it has implications for the kinds of lives we can live and the kind of education the society can expect for most of its children. I want to suggest that there are three primary reasons for addressing the debt—(a) the impact the debt has on present education progress, (b) the value of understanding the debt in relation to past education research findings, and (c) the potential for forging a better educational future.

The Impact of the Debt on Present Education Progress

In a recent news article in the business section of the *Cleveland Plain Dealer,* I read that affluent investors are more likely to be educated, married men (Torres, 2006). The article continued by talking about how Whites make up 88% of wealthy investor households, while Blacks and Latina/os make up only 3%. Asian Americans, who are 3.7% of the adult population, make up 5% of wealthy investors. But more salient than wealthy investor status to me was a quote in the article from former Federal Reserve Chairman Alan Greenspan: "My biggest fear for this country's future, competitively speaking, is that we're doing a poor job in education. If we can resolve our educational problems, I think we will maintain the very extraordinary position the United States holds in the world at large" (Torres, p. G6).

As I was attempting to make sense of the deficit/ debt metaphor, educational economist Doug Harris (personal communication, November 19, 2005) reminded me that when nations operate with a large debt, some part of their current budget goes to service that debt. I mentioned earlier that interest payments on our national debt represent the third largest expenditure of our national budget. In the case of education, each effort we make toward improving education is counterbalanced by the ongoing and mounting debt that we have accumulated. That debt service manifests itself in the distrust and suspicion about what schools can and will do in communities serving the poor and children of color. Bryk and Schneider (2002) identified "relational trust" as a key component in school reform. I argue that the magnitude of the education debt erodes that trust and represents a portion of the debt service that teachers and administrators pay each year against what they might rightfully invest in helping students advance academically.

The Value of Understanding the Debt in Relation to Past Research Findings

The second reason that we must address the debt is somewhat selfish from an education research perspective. Much of our scholarly effort has gone into looking at educational inequality and how we might mitigate it. Despite how hard we try, there are two interventions that have never received full and sustained hypothesis testing—school desegregation and funding equity. Orfield and Lee (2006) point out that not only has school segregation persisted, but it has been transformed by the changing demographics of the nation. They also point out that "there has not been a serious discussion of the costs of segregation or the advantages of integration for our most segregated population, white students" (p. 5). So, although we may have recently celebrated the 50th anniversary of the *Brown* decision, we can point to little evidence that we really gave *Brown* a chance. According to Frankenberg, Lee, and Orfield (2003) and Orfield and Lee (2004), America's public schools are more than a decade into a process of resegregation. Almost three-fourths of Black and Latina/o students attend schools that are predominately non-White. More than 2 million Black and Latina/o students—a quarter of the Black students in the Northeast and Midwest—attend what the researchers call apartheid schools. The four most segregated states for Black students are New York, Michigan, Illinois, and California.

The funding equity problem, as I illustrated earlier in this discussion, also has been intractable. In its report entitled *The Funding Gap 2005*, the Education Trust tells us that "in 27 of the 49 states studied, the highest-poverty school districts receive fewer resources than the lowest-poverty districts. . . . Even more states shortchange their highest minority districts. In 30 states, high minority districts receive less money for each child than low minority districts" (p. 2). If we are unwilling to desegregate our schools *and* unwilling to fund them equitably, we find ourselves not only backing away from the promise of the *Brown* decision but literally refusing even to take *Plessy* seriously. At least a serious consideration of *Plessy* would make us look at funding inequities.

In one of the most graphic examples of funding inequity, new teacher Sara Sentilles (2005) described the southern California school where she was teaching:

> At Garvey Elementary School, I taught over thirty second graders in a so-called temporary building. Most of these "temporary" buildings have been on campuses in Compton for years. The one I taught in was old. Because the wooden beams across the ceiling were being eaten by termites, a fine layer of wood dust covered the students' desks every morning. Maggots crawled in a cracked and collapsing area of the floor near my desk. One day after school I went to sit in my chair, and it was completely covered in maggots. I was nearly sick. Mice raced behind cupboards and bookcases. I trapped six in terrible traps called "glue lounges" given to me by the custodians. The blue metal window coverings on the outsides of the windows were shut permanently, blocking all sunlight. Someone had lost the tool needed to open them, and no one could find another . . . (p. 72)

Rothstein and Wilder (2005) move beyond the documentation of the inequalities and inadequacies to their *consequences*. In the language that I am using in this discussion, they move from focusing on the gap to tallying the debt. Although they focus on Black–White disparities, they are clear that similar disparities exist between Latina/os and Whites and Native Americans and Whites. Contrary to conventional wisdom, Rothstein and Wilder argue that addressing the achievement gap is not the most important inequality to attend to. Rather, they contend that inequalities in health, early childhood experiences, out-of-school experiences, and economic security are also contributory and cumulative and make it near-impossible for us to reify the achievement gap as *the* source and cause of social inequality.

The Potential for Forging a Better Educational Future

Finally, we need to address what implications this mounting debt has for our future. In one scenario, we might determine that our debt is so high that the only thing we can do is declare bankruptcy. Perhaps, like our airline industry, we could use the protection of the bankruptcy laws to reorganize and design more streamlined, more efficient schooling options. Or perhaps we could be like developing nations that owe huge sums to the IMF and apply for 100% debt relief. But what would such a catastrophic collapse of our education system look like? Where could we go to begin from the ground up to build the kind of education system that would aggressively address the debt? Might we find a setting where a catastrophic occurrence, perhaps a natural disaster—a hurricane—has completely obliterated the schools? Of course, it would need to be a place where the schools weren't very good to begin with. It would have to be a place where our Institutional Review Board and human subject concerns would not keep us from proposing aggressive and cutting-edge research. It would have to be a place where people were so desperate for the expertise of education researchers that we could conduct multiple projects using multiple approaches. It would be a place so hungry for solutions that it would not matter if some projects were quantitative and others were qualitative. It would not matter if some were large-scale and some were small-scale. It would not matter if some paradigms were psychological, some were social, some were economic, and some were cultural. The only thing that would matter in an environment like this would be that education researchers were bringing their expertise to bear on education problems that spoke to pressing concerns of the public. I wonder where we might find such a place?

Although I have tried to explain this notion of education debt, I know that my words are a limited way to fully represent it. How can I illustrate the magnitude of this concept? In his 1993 AERA Presidential Address, "Forms of Understanding and the Future of Educational Research," Elliot Eisner spoke of representation—not the mental representations discussed in cognitive science, but "the process of transforming the consciousness into a public form so that they can be stabilized, inspected, edited, and shared with others" (p. 6). So we must use our imaginations to construct a set of images that illustrate the debt. The images should remind us that the cumulative effect of poor education, poor housing, poor health care, and poor government services create a bifurcated society that leaves more than its children behind. The images should compel us to deploy our knowledge, skills, and expertise to alleviate the suffering of the least of these. They are the images that compelled our attention during Hurricane Katrina. Here, for the first time in a very long time, the nation—indeed the world—was confronted with the magnitude of poverty that exists in America.

In a recent book, Michael Apple and Kristen Buras (2006) suggest that the subaltern can and do speak. In this country they speak from the barrios of Los Angeles and the ghettos of New York. They speak from the reservations of New Mexico and the Chinatown of San Francisco. They speak from the levee breaks of New Orleans where they remind us, as education researchers, that we do not merely have an achievement gap—we have an education debt.

REFERENCES

Altonji, J., & Doraszelski, U. (2005). The role of permanent income and demographics in Black/White differences in wealth. *Journal of Human Resources, 40*, 1–30.

Anderson, J. D. (1989). *The education of Blacks in the South, 1860–1935.* Chapel Hill, NC: University of North Carolina Press.

Anderson, J. D. (2002, February 28). *Historical perspectives on Black academic achievement.* Paper presented for the Visiting Minority Scholars Series Lecture. Wisconsin Center for Educational Research, University of Wisconsin, Madison.

Apple, M. W. (1990). *Ideology and curriculum* (2nd ed.). New York: Routledge.

Apple, M. W., & Buras, K. L. (Eds.). (2006). *The subaltern speak: Curriculum, power and education struggles.* New York: Routledge.

Au, K. (1980). Participation structures in a reading lesson with Hawaiian children. *Anthropology and Education Quarterly, 11*(2), 91–115.

Banks, J. A. (2004). Multicultural education: Historical development, dimensions, and practices. In J. A. Banks & C. M. Banks (Eds.), *Handbook of research in multicultural education* (2nd ed., pp. 3–29). San Francisco: Jossey-Bass.

Bell, D. (1994). *Confronting authority: Reflections of an ardent protester.* Boston: Beacon Press.

Bereiter, C., & Engleman, S. (1966). *Teaching disadvantaged children in preschool.* Englewood Cliffs, NJ: Prentice Hall.

Bowen, W. G., & Bok, D. (1999). *The shape of the river.* Princeton, NJ: Princeton University Press.

Brice Heath, S. (1983). *Ways with words: Language, life and work in communities and classrooms.* Cambridge, UK: Cambridge University Press.

Brown v. Board of Education 347 U.S. 483 (1954).

Bryk, A., & Schneider, S. (2002). *Trust in schools: A core resource for improvement.* New York: Russell Sage Foundation.

Bureau of Indian Affairs, Office of Indian Education Programs. (2006). *School Report Cards: SY 2004–2006.* Retrieved February 5, 2006, from http://www.oiep.bia.edu

Christensen, J. R. (Ed.). (2004). *The national debt: A primer.* Hauppauge, NY: Nova Science Publishers.

Clark, K. B. (1965). *Dark ghetto: Dilemmas of social power.* Hanover, NH: Wesleyan University Press.

Cochran-Smith, M. (2004). Multicultural teacher education: Research, practice and policy. In J. A. Banks & C. M. Banks (Eds.), *Handbook of research in multicultural education* (2nd ed., pp. 931–975). San Francisco: Jossey-Bass.

Cohen, S. (1972). *Folk devils and moral panics: The creation of mods and rockers.* London: McGibbon and Kee.

Coleman, J., Campbell, E., Hobson, C., McPartland, J., Mood, A., Weinfeld, F. D., et al. (1966). *Equality of educational opportunity.* Washington, DC: Department of Health, Education and Welfare.

Cornbleth, C., & Waugh, D. (1995). *The great speckled bird: Multicultural politics and education.* Mahwah, NJ: Lawrence Erlbaum.

Delpit, L. (1995). *Other people's children: Cultural conflict in the classroom.* New York: Free Press.

Deutsch, M. (1963). The disadvantaged child and the learning process. In A. H. Passow (Ed.), *Education in depressed areas* (pp. 163–179). New York: New York Bureau of Publications, Teachers College, Columbia University.

Education Commission of the States. (2005). *The nation's report card.* Retrieved January 2, 2006, from http://nces.ed.gov/nationsreportcard

Education Trust. (2005). *The funding gap 2005.* Washington, DC: Author.

Eisner, E. W. (1993). Forms of understanding and the future of educational research. *Educational Researcher, 22*(7), 5–11.

Farrow, A., Lang, J., & Frank, J. (2005). *Complicity: How the North promoted, prolonged and profited from slavery.* New York: Ballantine Books.

Ferg-Cadima, J. (2004, May). *Black, White, and Brown: Latino school desegregation efforts in the pre– and post–Brown* v. Board of Education *era.* Washington, DC: Mexican-American Legal Defense and Education Fund.

Foster, M. (1996). *Black teachers on teaching.* New York: New Press.

Frankenberg, E., Lee, C., & Orfield, G. (2003, January). *A multiracial society with segregated schools: Are we losing the dream?* Cambridge, MA: The Civil Rights Project, Harvard University.

Freeman, C., & Fox, M. (2005). *Status and trends in the education of American Indians and Alaska natives* (No. 2005-108). U.S. Department of Education, National Center for Education Statistics. Washington, DC: U.S. Government Printing Office.

Fultz, M. (1995). African American teachers in the South, 1890–1940: Powerlessness and the ironies of expectations and protests. *History of Education Quarterly, 35*(4), 401–422.

Gay, G. (2004). Multicultural curriculum theory and multicultural education. In J. A. Banks & C. M. Banks (Eds.), *Handbook of research in multicultural education* (2nd ed., pp. 30–49). San Francisco: Jossey-Bass.

Gill, D. W. (2000). *Being good: Building moral character.* Downers Grove, IL: Intervarsity Press.

Goode, E., & Ben-Yehuda, N. (1994a). Moral panics: Culture, politics, and social construction. *Annual Review of Sociology, 20,* 149–171.

Goode, E., & Ben-Yehuda, N. (1994b). *Moral panics: The social construction of deviance.* Oxford: Blackwell.

Gordon, J. S. (1998). *Hamilton's blessing: The extraordinary life and times of our national debt.* New York: Penguin Books.

Grant, C. A. (2003). *An education guide to diversity in the classroom.* Boston: Houghton Mifflin.

Grofman, B., Handley, L., & Niemi, R. G. (1992). *Minority representation and the quest for voting equality.* New York: Cambridge University Press.

Hall, S., Critcher, C., Jefferson, T., Clarke, J., & Roberts, B. (1978). *Policing the crisis: Mugging, the state, and law and order.* London: Macmillan.

Hampton, H. (Director). (1986). *Eyes on the prize* [Television video series]. Blackside Productions (Producer). New York: Public Broadcasting Service.

Hess, R. D., & Shipman, V. C. (1965). Early experience and socialization of cognitive modes in children. *Child Development, 36,* 869–886.

Hunter-Gault, C. (Writer). (1997, May 16). An apology 65 years late [Television series episode]. In Lee Koromvokis (Producer), *Online News Hour.* Washington,

DC: Public Broadcasting Service. Retrieved February 2, 2006, from http://www
.pbs.orglnewshourlbblhealthl may97/tuskegee_5-16 html

Irvine, J. J. (2003). *Educating teachers for diversity: Seeing with a cultural eye.* New
York: Teachers College Press.

Jefferson, T. (1816, July 21). *Letter to William Plumer. The Thomas Jefferson Paper
Series. 1. General correspondence, 1651–1827.* Retrieved September 11, 2006,
from http://rs6 wc.govlcgi-binlampage

King, J. (2000, May 1). *Clinton announces record payment on national debt.* Retrieved February 7, 2006, from http://archives.cnn.com/2000/ALLPOLITICS
/stories/05/01/clinton.debt

Kozol, J. (2005). *The shame of the nation: The restoration of apartheid schooling in
America.* New York: Crown Publishing.

Ladson-Billings, G. (1994). *The dreamkeepers: Successful teachers of African American children.* San Francisco: Jossey-Bass.

Ladson-Billings, G. (2004). Landing on the wrong note: The price we paid for
Brown. Educational Researcher, 33(7), 3–13.

Lakoff, G., & Johnson, M. (1980). *Metaphors we live by.* Chicago: University of
Chicago Press.

Lee, C. D. (2004). African American students and literacy. In D. Alvermann & D.
Strickland (Eds.), *Bridging the gap: Improving literacy learning for pre-adoles-
cent and adolescent learners, Grades 4–12.* New York: Teachers College Press.

Lee, J. (2002). Racial and achievement gap trends: Reversing the progress toward
equity. *Educational Researcher, 31(1),* 3–12.

Lesiak, C. (Director). (1991). *In the White man's image* [Television broadcast]. New
York: Public Broadcasting Corporation.

Margo, R. (1990). *Race and schooling in the American South, 1880–1950.* Chicago:
University of Chicago Press.

Mendez v. Westminster 64F. Supp. 544 (1946).

Miller, J. (2005, September 22). New Orleans unmasks apartheid American style
[Electronic version]. *Black Commentator, 151.* Retrieved September 11, 2006,
from http://www.blackcommentator.com/151I 151_milkr_new_orleans.html

National Center for Education Statistics. (2001). *Education achievement and Black–
White inequality.* Washington, DC: Department of Education.

National Governors' Association. (2005). *Closing the achievement gap.* Retrieved
October 27, 2005, from http://www.subnet.nga.org/educlear/achievement/

National Voting Rights Act of 1965, 42 U.S.C. §§ 1973–1973aa-b.

Orfield, G., & Lee, C. (2004, January). Brown *at 50: King's dream or Plessy's night-
mare?* Cambridge, MA: The Civil Rights Project, Harvard University.

Orfield, G., & Lee, C. (2006, January). *Racial transformation and the changing nature
of segregation.* Cambridge, MA: The Civil Rights Project, Harvard University.

Plessy v. Ferguson 163 U.S. 537 (1896).

Podair, J. (2003). *The strike that changed New York: Blacks, Whites and the Ocean
Hill–Brownsville Crisis.* New Haven, CT: Yale University Press.

Popkewitz, T. S. (1998). *Struggling for the soul: The politics of schooling and the
construction of the teacher.* New York: Teachers College Press.

Robinson, R. (2000). *The debt: What America owes to Blacks.* New York: Dutton
Books.

Rothstein, R., & Wilder, T. (2005, October 24). *The many dimensions of racial inequality*. Paper presented at the Social Costs of Inadequate Education Symposium, Teachers College, Columbia University, New York.

Sentilles, S. (2005). *Taught by America: A story of struggle and hope in Compton*. Boston: Beacon Press.

Sleeter, C. (2001). *Culture, difference and power*. New York: Teachers College Press.

South Carolina v. Katzenbach 383 U.S. 301, 327–328 (1966).

Steele, C. M. (1999, August). Thin ice: "Stereotype threat" and Black college students. *Atlantic Monthly, 284,* 44–47, 50–54.

Takaki, R. (1998). *A larger mirror: A history of our diversity with voices*. Boston: Back Bay Books.

Torres, C. (2006, March 19). Affluent investors more likely educated, married men. *Cleveland Plain Dealer,* p. G6.

Tyack, D. (2004). *Seeking common ground: Public schools in a diverse society*. Cambridge, MA: Harvard University Press.

U.S. Department of Justice, Civil Rights Division. (2006, September 7). *Introduction to federal voting rights laws*. Retrieved September 11, 2006, from http://www.usdoj.gov/crtlvotinglintrolintro.htm

Wilcox, C. (1998). *Sugar water: Hawaii's plantation ditches*. Honolulu, HI: University of Hawaii Press.

Wolfe, B., & Haveman, R. (2001). Accounting for the social and nonmarket benefits of education. In J. Helliwell (Ed.), *The contribution of human and social capital to sustained economic growth and well-being* (pp. 1–72). Vancouver, BC: University of British Columbia Press. Retrieved September 11, 2006, from *http://www.oecd.org/dataoecd/5/19/1825109.pdf*

Woodson, C. G. (1972). *The mis-education of the Negro*. Trenton, NJ: Africa World Press. (Original work published 1933)

Zeichner, K. M. (2002). The adequacies and inadequacies of three current strategies to recruit, prepare, and retain the best teachers for all students. *Teachers College Record, 105*(3), 490–511.

CHAPTER 4

Through a Glass Darkly

The Persistence of Race in Education Research and Scholarship

For now we see through a glass darkly. . .

—I Corinthians 13:12

Then she began to look about and noticed that what could be seen from the old room was quite common and uninteresting, but that all the rest was as different as possible. . . .

—*Through the Looking Glass (And What Alice Found There)*, Lewis Carroll

This lecture begins with a woman. Her name is Cora Lyles Woodward. She was born in 1896 in a Fairfield County, South Carolina, town called Blair. Cora is at the center of this discussion because of the way race delimited her world and her possibilities and how her racial identification underscores the way "research" functions to serve ongoing narratives of superiority/inferiority, citizen/alien, intelligent/unintelligent, and human/inhuman for example. Much of our understanding of complex societies comes from an absolute reliance on the way the empirical accurately reflects reality. In Cora's case, the 1920s census tells us that she was a housewife married to Robert P. Woodward, mother of three, and designated by the census enumerator as a "mulatto"—child of mixed race (Black/White) parents. Ten years later, Cora shows up on the 1930s census again as a "housewife" and now mother of seven children. This time, the enumerator lists her as a "Negro." How did Cora's racial identity shift in 10 years? The simple answer that demographers provide is that the racial categories have changed. Ever since the United States Census Bureau began asking the question, "What is your race?" the available categories have been shifting and changing with White and Black as constant yet polar opposites. In between, there were categories like "Mongoloid," "Indian," "Mulatto," "Quadroon," and "Octoroon" (Lee, 1993). These last three categories are reminiscent of the Napoleonic categorizations that emerged out of Louisiana where, like blood quantum theories regarding "Indian-ness," blackness is being determined according to the perceived amount of "black blood" one has. Thus, a mulatto is the product of one White parent and one Black parent (e.g., President Obama, Halle Berry, Lenny Kravitz, Mariah Carey). A quadroon has one Black grandparent and an octoroon has one Black great grandparent. The point of these classifications was to codify issues of inheritance and social status along with maintaining the myth of White supremacy. It is interesting to note that citizens of Mexican descent were considered White and the basis for the famous Lemon Grove School District decision rested on the notion that Mexican Americans were White, not Black or American Indian (Ferg-Cadima, 2004).

But, Cora Lyles Woodward's racial identification change is not merely about the shift in federal racial classifications for it is important to recognize that Cora never fit the category of "mulatto." She was not the product of a White and Black union. Her mother was Black and her father reputedly Black and American Indian. However, visually she appeared to be solely African American. Why then, does the enumerator give her a more "privileged" identity than her husband Robert Preston Woodward who is identified throughout the census as "Negro"? My interest in the Woodwards is not merely academic. Robert and Cora Woodward were my grandparents but the puzzle of Cora's shifting racial identity also intrigues me as a scholar. My thesis for the purpose of this lecture is that Cora Woodward is granted an almost honorary whiteness because of the response to the U.S. Census form question no. 4 that asks about a person's literacy. While the form indicates that Robert is illiterate (I can attest that he was not), Cora's designation is literate. I want to argue that education and race—in this case, literacy and race—have been intricately linked for centuries and until we begin to unpack those linkages we will continue to struggle to make sense of how race operates in our research and scholarship.

RACE AND SOCIAL SCIENCE RESEARCH

One early clue to the link between race and education comes when as Anderson (1988) states, "between 1800 and 1835, most of the southern states enacted legislation making it a crime to teach enslaved children to read or write" (p. 2). This specific policy decision places a line between literacy and freedom, education and humanity. This is significant because as the 19th century was coming to an end, the English mathematician Sir Francis Galton first coined the term *eugenics*. He wrote, "Eugenics is the study of the agencies under social control that seek to improve or impair the racial qualities of future generations either physically or mentally" (Galton, 1883, frontispiece). Galton's ideas were well received in the United States and became foundational to the fledgling social sciences. In a 1921 *Good Housekeeping* magazine essay, then–vice president Calvin Coolidge wrote:

> There are racial considerations too grave to be brushed aside for any sentimental reasons. Biological laws tell us that certain divergent people will not mix or blend. The Nordics propagate themselves successfully. With other races, the outcome shows deterioration on both sides. Quality of mind and body suggests that observance of ethnic law is as great a necessity to a nation as immigration law. (p. 14)

Some might argue that sentiments like those expressed by Coolidge may have been common during the 1920s but that there must have been a firewall that existed between the nativism and racism of the culture and the science that the academy produced. Sadly, education and the social sciences did not rise above the popular beliefs regarding genetic inferiority attached to race and ethnicity. According to Selden (1999), colleges and universities "offering courses in eugenics increased from 44 in 1914 to 376 in 1928" (p. 14).

One of education research's major figures, Lewis Terman, Professor of Education at Stanford University and inventor of the Stanford-Binet Intelligence test, was a noted eugenicist. After serving the U.S. as a psychologist and intelligence test administrator during World War I, Terman advocated for the use of intelligence tests in schools. After administering his tests to Spanish-speakers and African Americans, Terman (1916) concluded:

> High-grade or border-line deficiency . . . is very, very common among Spanish-Indian and Mexican families of the Southwest and also among negroes. Their dullness seems to be racial, or at least inherent in the family stocks from which they come. . . . Children of this group should be segregated into separate classes. . . . They cannot master abstractions but they can often be made into efficient workers . . . from a eugenic point of view they constitute a grave problem because of their unusually prolific breeding. (pp. 91–92)

I highlight Terman here for a couple of reasons—first because he is such a fixture in the education research canon and second because as a Stanford School of Education alumna I know how much cognitive dissonance my very existence would present for him. We laud Terman for his longitudinal studies of giftedness that appear in the five-volume *Genetic Studies of Genius* (1925–1959) and I have known colleagues across the academy who identify proudly as "Termites." But rarely do we challenge the basis on which this work rests. Clearly no African American or Latino children were thought worthy for Terman's work. We do not discredit his sampling techniques despite his exclusion of entire groups of eligible subjects. Instead, we have used Terman's work as the basis for "gifted and talented" programs throughout the nation.

Our colleagues in sociology have openly declared that the ability to collect data and do scientific research on race is vital to their enterprise (American Sociological Association 2003). They issued their 2003 statement (which our own Executive Director, Dr. Felice Levine helped to draft) in response to a politically conservative movement to eliminate racial classification in state agencies such as schools, health institutions, prisons, etc. They assert, "When a concept is central to societal organization, examining how, when, and why people in that society use the concept is vital to understanding the organization and consequences of social relationships." Their statement argues that there are four primary areas of inquiry that interest sociologists regarding racial classification:

- A sorting mechanism for mating, marriage, and adoption.
- A stratifying practice for providing or denying access to resources.
- An organizational device for mobilization to maintain or challenge systems or racial stratification.
- A basis for scientifically investigating proximate cases.

But it is not merely the professional association statement of sociology that helps us understand the field's link to race as a central concept. Howard Winant (2000) argues, "race has always been a significant sociological theme, from the founding of the field and the formulation of the 'classical' theoretical statements to the present." The seminal work in 20th-century racial theorizing comes from pioneering work by W. E. B. Du Bois in his study of Black life in Philadelphia (1998 [1899]). His conceptualization of "the veil" and his understanding of racial dualism or "double consciousness" provide both theoretical sophistication and empirical rigor to the study of race in sociology. Additionally, sociologists at the Chicago School produced a large body of work on race that demonstrates a melding of pragmatism and progressivism. The Chicago School scholars receive credit for breaking from the notion of racial biologism to assert strongly that race was socially constructed. Indeed, it was the research of a sociologist, Kenneth Clark, and his wife Mamie that brought about the civil rights victory known as *Brown* as he testified about the social psychological harm of segregation on behalf of the plaintiff.

In "The Dark Side of the Force: One Hundred Years of the Sociology of Race," Winant (2007) details the genealogy of race in sociology over the last 100 years and points out the field's linkage to the broader sociopolitical trends. He argues "politically the field can be divided . . . in three parts: mainstream, insurgent, and reactionary." While these explanations are too complex for the space allotted to this lecture, I do want to underscore

Winant's assertion, "the field of sociology is necessarily part of the problem it is trying to explain" (p. 537).

I take Winant's assertion as a relevant segue to another social science that informs education—anthropology. As someone who was trained in anthropology and a member of the American Anthropological Association (AAA), I have watched carefully the ways that race was taken up in the field. For more than 3 years, AAA has conducted a public education project titled, "Race: Are We So Different?" This project garnered more than 4 million dollars in grant support. More than 1.5 million people have walked through the 5,000-square-foot exhibit that explores the science, history, and lived experiences of race and racism in our nation and has traveled to 14 museums across the U.S. For those who know the field of anthropology, this heavy investment in debunking prevailing thinking about race is justified since anthropology is so heavily implicated in forming our ideas and thinking about race.

Anthropology emerged after the age of Western European exploration as "the study of humans" and that study was almost always focused on the people in European colonies. Thus, anthropology was conceived as a study of "the other." Anthropologist Audrey Smedley (1993) points out that race began as a folk classification—"ideologies, distinctions, and selective perceptions that constitute a society's popular imagery and interpretations of the world" (p. 25). But, by the mid- to late 18th century naturalists and other learned men "gave credence and legitimacy [to race] as a supposed product of scientific investigations" (p. 26). Race was regularly on display in World's Fairs and Exhibitions with the classification and ranking of various ethnic and cultural groups. In the past, anthropologists regularly provided the so-called science for these classifications and rankings. The major influence of anthropology on our thinking about race was in the formation of race as a worldview.

Race as a worldview conceives of human populations as inherently unequal and according to Smedley (1993) in the early decades of the 19th century, race in North America contained five ideological components that form a structure of hierarchy and inequality. These elements are:

- Universal classification of human groups as exclusive and discrete biotic entities;
- Imposition of a non-egalitarian ethos that requires the ranking of these groups in relation to each other;
- A belief that the outer physical characteristics of human populations were surface manifestations of inner qualities such as intellect, morality, and temperament;
- A belief that all these characteristics, both outer and inner, were heritable;

- Each exclusive group (or race) was created unique and distinct by nature or by God, so that the imputed differences, believed fixed and unalterable, could never be bridged or transcended (p. 27).

RACE AND EDUCATION RESEARCH

Finally, we arrive at the point to connect race with education research. Because education is a field heavily dependent on the social science disciplines it is logical to assume that it contains some of the shortcomings of those disciplines regarding a concept like race. Education research borrows psychology's notions of normal and exceptional individuals, sociology's notions of normal and exceptional groups such as families and communities, as well as institutions and anthropology's notions of normal and exceptional cultures with implicit beliefs about the classification and ranking of cultural groups.

As a young scholar, I was deeply disturbed by the way race was dealt with in my graduate studies. The research was quick to establish categories like race, class, and gender as logical ways to consider human variation and to promote notions of superiority and inferiority within those categorical boundaries. I also found it puzzling that so many education research findings and innovations were linked to race without clear attribution of how race helped move and develop the field. For example, Elizabeth Cohen's (1994) path-breaking work on status equalization led to almost everything we know about cooperative grouping in instruction. Cohen was clear that her work was important for helping the desegregation efforts. Subsequent scholars seem to dismiss or ignore the role race played in helping us understand classroom dynamics and cooperative grouping.

Large portions of the research done on Title I of the Elementary and Secondary Education Act of 1965 rely on schooling experiences of racialized groups in Head Start, Follow Through, and other compensatory programming. Even the beloved "Sesame Street" children's television program has relied heavily on the lives and day-to-day experiences of children of color. A page on a Georgetown University early childhood website describing the show states, "devised in 1968 as a program designed to enhance school readiness in low-income and minority children, Sesame Street was the first television series to attempt to teach an educational curriculum to its viewers" (retrieved electronically on September 22, 2011, from http://elp.georgetown.edu/linktext.cfm?lid=8). A similar model was used for older elementary-age children in "The Electric Company," a Children's Television Workshop program that ran for six seasons.

In my dissertation (Ladson, 1983), I focused on Black students' conceptualizations of themselves as citizens because an article on the National Assessment of Educational Progress citizenship objectives test declared that they were poorer citizens than their White counterparts. I found this characterization hyperbolic given the long history of African Americans' dedication to the nation from fighting in every war since the American Revolution to literally dying for the franchise. This research was the beginning of my understanding of the paradigmatic and epistemologic challenges research aimed at unpacking race must confront.

Years later as a part of my Spencer postdoctoral fellowship, I was still plagued with the paradigmatic issue. Since much of the literature is fixated on failure and what is wrong with African American and other students of color, I had the temerity and unmitigated gall to ask, "What is right with African American students and what happens in those classrooms where teachers are successful with them?" The first roadblock I encountered was that almost all of the education research literature on African American students was organized around failure. I sat before a computer terminal and entered the search terms, "Black education" and African American education. Within two clicks of the computer I saw the cross references, "see culturally deprived; see culturally deficient." Our entire field was resting on a deficit paradigm that makes it difficult to uncouple the work we want to do from the centuries of work handed down from ideological positions that emerged from constitutive disciplines that insist on the inferiority of entire groups of people. So I had to begin without the help of conventional education research literature and reach for existence proofs as the evidentiary basis on which to make claims of African American excellence and success. That is not a particularly hard case to make. If W. E. B. Du Bois could earn a Ph.D. in history from Harvard in 1895 (the first African American to do so), if Carter G. Woodson could earn a Ph.D. in history from Harvard in 1912 (the second African American to do so), if Anna Julia Cooper could come out of slavery and become teacher and school principal, and if George Washington Carver could come out of slavery and complete a master's degree in botany from Iowa State and go on to be one of the nation's most prolific scientists then we know that discourses about African American intellectual inferiority cannot stand in the face of these amazing biographies.

However, I know that certain analyses suggest that people like those previously mentioned reflect what we in research call "outliers." They become the exceptions that prove the rule. So, we need a greater sample for empirical and statistical power. For this, I point to the 105 Historically Black Colleges and Universities (HBCUs) in this country. All but 6 of these institutions were founded in former slave states. Most were established at the end of the Civil War, with the exception of Cheyney University of Pennsylvania, established in 1837, Lincoln University in Pennsylvania, established in 1854, and Wilberforce University in Ohio, established in 1856.

So desperate for education were the newly emancipated African Americans that they started these schools in boxcars (Atlanta University), church basements (Spelman College), and on garbage dumps

(Bethune-Cookman). These institutions started in meager circumstances with limited resources produced some of the nation's best minds—W. E. B. Du Bois, Thurgood Marshall, Martin Luther King Jr., and Toni Morrison. Even today, HBCUs produce 50% of the Black teachers and 70% of Black dentists. I knew that African American success and excellence was both possible and a reality.

My research on successful teachers of African American students allowed me to build the theory of culturally relevant pedagogy (Ladson-Billings, 1995) where we could see that success in a classroom of African American students rests on three propositions: focus on student learning, development of cultural competence, and promotion of sociopolitical consciousness. It did not rest on tinkering with the curriculum or demanding absolute quiet or having everyone wear a uniform. It rests on a teacher who believes deeply in the intellectual capability of the student and his or her own efficacious abilities. When I was first asked "why African American students and success," I immediately responded, "Why not?" If we can improve the system for what the Bible calls "the least of these," it seems reasonable that it will provide a way to improve it for all others. Interesting, the question of "why African Americans" has never come up among my colleagues in Sweden, Japan, the UK, or Brazil. They are only interested in the portability of the theory for struggling students in their countries.

As my work on culturally relevant pedagogy was starting to get some recognition, I found myself grappling with a new theoretical issue that was more likely to bring less sanguine responses—critical race theory. The title of this lecture is "Through a Glass Darkly: The Persistence of Race in Education Research." I chose the title because I believe much of what we do in education research regarding race is cloudy and imprecise. We are using crude measures to sort and slot people into categories—Black, White, Latino, immigrant, English-speaking, low-income, disabled, first-generation, etc.—as if we don't live our lives across multiple categories of being or as if some of the categories that are most salient in our lives aren't invisible. We know little about things like the faith commitments of students. We know little about the way family structure and relations affect students—here I am not merely talking about things like one- versus two-parent households or number of siblings. Rather, I am talking about things like family cohesion and fictive and actual kin networks. For example, I was in a household with only one sibling, my brother, but I attended high school with 11 first cousins. Those many kin relations made me wary of misbehaving—there were far too many witnesses. We know little about the role of sponsorship in student success. In her outstanding work on literacy, Brandt (1998) argues for a concept of "sponsors of literacy" in which "sponsors . . . are any agents, local or distant, concrete or abstract, who enable, support, teach, model, as well as recruit, regulate, suppress, or withhold literacy—and gain advantage by it in some way" (p. 166).

Extremely important to me as a researcher is the impact of race—explicitly and implicitly manifested—on learning. Does the race of the teacher and other classmates matter for learners? Does the race of the students, their parents, and administrator matter to teachers? And if so, HOW does it matter? Does it matter in ways that enhance or thwart student learning and academic achievement? While culturally relevant pedagogy has been the site of most of my empirical work, it is my theoretical foray into critical race theory that has drawn the most skepticism and ire from colleagues and others.

Critical race theory (CRT) comes from legal scholarship that argues that racism is normal, not aberrant, in U.S. society (Delgado & Stefancic, 2001). CRT uses storytelling or more accurately counternarratives to weave legal truths in fanciful and oppositional ways. It also uses critical social science and scholarship from Black studies, Latino studies, Asian American studies, and feminist studies to explore the ways race continues to have power and predictive value. One of the hallmarks of critical race theory work is the chronicle. Here, the scholar tells a tale—a moral story or parable—to illustrate a deeper truth. All CRT chronicles are based on actual events or legal cases. The one I have constructed follows that pattern. So, as I close I leave you with "The Chronicle of the Best Black Students":

Barry and Bonnie Black were an African American couple who had dreams and aspirations. They were going somewhere. During the first years of their marriage they scrimped and saved so they could buy a lovely old home in the city's historic district. On the day they moved in, they had to pinch themselves as they walked through the home filled with original fireplaces and stately hardwoods. As they made it to the third floor attic area, they discovered that the previous owners had left behind some possessions. One that caught Bonnie's eye appeared to be an ancient lamp—the kind you saw in movies from somewhere in Turkey or Pakistan. When Barry noticed the lamp, he smiled at Bonnie and asked, "You don't suppose if we rub it we'll produce a genie do you?" Bonnie giggled and said, "It couldn't hurt!" Barry picked up the lamp and began to rub, "Let's see, I think I'll ask to get this big mortgage paid off," he quipped. No sooner than the words left his mouth a cloud of smoke and indeed a genie appeared. "Your wish is my command," bellowed the genie. Barry and Bonnie grabbed each other and stood with their mouths agape. "What in the world?" started Bonnie. "C'mon, c'mon I don't have all day," replied the genie. "Let's hear your wish." Barry seemed to compose himself and said, "Wish . . . I thought we're supposed to get three wishes." "You people watch too many movies. We're in the middle of a recession. You get ONE wish," replied their ephemeral guest. Barry and Bonnie looked at each other for what seemed an eternity and then in unison they said, "We'd like to have the 'best Black children'!"

Sure enough when the couple's first baby, Bonita was born, she looked like the best Black child. She was beautiful, alert, and in perfect health. As the years progressed, the couple had two additional children, and while they did not get three wishes it appeared that they got the three best Black children ever. Barry and Bonnie delighted in raising Bonita, Barak, and Belinda . . . their best Black children.

By the time Bonita arrived at George Washington Community High School, she had proven herself to be a model student. She excelled in the classroom and in the arts. Although she was the only African American in the school she was well liked and a stellar student. In her senior year, Bonita was taking all Advanced Placement courses and was first violinist in the school's symphony orchestra. When the grade chairman calculated the grades, it was apparent that Bonita was the class valedictorian. Barry and Bonnie gushed with pride and said to each other, "We do have the best Black children." A few days before graduation the principal summoned Bonita to the office. She felt certain he wanted to give her some special congratulatory words. However, once in the office the principal informed Bonita that the school was going to "go in a different direction" this year and have "co-valedictorians." "I don't understand," Bonita remarked. "I was clearly the best student in the graduating class." " I know," smiled the principal. "We just thought it would be fair to be a bit more inclusive!"

Although puzzled about what happened with Bonita and the valedictory address, the Blacks knew that son Barak would have an amazing high school career. The moment Barak set foot in Washington High, he was a star. He was a brilliant student with drop-dead good looks and amazing athletic ability. Barak was captain of both the debate team and the football team. In his senior year, he ran for Homecoming King and to no one's surprise he won handily. Barak was elated about this honor. He would lead the homecoming parade by riding in a sleek convertible seated beside a beautiful Homecoming Queen. Would it be Stacey, the cheerleader, or Lizzie, the beautiful brainiac in his physics class? Either way, he'd be looking good as he led the parade, led his team to a victory, and received the accolades of his classmates at the big homecoming dance. The only thing better than this would be getting into Stanford, where he could excel in engineering and on the football field.

Two days before the big homecoming festivities, Barak received a summons to the principal's office. Like his sister before him, Barak assumed the call was to commend him for his excellence. However, once again one of the best Black children would hear disappointing news. "Congratulations, son," the principal began. I am sure your parents are quite proud of you. "Yes, sir, they are," responded Barak. "Well, we here at Washington High are also proud. However, we're going to make a little change in the homecoming parade and dance this year. You will be our king, but there won't be a homecoming queen." "Why not?" exclaimed Barak. "Did the homecoming queen get ill? Can't the first runner-up take her place?" "Errr, no, I don't think that's going to happen, son," the principal replied. "You're a big handsome guy and you're going to look great sitting in that car. In fact, you get to choose what you want to wear, instead of having to coordinate with some girl. You can wear a tuxedo, or go casual, or hey . . . you could wear your football jersey since you'll be starring in the game after the parade. That's gonna be something special."

When Barak told his parents what happened, they looked at each other knowingly and sighed a huge sigh. "Here we go again," Barry remarked.

When time came for Barry and Bonnie to send their third best Black child, Belinda to George Washington Community High School, Bonnie told Barry she had another idea in mind. "I was thinking, dear," she began, "what if we sent Belinda to Carver High School where we attended?" "George Washington Carver High?" Barry questioned. "Yes . . . we know Belinda is exceptionally smart like our other two children, artistically gifted like Bonita AND athletically exceptional like Barak. Belinda will excel no matter where she goes and we can ensure that she has enough enrichment opportunities to make up for possible shortcomings at the school. At least we will not have to see another disappointed kid when her excellence rises above the others." "You may have a point," Barry replied. "We could give it a try and if things don't seem to be working she can always transfer back here to George Washington Community High School."

Belinda was surprised her parents enrolled her in Carver High but within a few weeks she was among the most popular kids at the school. Her phone was constantly ringing and she had more dates than she could keep up with. She was captain of the debate team, head cheerleader during football season, starting point guard on the girls' basketball team, and class president. By the time she had completed four years at Carver, Belinda had held every major office in the student government. She had scores of friends and was much loved by the teachers and administrators. She loved going to school and her 4.0 grade point average made her a shoe in for valedictorian and the university of her choice.

In Spring when colleges and universities began sending out their admissions decisions, the Black family's mailbox was inundated with acceptances. However, Belinda's first choice, the state's elite public university sent a very thin envelope with a letter that began ". . . we regret to inform you . . ." Barry and Bonnie could not believe it. Why on earth would the state university reject her? Her profile was stellar. What could have happened? Determined not to have another disappointed best Black child, Barry and Bonnie contacted elite state university to see if there was some mistake. They learned that although Belinda had a fantastic profile, her 4.0 grade point average was eclipsed by the better than 4.0 averages of her White counterparts. George Washington Carver High School did not offer any advanced placement courses to allow Belinda to build a GPA that was greater than 4.0.

So, despite raising three of the best Black children, Barry and Bonnie could not shield their children from the endemic racism that was a part of the society. They tried playing by the rules and that did not work. They tried an alternative strategy and that did not work. Their children like millions of Black and Brown children had to learn the gritty reality—despite how hard we try, race still matters.

However, in addition to the salience of race I want to underscore the reality that all parents send their best children to school . . . regardless of their race, ethnicity, gender, language, immigrant status, or ability. They don't have a set of spare, better children tucked away in a china cabinet. The children who walk through the doors of the nation's schools are the best Black, Brown, Yellow, Red, and White children we have and until we truly recognize and embrace that reality we will continue to look through a glass darkly.

REFERENCES

American Sociological Association. (2003). *The importance of collecting data and doing social scientific research on race*. Washington, DC: Author.

Anderson, J. D. (1988). *The education of Blacks in the south, 1860–1935*. Chapel Hill: University of North Carolina Press.

Brandt, D. (1998). The sponsors of literacy. *College Composition and Communication, 49*, 165–185.

Cohen, E. (1994). *Designing groupwork: Strategies for heterogeneous classrooms*. New York, NY: Teachers College Press.

Delgado, R., & Stefancic, J. (2001). *Critical race theory: An introduction*. New York: New York University Press.

Du Bois, W. E. B. (1998). *The Philadelphia Negro: A social study*. Philadelphia: University of Pennsylvania Press. (Original work published 1899)

Ferg-Cadima, J. A. (2004). Black, white and brown: Latino school desegregation efforts in the pre- and post–*Brown vs. Board of Education* era. Washington, DC: MALDEF.

Galton, F. (1883). *Inquiries into human faculty and its development*. London: Macmillan.

Ladson, G. (1983). *Citizenship and values: An ethnographic study of citizenship and values in a predominately Black school setting* (Unpublished doctoral dissertation). Stanford University, Stanford, CA.

Ladson-Billings, G. (1995). Toward a theory of culturally relevant pedagogy. *American Educational Research Journal, 32*, 465–491.

Lee, S. M. (1993). Racial classifications in the U.S. census: 1890–1990. *Ethnic and Race Studies, 16*, 75–94.

Selden, S. (1999). *Inheriting shame: The story of eugenics in America*. New York, NY: Teachers College Press.

Smedley, A. (1993). *Race in North America: Origins and evolution of a worldview*. Boulder, CO: Westview.

Terman, L. M. (1916). *The measurement of intelligence*. Boston, MA: Houghton Mifflin.

Terman, L. M. (1925–1959). *Genetic studies of genius* (Vols. I–V). Stanford, CA: Stanford University Press.

Winant, H. (2000). Race and race theory. *Annual Review of Sociology, 26,* 169–185.

Winant, H. (2007). The dark side of the force: One hundred years of the sociology of race. In C. Calhoun (Ed.), *Sociology in American: A history* (pp. 535–571). Chicago, IL: University of Chicago Press.

CHAPTER 5

New Directions in Multicultural Education

Complexities, Boundaries, and Critical Race Theory

The Sunday, May 20, 2001, headline on the *Chicago Tribune* read, "A Multicultural State for Sears." The subheading pointed out that Sears, one of the largest retailers in the United States, was targeting Black and Latino consumers. (In this chapter, the term *Black* designates all individuals of African descent. In cases where the reference is solely to Blacks who also have a U.S. heritage, the term is *African American*.) The ease with which a major newspaper used the term *multicultural* tells us something about how power and domination appropriate even the most marginal voices. Multicultural has made it to Main Street.

This chapter examines the ways current ideas about the term *multicultural* must give way to new expressions of human and social diversity. It argues for reconceptualized views of difference that often are forced to operate in old social schemes. Placed in a linear chronology, this chapter would necessarily cover a large volume, not a chapter. Thus the liberty taken with this discussion is to appropriate a metaphor—jazz—to scaffold the changing, often conflicting, developments and iterations of this field we call multicultural education.

Carl Engel's discussion of jazz in 1922 pointed out that "good jazz is a composite, the happy union of seemingly incompatible elements. . . . It is the upshot of a transformation . . . and culminates in something unique, unmatched in any other part of the world" (p. 6). Engel further asserts that "jazz is rag-time, plus 'Blues,' plus orchestral polyphony; it is the combination . . . of melody, rhythm, harmony, and counterpoint" (p. 8). Finally,

> Jazz is abandon, is whimsicality in music. A good jazz band should never play, and actually never does play, the same piece twice in the same manner. Each player must be a clever musician, an originator as well as an interpreter, a wheel that turns hither and thither on its own axis without disturbing the clockwork." (p. 9) (A number of these jazz references come from the *Atlantic*

Monthly's jazz archives, which can be found on the Internet at www.theatlantic
.com/unbound/jazz.)

Indeed, what we now call multicultural education also is a composite. It
is no longer solely race, or class, or gender. Rather, it is the infinite permutations that come about as a result of the dazzling array of combinations
human beings recruit to organize and fulfill themselves. Like jazz, no human
being is ever the same in every context. The variety of "selves" we perform
have made multicultural education a richer, more complex, and more difficult enterprise to organize and implement than previously envisioned. In
1955, Arnold Sundgaard pointed out:

> A song of itself is not jazz, no matter what its origin. Jazz is what the jazzmen
> [*sic*] searching together bring to it, take from it, find within it. . . . Much is left
> free for improvisation, and no precise method of notation has been developed
> to indicate its rhythmic and emotional complexities. . . . The song and its ar-
> rangement become . . . a means to an end. The music used . . . is somewhat
> incidental to the inspired uses to which it is put. For this reason jazz . . . thrives
> on endless exploration and ceaseless discovery. (pp. 1–2)

Again, like jazz, multicultural education is less a thing than a process. It
is organic and dynamic, and although it has a history rooted in our traditional notions of curriculum and schooling its aims and purposes transcend
all conventional perceptions of education. Early attempts at multicultural education were rooted in what Hollinger (1995) called the ethnoracial
pentagon, that is, African Americans, Asian Americans, Latinas/os, Native
Americans, and European Americans. These static categories held some political sway but began to lose their social and symbolic meanings because
of the changes in the everyday lives of most people. Racial and ethnic inequity and discrimination had played significant roles in contouring the U.S.
landscape. But demographic shifts, a growing understanding of the multiple
identities that people inhabit and embrace, and an awareness of other forms
of oppression made the ethnoracial distinctions a limited way to talk about
multiculturalism and multicultural education.

Perhaps the limitation in this thinking about multiculturalism stems
from limited thinking about the term *culture*. Most common definitions of
culture describe it either as "an aesthetic phenomenon" (Coffey, 2000, p.
38) or a particular way of life that includes knowledge, values, artifacts, beliefs, and other aspects of human endeavor peculiar to any group or groups
of people (Williams, 1976). It is this latter definition that has come to be associated with multiculturalism. However, Coffey (2000) cites Tony Bennett
in describing new thinking about culture:

[It] is more cogently conceived . . . when thought of as a historically specific set of institutionally embedded relations of government in which the forms of thought and conduct of extended populations are targeted for transformation—in part via the extension through the social body of the forms, techniques, and regimens of aesthetic and intellectual culture. (Bennett, 1992, p. 26)

Bennett's (1992) work is informed by Foucault's (1991) writing on governmentality and argues that culture is created through the processes of social management, and that it is both the object and the instrument of government. This definition does not negate the materiality of culture (that is, the objects and practices of culture) but expands conventional notions of culture to include the way both specialized and everyday practices are marked as culture. The very human endeavors that may be seen as normal or commonsensical are culturally bounded. Multiculturalism cannot be seen merely as a study of the other, but rather as multiple studies of culture and cultural practices in the lives of all humans.

Another theme of this chapter is that the notion of America, like jazz, does not lend itself easily to definition and prescription. Ward and Burns (2000) link jazz to America:

It is America's music—born out of a million American negotiations: between having and not having; between happy and sad, country and city; between black and white and men and women; between the Old Africa and the Old Europe—which could only have happened in an entirely New World.

It is an improvisational art, making itself up as it goes along—just like the country that gave it birth.

It rewards individual expression but demands selfless collaboration.

It is forever changing but nearly always rooted in the blues.

It has a rich tradition and its own rules, but it is brand-new every night.

It is about just making a living and taking terrible risks, losing everything and finding love, making things simple and dressing to the nines.

It has enjoyed huge popularity and survived hard times, but it has always reflected Americans—all Americans—at their best. (p. xxi)

I argue that this multilayered, eclectic description of America is similarly evident in new notions of multicultural education. The early beginnings of multicultural education (see J. A. Banks, 2003) are reminiscent of the early beginnings of jazz. Scholars as far back as George Washington Williams in the 1880s and W. E. B. Du Bois in the first decades of the 20th century began to articulate a new vision of history that positioned African Americans as fully human cultural agents. The dissonance caused by this "new" vision of history parallels the dissonance from early jazz stirrings. The editor of *Etude* magazine (cited in Ward & Burns, 2000) asserted that the music was "syncopation gone mad. . . . Whether it is simply a passing phase of our decadent art culture or an infectious disease which has come to stay . . . time alone can tell" (pp. 14–15).

However, by the 1960s and 1970s social movements concerning the rights of African Americans, Latinas/os, Native Americans, Asian Americans, women, and the poor were sweeping across America. By appropriating the language of civil rights and the strategy of legal remedies, various groups were able to make use of existing laws and push for new ones that recognized their basic humanity. The parallel moment in jazz was roughly between 1917 and 1924, or the emergence of the jazz age. It was during this era of World War I and the Roaring Twenties that jazz became clearly established in the United States. In 1926, R.W.S. Mendl stated that "jazz is the product of a restless age: an age in which the fever of war is only now beginning to abate its fury: when men and women, after their efforts in the great struggle, are still too much disturbed to be content with a tranquil existence" (quoted in Ward & Burns, 2000, p. 102).

In the Ward and Burns volume (2000), a quotation from Duke Ellington captures another central point of this discussion, that of freedom and liberation:

> Jazz is a good barometer of freedom. . . . In its beginnings, the United States of America spawned certain ideals of freedom and independence through which eventually jazz was evolved, and the music is so free that many people say it is the only unhampered, unhindered expression of complete freedom yet produced in this country. (p. vii)

Multicultural education, like America itself, is about the expression of freedom, but notions of freedom and liberation almost always involve contestation. The work of the social movements was taken up by theorists and practitioners to create new curriculum and instructional practices to reflect changes in the sociopolitical landscape. Work by James A. Banks, Gwendolyn Baker, Carl Grant, and Geneva Gay built on the ethnic studies work of scholars such as Carlos Cortés, Jack Forbes, Asa Hilliard, Barbara Sizemore, and others to create rubrics for curriculum designers and teachers who took on the task of aligning school curricula with emerging scholarly evidence about the histories, cultures, lives, and experiences of various peoples. More important, this work challenged old perceptions of America as a "White" country.

Today it is almost impossible to walk into an elementary school in the United States and not find representation of "multicultural America." These representations take the form of characters in reading books, bulletin board displays, assembly programs, and even school supplies (Crayola crayons offers what it calls a "multicultural" crayon set purportedly with hues that represent various skin colors). But it is just this commonality (as expressed earlier in the Sears store example) that has forced scholars and activists to begin pushing the boundaries of multicultural education and argue against the ways dominant ideologies are able to appropriate the multicultural discourse (McCarthy, 1988; Wynter, 1992). At the secondary school level, there is an array of courses (typically electives) and clubs that acknowledge the cultural contributions of various groups formerly ignored by the school curriculum. However, these efforts typically represent what King (2001) calls "marginalizing knowledge," which "is a form of curriculum transformation that can include selected 'multicultural' curriculum content that simultaneously distorts both the historical and social reality that people actually experienced This form of marginalizing inclusion is justified in the (indivisible) interest of 'our common culture'" (p. 274).

McLaren (1994, 2000) introduces the notions of "critical multiculturalism" and/or "revolutionary multiculturalism" to interrupt the diversity discourse that emerged to supplant and subvert the original intentions of theorists who set out to create a pedagogy of liberation and social justice. King (2001) calls for "deciphering culture-centered knowledge" that leads to "changed consciousness and cognitive autonomy [that] can be a foundation for curriculum transformation" (p. 276). This "new multiculturalism," like the new jazz ushered in by alto saxophonist Ornette Coleman, represents a "permanent revolution" (Davis, 1985, p. 1). In his discussion of Coleman's work, Davis said:

> What must have bothered musicians . . . more than the unmistakable southern dialect of Coleman's music was its apparent formlessness, its flouting of rules that most jazz modernists had invested a great deal of time and effort in mastering. In the wake of bebop, jazz had become a music of enormous harmonic complexity. By the late 1950s it seemed to be in danger of becoming a playground for virtuosos, as the liberating practice of running the chords became routine. If some great players sounded at times as though they lacked commitment and were simply going through the motions, it was because the motions were what they had become most committed to. (p. 4)

Critical multiculturalism that relies on a deciphering knowledge seeks to push past going through the motions of multiculturalism. The remainder of this chapter discusses a rubric for thinking about multicultural education, the extant tensions within the field, a rearticulation of race, and a look at current trends in multicultural education.

A RUBRIC FOR THINKING ABOUT MULTICULTURAL EDUCATION

The discomfort is also there, of course, in the music's structure. Rather than following standard chord progressions and traditional solo structures, large portions of the ensemble's repertoire are devoted to impromptu explorations of a semiotic freedom (Heble, 2000).

Banks (2003) puts forth five dimensions of multicultural education that help us understand its comprehensive and multifaceted nature: content integration, knowledge construction, prejudice reduction, equity pedagogy, and an empowering school culture (see Banks for a full explanation of these elements). This chapter focuses more directly on the knowledge construction aspect of his dimensions because new notions of knowledge, what is knowable—or the epistemological basis of a discipline or area of study—determines its theoretical, conceptual, methodological, and pedagogical trajectory. Gordon (1997) reminds us that "mainstream social science knowledge is grounded in the standards for knowledge production that have developed in the physical sciences (Keto, 1989), in which the main purpose of research is seen as seeking universal 'truths,' generalizations one can apply to all—'totalizing schemas'" (p. 47).

Gordon further asserts that epistemological paradigms emerging from the experiences of people of color and women offer a challenge to these mainstream perspectives.

Culturally centered research (here the term *cultural* refers to a variety of human groupings: race, ethnicity, gender, social class, ability, sexuality, and religion) argues against the claims of universality and objectivity of knowledge that mainstream research presumes. It recognizes that both the knower and the known have particular standpoints grounded in historical, political, social, and economic contexts. Thus it is important to make clear the frame of reference from which the researcher works and understands the world. Gordon (1997) argues that this challenge to mainstream research has caused an "epistemological crisis" (p. 49). However, mainstream scholars have found ways to construe multicultural education as a part of the dominant paradigm. Both McLaren (1994) and King (2001) provide clear examples of this.

McLaren (1994) argues that multiculturalism has taken on a variety of forms that move it away from ideals of liberation and social justice. He terms these forms conservative (or corporate) multiculturalism, liberal multiculturalism, and left-liberal multiculturalism. McLaren is careful to identify these forms as heuristic devices, not meant to serve as essentialized and fixed categories but rather as useful categories to describe an array of thought and practice evident in schools and society today. One reason these categories become important is, as McLaren states, that "multiculturalism without a transformative political agenda can be just another form of accommodation to the larger social order" (p. 53).

Conservative or corporate multiculturalism is a strategy for disavowing racism and prejudice without conceding any of the power or privilege the dominant class enjoys. For example, the approach of the Sears store mentioned in the beginning of this chapter represents the way corporate interests have attempted to mobilize the multicultural rhetoric to promote consumption (and perhaps exploitation of workers). Their message, like that of Glazer (1997), is that we are all multiculturalists now. Corporate or conservative multiculturalism has a veneer of diversity without any commitment to social justice or structural change. Like King's (2001) description of marginalizing knowledge, conservative multiculturalism is a "form of curriculum transformation that can include selected 'multicultural' curriculum content that simultaneously distorts both the historical and social reality that people actually experienced" (p. 274). So even though students might see representations of various groups in their texts and school curriculum, how those people are represented may be conservative or marginalizing. A typical textbook strategy for accomplishing this is to place information about racially and ethnically subordinated peoples in a special features section while the main text, which carries the dominant discourse, remains uninterrupted and undisturbed by "multicultural information."

The second type of multiculturalism McLaren (1994) identifies is liberal multiculturalism. This rests on a perspective of "intellectual sameness among the races . . . or the rationality imminent in all races that permits them to compete equally in a capitalist society" (p. 51). In King's (2001) analysis, this might be thought of as "expanding knowledge." This represents a kind of curriculum transformation, but the "rotation in the perspective of the subject can multiculturalize knowledge without changing fundamentally the norm of middle-classness in the social framework's cultural model of being" (p. 275). This type of multiculturalism finds a ready home in the academy because it tries to address the concerns of all groups equally without disturbing the existing power structure. Thus most campuses offer programs and activities directed at African Americans, Latinas/os, Asian Americans, Native Americans, women, gays, lesbians, the disabled, and other identified groups. However, these programs and groups operate in isolation from each other, and the campus community rarely calls into question the way White middle-class norms prevail.

The perspectives of liberal multiculturalism are similar to what Sleeter and Grant (1987) identified as a human relations approach to multicultural education. Here emphasis on human sameness fails to reveal the huge power differentials that exist between the White middle class and other groups in U.S. society. By acknowledging the existence of various groups while simultaneously ignoring the issues of power and structural inequity, liberal multiculturalism functions as a form of appeasement. As previously stated, liberal multiculturalism argues for intellectual sameness among distinctive cultural groups. This form of multiculturalism also holds on to notions of meritocracy and argues for equal opportunities to compete in a capitalist market economy. This thinking fails to recognize the structural and symbolic practices that militate against the ability of the poor, women, and non-White ethnic and cultural groups to access (and succeed in) the society.

For example, Conley (2000) describes his growing up poor in a New York housing project that was almost all Black and Latino. Even here, his

White skin privilege prevailed. All of his Black classmates were regularly struck by teachers for misbehavior, but "everyone involved, teacher and students, took it for granted that a Black teacher would never cross the racial line to strike a White student" (Conley, p. 45). Later, as a sociology professor, Conley began to ask his students a simple question: how they got their first job. Almost all of his African American and Latina/o students reported that they searched the newspaper classified advertisements or responded to help wanted signs in store and business windows to search for work. Almost none of the White students found their first jobs that way. Instead, family, friends, and other familiar connections meant that employment came to them.

It is important to point out that the advantage of White skin privilege is not totally invisible to Whites. Hacker (1992) asked his White students at Queens College how much they would want in the way of "compensation" if they were to become Black for the next 20 years. Hacker reminded the students that they would suffer no loss of resources, intellect, or social status in this hypothetical skin change experiment. Still, students reported that they would want $1 million in compensation. Thus White college students believe their White skin is worth at least $50,000 a year.

Sims (1982) gave curriculum examples of liberal multiculturalism in her description of children's fiction. She categorized those books that merely colored in the faces of children while maintaining a story line that gave no indication of the characters' racial and cultural experiences as "culturally neutral." Classics such as Ezra Jack Keats's *A Snowy Day* or *Whistle for Willie* are prototypical examples of such books. The story purports to be a universal one, where the characters' racial identity adds nothing to the story line. Rather, such books attempt to underscore the human commonality rather than differences.

A third approach to multiculturalism is what McLaren (1994) calls "left-liberal multiculturalism." This form of multiculturalism emphasizes cultural differences to the point of exoticism. According to McLaren, "the left liberal position tends to exoticize 'otherness' in a nativistic retreat that locates difference in a primeval past of cultural authenticity" (p. 51). The reliance on separate and distinct campus programs of identity politics fosters this essentialized notion of culture. Few, if any, programs in ethnic studies, gender, sexuality, or disability integrate across identities; rarely are there Black women's studies programs or Latino gay programs.

Current academy relations treat identity politics as monolithic and essentialized. Even within programs, there is often little room for perspectives that stretch the epistemological and ideological boundaries. Dyson (1994) argues that "contemporary African American culture is radically complex and diverse, marked by an intriguing variety of intellectual reflections, artistic creations, and social practices" (p. 218). Surely the same can be said of every other cultural group. Scholars such as Lowe (1996), Anzaldúa (1987), and Warrior (1995) examine the complexities of ethnic identities within Asian American, Latina/o, and American Indian groups, respectively.

In speaking of the cultural complexities of Black identities and cultures, Gilroy (1993) urges people of African descent (particularly those in the Diaspora) to avoid the "lure of ethnic particularism and nationalism" (p. 4) in favor of "global, coalitional politics in which anti-imperialism and anti-racism might be seen to interact" (p. 4). Further, Gilroy encourages people of various racial and cultural identities to break out of linear, absolutist renderings of their cultural selves that often characterize ethnic studies agendas. Instead, Gilroy points back to Du Bois's (1953/1989) powerful notion of double consciousness as an appropriate rubric for understanding the identity challenge of all peoples who suffer the oppression of dominant culture norms and constraints. McKay and Wong (1996) provide another compelling example of the way people eschew the ethnic, racial, and/ or cultural boundaries established by totalizing discourses, to act in ways that more accurately reflect current identities. In their study of adolescent Chinese immigrants, they found that the students had different motivations for learning (or not learning) English, tied to their identities and influenced by economic status, peer groups, neighborhoods, and academic ability.

Finally, McLaren (1994) offers a notion of critical multiculturalism. Here he calls for a restructuring of the social order through a radical approach to schooling. McCarthy (1988) suggests that because multiculturalism originates in the liberal pluralist paradigm it is limited in its ability to create long-lasting substantive social change. Instead, from McCarthy's perspective multicultural education represents a "curricular truce" (p. 267) that was designed to pacify the insurgent demands of African Americans, Latinas/os, Asian Americans, and Native Americans during the 1960s and 1970s.

King (2001) offers what she terms "deciphering knowledge" as an emancipatory form of cultural knowledge. Drawing heavily on the work of Sylvia Wynter (1989, 1992) and novelist Toni Morrison (1989, 1991), King asserts that deciphering knowledge is "aimed at changed consciousness and cognitive autonomy" as the "foundation for curriculum transformation" (p. 276). Though not specifically postmodern, this work engages Foucault's notion (1972) of the archaeology of knowledge to reveal the discursive practices that support the racial and power ideologies that contour the social order. Such work examines both the explicit and implicit texts to articulate meaning and intentions. For example, Morrison's (1991) examination of classics from the American literary canon exposes how race was configured throughout the texts without ever having to use the familiar terms and codes. A much less sophisticated example of "text" can be seen in everyday advertising and media representations. For example, when George Herbert Bush ran for president in 1988 his campaign aired what came to be known as the "Willie Horton ad." The literal representation of the ad was one of a particular criminal,

Willie Horton, who was released from jail by Mr. Bush's opponent, only to kill again. Applying deciphering knowledge to the ad/text allows us to see the way Horton was a proxy for the supposed danger and criminality of African American men. On the opposite end of the spectrum is the way that various ethnic and cultural groups members are recruited to represent a form of "contained diversity." For example, high-level government officials and appointees can be used to reflect a commitment to diversity regardless of their lack of interest or personal commitment to social justice and transformative social change. Deciphering knowledge helps people see through the veneer of inclusion to the ways in which diversity or multiculturalism is being manipulated to maintain and justify the status quo.

Another example of critical multiculturalism and deciphering knowledge is the postcolonial project. Smith (1999) points out that from the perspective of the colonized, the very term *research* is linked to European imperialism and colonialism. This notion was established earlier by Fanon (1963, 1967), who explained the ways European education creates a sense of alienation and self-negation in the colonized. Writing from a place of "alterity" (Wynter, 1992), those who are positioned as "others" see the social framework from another perspective, not unlike Du Bois's (1953/1989) double-consciousness:

> the Negro is a sort of seventh son, born with a veil, and gifted with second sight in this American world—a world which yields him no true self consciousness, but only lets him see himself through the revelation of the other world. It is a peculiar sensation, this double consciousness, this sense of always looking at one's self through the eyes of others, of measuring one's soul by the tape of a world that looks on in amused contempt and pity. (p. 3).

TENSIONS WITHIN THE FIELD

[John] Coltrane seemingly forsook lyricism for an unfettered quest for ecstasy. The results remain virtually indescribable, and they forestall criticism with the furious directness of their energy. Yet, their effect depends more on the abandonment of rationality, which most listeners achieve only intermittently if at all.

—Strickland (1987)

For the sake of argument, let us presume that we agree that McLaren's (1994) critical multiculturalism and King's (2001) deciphering knowledge are indeed what we mean when we refer to multiculturalism. Such agreement does not necessarily resolve tensions within the field of multiculturalism. Although multicultural education began as a challenge to the inequities that students of color experienced in school and society, it soon became an umbrella movement for a variety of forms of difference—particularly race, class, and gender. Within each category of difference, other issues emerged: linguistic, ethnic and cultural, sexual orientation, and ability.

The work of feminists gave rise to demands for social equity for women and supported an epistemological challenge to the academy. Work by Gilligan (1977), Noddings (1984), Lather (1991), Code (1991), and others challenged the notion that conventional positivist paradigms represent the full spectrum of social and educational experiences. Feminist scholars demanded that new forms of scholarship be represented in the academy. Thus gender work became another task of the multicultural project. Schmitz, Butler, Rosenfelt, and Guy-Sheftall (2001) point out that there exists a "continuing tension in feminist scholarship, the tension between an emphasis on equality . . . and an emphasis on difference" (p. 710). I would argue that this tension runs deeper because of the complex and multiple identities women assume. Jaimes and Halsey (1992) suggest that the work of Native American women is one of sovereignty over Western feminism. Similarly, African American women such as Audrey Lourde, bell hooks, Alice Walker, and Patricia Hill Collins have asked about the place of Black women and their particular issues in the feminist discourse. Although Frankenberg (1993) has clearly acknowledged that race shapes White women's lives, many others have ignored race and class in their discussions of feminist work. Trinh T. Minh-ha (1989) argues that we cannot think of race and gender as separate and distinct identities because this creates dichotomous thinking that serves the interests of the dominant order:

> Many women of color feel obliged [to choose] between ethnicity and womanhood: how can they? You never have/are one without the other. The idea of two illusorily separated identities, one ethnic, the other woman (or most precisely female), partakes in the Euro-American system of dualistic reasoning and its age–old divide-and-conquer tactics. . . . The pitting of anti-racist and anti-sexist struggles against one another allows some vocal fighters to dismiss blatantly the existence of either racism or sexism within their lines of action, as if oppression only comes in separate, monolithic forms. (p. 105)

Perhaps the emblem of the fissure between race and gender in the United States was the O. J. Simpson trial (see Morrison & Lacour, 1997). Feminists (many of the more vocal ones were White) advocated constructing the trial around the worrisome women's issue of domestic violence. However, both Simpson's defense team and segments of the African American community saw the trial as an opportunity to underscore the way the justice system (and the society) uses a racial measurement to determine the kind of available justice defendants receive.

Another point of tension for feminists is around class issues. The seemingly stunning efforts of the women's movement to help women gain access to middle-class positions in the corporate sector, the academy, and social services pale in comparison to the continued problems of women in poverty, women's health, and child support and care. Women of color often find themselves in poverty alongside men of color (James & Busia, 1993). Thus their social and political allegiances are complex and multiple. Recognizing the masculinist discourse of the 1960s civil rights movement (both the nonviolence of Martin Luther King and the self-determination of the Black Panther Party), African American women still understand the need to work with African American men who are locked out of economic opportunities right along with them.

Still another source of tension regarding multiculturalism and feminism is in the global realm. In an edited volume entitled *Is Multiculturalism Bad for Women?* (Okin, Cohen, Howard, & Nussbaum, 1999), Okin raises important questions about ways that group rights may trump women's rights on issues of polygamy, genital mutilation, forced marriage, differential access for men and women to health care and education, disparate rights of ownership, and unequal vulnerability to violence. Her main argument is that some group rights can endanger women. However, there are non-Western feminists who challenge the essentialized and stereotypical representations of women within their cultures (Afsaruddin, 1999). These feminists offer a variety of perspectives, some of which challenge notions of moral universalism and the imposition of Western standards on all women in all circumstances. Afsaruddin points out that the lives of women in Muslim societies are not uniform, unchanging, or monolithic. Rather than accept the idea that feminism is incompatible with Islam, Afsaruddin asserts that Western readings of Muslim traditions such as veiling by educated women in urban centers may be "the farthest thing from tradition" (p. 23). The meaning of the veil in these contexts may reflect Muslim women's decision to claim both private and public identities on their own terms.

It is not just feminism and its warrants on equity and social justice that have caused a sort of "family feud" in multiculturalism, but also the new studies that emerged around linguistic diversity, immigrant status, social class, ability, and sexuality. Although these varied and multiple identity categories do not compete as they are embodied in single individuals (for example, a Mandarin-speaking disabled lesbian Asian American woman), politically the categories are pitted against each other and compete for primacy on academic and policy agendas. Reed (1997) and Palumbo-Liu (1995) grapple with the intercultural and intracultural struggles that emerge from our increasing diversity. Tensions between older and newer immigrant communities (for instance, Chinese American, Vietnamese, Laotian, and Hmong immigrants), tensions between immigrant communities and constitutive communities of color (such as Korean Americans and African Americans), and tensions resulting from biracial and multiracial identities all are examples of the changing cultural landscape. Political issues like those that emerged in California around undocumented workers (Proposition 187), affirmative action (Proposition 209), and bilingual education (the Unz Amendment) often reveal fissures and fractures in loosely aligned coalitions of oppressed peoples.

Of course, the tensions of class and economic asymmetry continue to plague discussions of multiculturalism. Because so much of the debate has centered on equal access and improved achievement in schools (Banks & Banks, 2001; Grant & Sleeter, 1997), a major interpretation of the project has been one of gaining access to the extant economic order. Sleeter & Grant (1987) analyzed the various forms multicultural education takes and concluded that only those that included a social reconstructionist perspective could be legitimately seen as multicultural. However, few expressions of multicultural education in school take on the critique of capitalism as systemically inequitable (McCarthy, 1993; Olneck, 1990). Increasing disparities between the rich and poor, the concentration of wealth in the hands of a few, and a burgeoning underclass (Collins & Yeskel, 2000) make very real Justice Brandeis's comment that "you can have great wealth concentrated in the hands of a few, or democracy. But you cannot have both" (Goldman, 1953, p. xi). These economic disparities occur both internationally and intranationally. Thus the concerns of a middle-class White woman or a middle-class African American man seem to take on less urgency in the face of the exploitation of Latin American and Southeast Asian workers who toil for pennies a day to make high-priced basketball shoes or baseballs. The cries of environmentalists to save the rain forests meet with hostilities from starving indigenous peoples. As Nobel Prize–winning economist Amatrya Sen (1995) argues, everyone is for equality; it's just that what constitutes equality for one is not the same as for another. For instance, amid the affirmative action debate, both sides lay claim to the rhetoric of equality. Those on the left insist that the need to redress past wrongs is the only way to ensure the disruption of the cycle of inequity (Bell, 1987; Crenshaw, 1988). Those on the right insist that granting special preferences only furthers inequity (see, for example, arguments advanced by McWhorter, 2001; Sowell, 1984; and Steele, 1990).

In the face of the events that occurred in the United States on September 11, 2001 (reference is to the attack on the World Trade Center in New York City; the Pentagon in Washington, D.C.; and the downed airplane in Pennsylvania), new fault lines have been drawn concerning diversity, inclusion, and democracy. Despite the longstanding presence of Muslims in the United States, the national gaze on Islam cast the religion in quite a different light. Now, those who practice Islam are configured in a narrow outline: Arab, Middle Eastern, religious fundamentalist, terrorist, fanatic. They have become the new "other" in the same way that American Indians, African Americans, Latinos, and Asian Americans were at various points in our history. Of course, this current depiction of Muslims narrows and limits the full spectrum of people who practice the religion. For instance, there are 1,209 mosques in the United States, the typical mosque is ethnically diverse, and 30 percent of Muslims in this country are African Americans (U.S. Department of State, 2001). So although Muslims of Middle Eastern origin have been made the proxy for all who practice Islam, the empirical evidence reveals that adherents to the faith are as diverse and complex as any other human group (Eck, 2001).

What does a critical resistant multiculturalism look like in a community where African American Christians, Yemeni immigrant Muslims, Orthodox Jews, Korean Buddhists, and Spanish-speaking Chicana/o Catholics all must vie for rights and opportunities? What happens when among this group there are feminists and gays, lesbians, and bisexuals at odds with some of the religious tenets of one or more of these groups? It is this "big tent" multiculturalism that has rendered much of what happens in the name of multiculturalism ineffective. The Democratic Party in the United States refers to itself as a big tent party because it purports to include everyone; unfortunately, this inclusion has not considered what happens when some groups under the tent are at odds with others.

What one group perceives as the multicultural agenda is something else for another. Victims of racism and ethnic discrimination and violence worry that attention to other forms of human diversity dilutes multicultural education's ability to address their concerns. Feminists and other proponents of gender equity may feel marginalized within the multicultural education discourse. The complexity of identities that individuals experience makes it difficult to craft a multicultural mission that speaks to the specificity of identity. However, attempts to be all things to all people seem to minimize the effective impact of multicultural education as a vehicle for school and social change.

The identity politics of multicultural education is cast as a struggle for rights. The discussion of various groups within the rhetoric of rights provides a new way to think about these conflicts. The next section discusses Critical Race Theory as a way to formulate a rights-based discourse. It is important to note that by taking up Critical Race Theory as a theoretical framework, one is not necessarily privileging race over class, gender, or other identity category. Critical Race Theory is a complex legal and intellectual tool for making sense of all forms of human inequity. The strategies it deploys can be used by scholars working on issues of gender, class, ability, and other forms of human difference. Its use in this chapter is as an exemplar of new scholarship. The references made here are specifically to race because of the body of scholarship that has emerged in this area.

CRITICAL RACE THEORY AS A MULTICULTURAL HEURISTIC

I did not come to America to interpret Wagner for the public. I came to discover what young Americans had in them and to help them express it. I am now satisfied that the future of music in this country must be founded upon what are called the Negro melodies. In the Negro melodies of America I discovered all that is needed for a great noble school of music. They are pathetic, tender, passionate, melancholy, solemn, religious, bold, merry, gay, or what you will.

—Antonín Dvořák, 1892 (cited in Ward & Burns, 2000, p. 10)

It may seem strange to return to a discussion of race after going to great lengths to explain the human complexity with which we are now faced. However, this argument is not about race as positivist social science defines it or how notions of liberalism embrace it. Rather, Critical Race Theory (CRT) is about deploying race and racial theory as a challenge to traditional notions of diversity and social hierarchy.

Although we are just beginning to see CRT in education (Ladson-Billings, 1998; Ladson-Billings & Tate, 1995; Tate, 1997), it has its beginnings in the 1970s with the early work of legal scholars Derrick Bell and Alan Freeman and their growing dissatisfaction with the slow pace of racial reform in the United States (Delgado, 1995). Soon they were joined by others; by the mid-1990s legal scholars had written more than 300 leading law review articles and a dozen books on the topic.

CRT incorporates scholarship from feminism, continental social and political philosophy, postmodernism, cultural nationalism, and a variety of social movements. Cornel West (1995) identifies CRT as

> an intellectual movement that is both particular to our postmodern (and con-servative) times and part of a long tradition of human resistance and liberation. On the one hand, the movement highlights a creative—and tension ridden— fusion of theoretical self-reflection, formal innovation, radical politics, existen-tial evaluation, reconstructive experimentation and vocational anguish. But, like all bold attempts to reinterpret and remake the world to reveal silenced suffering and to relieve social misery, Critical Race Theorists put forward novel readings of a hidden past that disclose the flagrant shortcomings of the treach-erous present in the light of unrealized—though not unrealizable—possibilities for human freedom and equality. (pp. xi–xii)

CRT begins with a number of premises. First and foremost is the proposi-tion that "racism is normal, not aberrant, in American society" (Delgado, 1995, p. xiv). Because racism is such an integral part of our society, "it looks ordinary and natural to persons in the culture" (p. xiv). For instance, from time to time instances of racist behavior are exposed in "surprising" places such as corporate boardrooms (see, for example, White, 1996). These incidents are followed by public outrage and demands for redress. However, these instances keep happening over and over because they are normal, ordinary features of the society. Similarly, sexism, patriarchy, heterosexism, able-ism, classism, linguisticism, and other forms of hierarchy that come from dominance and oppression are also normal. Thus the theory's identification of racism as normal provides an important tool for identifying other such "normal, ordinary" thinking in the society.

A second aspect of CRT is the use of storytelling to challenge racial (and other) oppression. The significance of this storytelling is not merely to exhibit another form of scholarship but rather to use stories to "analyze the myths, presuppositions, and received wisdoms that make up the common culture about race" (Delgado, 1995, p. xiv). CRT storytelling begins with the premise that a society "constructs social reality in ways that promote its own self-interest (or that of elite groups)" (p. xiv). Thus, it is the responsibility of CRT theorists to construct alternative portraits of reality—portraits from subaltern perspectives.

A third aspect of CRT is Derrick Bell's (1980) concept of interest convergence. Here Bell argues that a society's elites allow or encourage advances by a subordinated group only when such advances also promote the self-interest of the elites. Two examples of interest convergence are the way affirmative action policies are enacted and the specific instance of the state of Arizona and the Martin Luther King, Jr., holiday. Despite all of the conservative arguments against affirmative action, an analysis of affirmative action policies indicates that White women, because of their large number, are the major beneficiaries of affirmative action (U.S. Census Bureau, 2000). However, most White women have some relationship to White men, whether as spouses, partners, siblings, parents, or children. This means that White men and White children can share the financial and social benefits that White women enjoy as a result of affirmative action. Thus the interests of women and people of color converge with that of White men who receive the ancillary benefit of White women's improved labor conditions.

In the specific case of the state of Arizona and Martin Luther King, Jr., Day, then-governor Evan Mecham argued that the state could not afford to observe the holiday. However, after threatened boycotts from tourists, various African American civil rights groups, and the National Basketball Association, the state reversed its decision. It did not have a change of heart about the significance of honoring Martin Luther King, Jr.; rather, the potential loss of revenue meant that the state had to have its interests converge with that of African Americans.

CRT theorists have also tried out new forms of writing. Since some are postmodernists, they believe that form and substance are intimately linked. They use biography, autobiography, narratives, and counternarratives to

expose the way traditional legal scholarship uses circular and self-serv-
ing doctrines and rules to bolster its arguments. Most mainstream legal
scholarship embraces universalism over particularism, but CRT responds
to a "call to context" (Delgado, 1995, p. xv) and a critique of liberalism,
which is a system of civil rights litigation and activism that depends on
incremental change, faith in the legal system, and hope for progress.

Although a number of the more prominent names in CRT are African
Americans (Derrick Bell, Robin Barnes, Kimberlé Crenshaw, Lani Guinier,
Cheryl Harris, Charles Lawrence, Patricia Williams), Latina/o scholars
(and other scholars of color) also have served as important architects of
this movement. Richard Delgado, Ian Haney López, Michael Olivas, Gerald
Torres, Margaret Montoya, Mari Matsuda, Robert Chang, Leslie Espinoza,
Jayne Chong-Soon Lee, and Lisa Ikemoto all have written important law
review articles that sculpt the body of knowledge we have come to know as
Critical Race Theory. This work is not just about the Black-White binary.
The group known as the LatCrits (see Delgado, 1992, 2000; and Olivas,
1995) are developing a stream of CRT focused on language and immigration issues. Other CRT scholars work primarily on issues facing women of
color; there are still other scholars (Grillo & Wildman, 1995; Haney López,
1995) who focus on making systems of privilege more apparent. Through
their work they examine the social construction of Whiteness and how
Whiteness becomes the default racial identity—never occupying a space of
otherness or difference.

For those who think that CRT is only about race, in the narrowest sense
of the term, Delgado (2000) has an important response:

> Minority groups in the United States should consider abandoning all binaries,
> narrow nationalisms, and strategies that focus on cutting the most favorable
> possible deal with whites, and instead set up a secondary market in which they
> negotiate selectively with each other. . . . The idea would be for minority groups
> to assess their own preferences and make tradeoffs that will, optimistically,
> bring gains for all concerned. Some controversies may turn out to be poly-
> centric, presenting win-win possibilities so that negotiation can advance goals
> important to both sides without compromising anything either group deems
> vital. . . .
>
> Ignoring the siren song of binaries opens up new possibilities for coalitions
> based on level-headed assessment of the chances for mutual gains. It liberates
> one from dependence on a system that has advanced minority interests at best
> sporadically and unpredictably. It takes interest convergence to a new dimen-
> sion. (p. 306)

Although CRT's relationship to law is evident, its use in education represents a new dimension and challenge to liberal orthodoxy in the field.
However, several scholars have attempted to address the way CRT creates

a new way to analyze and critique current practices in schooling and education (Ladson-Billings, 1998; Ladson-Billings & Tate, 1995; Parker, Deyhle, & Villenas, 1999; Tate, 1997; Taylor, 1998). CRT connections to issues like school funding (Kozol, 1991) and school desegregation (Shujaa, 1996) are fairly evident. But other aspects of schooling are amenable to a CRT analysis, for example, curriculum, instruction, and assessment.

Curriculum

CRT sees the official knowledge (Apple, 1993) of the school curriculum as a culturally specific artifact designed to maintain the current social order. As Swartz (1992) suggests:

> Master scripting silences multiple voices and perspectives, primarily legitimizing dominant, White, upper-class, male voicings as the "standard" knowledge students need to know. All other accounts and perspectives are omitted from the master script unless they can be disempowered through misrepresentation. Thus, content that does not reflect the dominant voice must be brought under control, *mastered*, and then reshaped before it can become a part of the master script. (p. 341)

This kind of master scripting means stories of people of color, women, and anyone who challenges this script are muted and erased. The muting or erasing of these voices is done subtly, yet effectively. Instead of omitting them altogether, they can be included in ways that distort their real meaning and significance (King, 1992). Examples of this muting and erasure are evident in the way cultural heroes are transformed in textbooks to make them more palatable to dominant constituencies. Rosa Parks becomes the tired seamstress rather than a lifelong community activist. Martin Luther King, Jr., becomes a sanitized folk hero who enjoyed the support of all "good" Americans rather than the FBI's public enemy number one who challenged an unjust war and economic injustice (Dyson, 2000). Che Guevara, the Black Panthers, Japanese American resistance to the internment camps, and countless other counternarratives rarely exist in the curriculum.

In addition to the content of the curriculum, CRT also raises questions about its quality. Many children of the dominant group have an opportunity for "enriched" and "rigorous" curriculum. Poor, immigrant, bilingual, and children of color usually are confined to the "basics." As Kozol (1991) observes:

> The curriculum [that the White school] follows "emphasizes critical thinking, reasoning and logic." The planetarium, for instance, is employed not simply for the study of the universe as it exists. "Children also are designing their own galaxies," the teacher says. . . .

"Six girls, four boys. Nine white, one Chinese. I am glad they have this class. But what about the others? Aren't there ten Black children in the school who could enjoy this also?" (p. 96)

Recent emphasis on testing in the nation's schools has meant that many schools serving subordinated students spend most of the day with no curriculum outside of test preparation. McNeil (2000) states that students experience "phony curricula, reluctantly presented by teachers in class to conform to the forms of knowledge their students would encounter on centralized tests" (p. 5).

Students who are not in the social, political, economic, and cultural mainstream find their access to high-quality curriculum restricted. Such restriction is a good example of CRT theorist Cheryl Harris's (1993) notion of use and enjoyment of property. Harris argues that Whiteness is a form of property that entitles Whites to rights of disposition, use and enjoyment, reputation and status—and the absolute right to exclude. The failure of many groups to participate in advanced classes and other school-sponsored enrichment activities is not by happenstance. The infrastructure and networks of Whiteness provide differential access to the school curriculum.

Instruction

Haberman (1991) describes what he terms the "pedagogy of poverty," reflecting the basic mode of teaching in schools serving poor urban students (who are likely to be students of color, immigrants, and children whose first language is not English). This pedagogy consists of "giving information, asking questions, giving directions, making assignments, monitoring seatwork, reviewing assignments, giving tests, reviewing tests, assigning homework, reviewing homework, settling disputes, punishing noncompliance, marking papers, and giving grades" (p. 291). According to Haberman, none of these functions is inherently bad, and in fact some might be beneficial in certain circumstances. But "taken together and performed to the systematic exclusion of other acts they have become the pedagogical coin of the realm in urban schools" (p. 291). Haberman contrasts this pedagogy of poverty with "good" teaching, which he says involves student engagement with issues important to their lives; explanations of human differences; major concepts and ideas; planning what they will be doing; applying ideals to their world; heterogeneous groups; questioning common sense; redoing, polishing, or perfecting their work; reflecting on their own lives; and accessing technology in meaningful ways. It is no surprise that the kinds of instruction students have access to breaks along racial fault lines.

McLaren (2000) calls for a critical pedagogy that is a "way of thinking about, negotiating, and transforming the relationship among classroom teaching, the production of knowledge, the institutional structure of the school, and the social and material relations of the wider community, society, and nation-state" (p. 35). Of course, critical pedagogy must be performed by critical pedagogues, and few, if any, teacher preparation programs systematically prepare such teachers.

CRT's project is to uncover the way pedagogy is racialized and selectively offered to students according to the setting, rather than to produce critical pedagogy. Ladson-Billings's (1994) writing on culturally relevant pedagogy describes the work of teachers whose sociopolitical consciousness infused their teaching in a community primarily serving African American students. These teachers understood the decidedly racial and political perspective of their work and unashamedly took on oppressive structures from the school administration and state mandates.

Assessment

Current cries for accountability almost always mean some form of testing, preferably standardized testing. The George W. Bush administration claims that it will "leave no child behind" through the use of "state-of-the-art tests" and argues that "teaching to the test is really teaching those things we have already decided every child should know and be able to do" (U.S. Department of Education, 2001, pp. 7–8). For the CRT theorists, most of the tests children of color, poor children, immigrant children, and limited-English-speaking children experience inevitably legitimize their deficiencies.

In the classroom, a poor-quality curriculum, coupled with poor-quality instruction, a poorly prepared teacher, and limited resources add up to poor performance on the so-called objective tests. CRT theorists point out that the assessment game is merely a validation of the dominant culture's superiority. In his "Chronicle of the Black Crime Cure," Bell (1987) tells a story of a Black street gang member who finds a magical stone that he ingests. Instantly, the gang member is converted. He stops all wrongdoing and begins fighting crime wherever he finds it. Then he distributes the magical stones to the rest of his band. They too become converts and fight crime everywhere. By some mechanism, the group is able to distribute the magic stones to every Black community in the country. Crime plummets. There are no more muggings, burglaries, rapes, or murders in the communities. However, all of the social barriers that supposedly were closed because of Black "criminal tendencies" remain intact. Jobs do not become available to Blacks. White neighborhoods do not welcome Blacks. Schools, which are now filled with well-behaved and eager Black children, continue to offer poor-quality teaching.

More important, the "Black Crime Cure," which to this point in the chronicle has been a perennial excuse for inequitable treatment and policies,

begins to undermine the crime industry. Police officers, judges, court workers, prison guards, and weapons manufacturers experience serious job cutbacks. Hundreds of millions of dollars are lost, and many begin to see how
the lack of Black crime undermines the social order. The cave that holds the
magical stones is mysteriously blown up.

The "Black Crime Cure" is a good example of a CRT narrative. Bell
has taken a fanciful story as a canvas on which to reveal the ways that race
and other social inequity are important tools for maintaining the privilege
of the dominant group. An analogous education story might be called
the "Achievement Gap Cure," where Black, Latino, and American Indian
families find a magical potion that allows their children to equal and ex-
ceed the academic performance of White middle-class students. Were this
to happen, the dominant group would be deeply affected. All the education positions in remediation and special education would be lost. Every
researcher who has made a career describing low performance and pre-
scribing remedies would have to develop a new research agenda. More
important, White middle-class parents would lobby for a new way to identify their children as superior. Such was the case in an upper-middle-class
California school community that tried to detrack mathematics courses
(Kohn, 1998). White middle-class parents vehemently opposed detracking
because there would be no way to determine how much better their children were than other children—and to keep their children from forming
social networks with the "others."

From a CRT perspective, current assessment schemes continue to in-
stantiate inequity and validate the privilege of those who have access to
cultural capital (Bourdieu, 1977). Indeed, the entire history of standardized testing has been one of exclusion and social ranking rather than di-
agnosis and school improvement. Intelligence testing, for example, has
been a way to legitimate the ongoing racism aimed at non-White peoples
(Aleinikoff, 1991; Gould, 1981). The history of the United States is replete
with examples of how people of color have been subordinated by "scientific" theories, each of which depends on racial stereotypes that make
the socioeconomic condition of these groups seem appropriate. Crenshaw
(1988) contends that the point of controversy is no longer that these stereotypes were developed to rationalize the oppression of people of color
but rather that they "serve a hegemonic function by perpetuating a my-
thology about both [people of color] and Whites even today, reinforcing
an illusion of a White community that cuts across ethnic, gender, and class
lines" (p. 1371).

The promise of CRT is that it can be deployed as a theoretical tool
for uncovering many types of inequity and social injustice—not just racial
inequity and injustice. Some aspects of this new scholarship are beginning
to appear in the current scholarly efforts in multiculturalism and multicultural education. Examples of this work are presented in the next section.

CURRENT TRENDS IN MULTICULTURALISM

My music is the spiritual expression of what I am—my faith, my knowledge, my being. . . . When you begin to see possibilities of music, you desire to do something really good for people, to help humanity free itself from its hang-ups.

—John Coltrane (quoted in Ward & Burns, 2000, p. 436)

The possibilities that this current era offers for multiculturalism and multi-cultural education seem endless. In addition to adding new areas such as dis-ability studies (Linton, 1998; Shakespeare, 1998) and queer studies (Fuss, 1991; Sedgwick, 1990), cultural studies, postcolonial, postmodern, and poststructuralist studies all attempt to push past conventional and essential-ized thinking about race, class, and gender. But these "new studies" are not unproblematic. Multicultural education's seeming allegiance to the triumvi-rate of race, class, and gender may have rendered it less useful to scholars and practitioners who have to work with the complexities of identities that do not fit into fixed categories. Thus cultural studies, with its multiple lenses and multilayered perspectives, began to fill this space. Unfortunately, the complexity of identity may also mean that some explanations offered by cultural studies are too diffuse and rhetorical to be meaningful in every-day lives, especially in pre-K–12 classrooms. Sometimes what is pushing up against an individual is racism or sexism, or class discrimination plain and simple. An argument about one's complex identity does not alleviate that oppression.

Similarly, although postcolonial theory serves as a useful rubric for scholarship, the people who live under these regimes ask, as Aboriginal ac-tivist Bobbi Sykes did most memorably,

> "What? Post-colonialism? Have they left?" (cited in Smith, 1999, p. 24). Smith further asserts that "there is also, amongst indigenous academics, the sneaking suspicion that the fashion of post-colonialism has become a strategy for rein-scribing or reauthorizing the privilege of non-indigenous academics because the field of 'post-colonial' discourse has been defined in ways which can still leave out indigenous peoples, our ways of knowing and our current concerns." (p. 24)

On the question of the postmodern, multiculturalism again offers an important challenge. Clearly oppressed peoples have argued about the con-tested nature of history and other social phenomena (Smith, 1999). West (1993) argues that postmodernism is attractive, for example, to Black in-tellectuals because it "speaks to the black postmodern predicament, defined by rampant xenophobia of bourgeois humanism predominant in the whole academy, the waning attraction to orthodox reductionist and scientific versions of Marxism, and the need for reconceptualization regarding the specificity and complexity of African American oppression" (p. 80). But as Smith points out, "there can be no 'postmodern' for us until we have settled some business of the modern" (p. 34).

Perhaps the place where these new trends can most help multiculturalism and multicultural education is methodology. Early scholarship in multiculturalism seemed to mimic mainstream scholarship, with its use of surveys, interviews, content analysis, and other apparently positivist approaches to research. Multiculturalism and multicultural education have access to more expanded methodologies such as narrative inquiry (Tierney, 1995), counterstories (Bell, 1998), historical ethnographies (Siddle Walker, 1996), autobiography, portraiture (Lawrence-Lightfoot & Davis, 1997), and a full range of indigenous projects: claiming, testimonies, celebrating survival, remembering, indigenizing, intervening, revitalizing, gendering, connecting, envisioning, reframing, restoring, returning, democratizing, naming, protecting, creating, and sharing (Smith, 1999). Fewer academic writers have taken up the challenge to "talk back" (hooks, 1989) in their own languages. Notable exceptions are the work of Ngugi Wa Thiong'o (1986) and Anzaldúa (1987), which use native languages to work against oppression. Wa Thiong'o asserted that "language carries culture and the language of the colonizer became the means by which the 'mental universe of the colonized' was dominated" (quoted in Smith, 1999, p. 36).

The other more present trend in multiculturalism and multicultural education is globalization. Even though multicultural education has always included some acknowledgment of international iterations (Moodley, 1983; Troyna & Williams, 1986; Verma & Bagley, 1982), like their U.S. counterparts they were local expressions of multiculturalism that deal primarily with the cultural landscape of particular nation states. Now with the increasing blurring of national geopolitical borders, notions of difference and otherness take on new meaning. Technological advances mean that the West can (and does) assert its hegemony over what people see and hear, how they speak, and ultimately what they think. Communication satellites, fiber optic cables, the Internet, and e-mail bring every corner of the world into our homes. Almost everywhere in the world, people have access to CNN, ESPN, and other U.S.-generated images and perspectives. Thus a worldwide vision of civilization, progress, aesthetics, standard of living, and advance reflects what the world of Western television and other media project.

In this more global environment, the question of group rights versus individual rights takes on new meaning (Kymlicka, 1995). Group and individual rights in South Africa shape up differently from such rights in Germany. Pan-ethnic rights signal new alignments and configurations. Despite the controversy over Huntington's (1997) assessment of realignment in world allegiances, he clearly raised some important questions about how culture may be positioned to trump nationality. Huntington argues that instead of national allegiances, the world is divided along what he terms civilizational allegiances. Thus Spanish speakers, regardless of their national residence, may demonstrate a strong affinity to each other in relation to other groups, or Muslims worldwide may cohere in opposition to Jews or Christians. However, it is equally important to avoid the single-explanation trap that substitutes culture for economy. Indeed, the melding of culture, economy, and politics makes for a new calculus where disruption in one part of the world causes tremors throughout the world. The breakup of the Soviet Union, war in the Balkans, the Palestinian-Israeli conflict, and famine in East Africa all work to configure nation-states in different ways. Previously "White" nations find their streets and communities home to immigrants from Black, Brown, and Yellow nations. Those nations that formerly talked about diversity and multiculturalism in the abstract now come face to face with multicultural, multilingual everyday lives.

The enduring question facing multicultural education is what to do as a school reform effort in the face of this rapid social and cultural change. Multicultural education faces pressure from forces of school reform and standardization on one end of the spectrum and the complexities and changes occasioned by globalization on the other. Gay (2001) points out the current lag between multicultural education theory and practice. Such a gap is likely to be exacerbated by the call for standardized tests as the primary measure of achievement as well as the sheer volume of new knowledge about the world and increasing global interactions. College and university programs seem to be moving in two directions related to these pressures. To conform to the demands of state and national external reviews, some programs of teacher preparation are developing standards-based programs (National Council for Accreditation of Teacher Education, 2002) that at least nominally address diversity. At the same time, more graduate programs include opportunities for advanced work in multicultural education, multiculturalism, and cultural studies.

Where multiculturalism and multicultural education go from here is difficult to predict. Will it follow the 1970s jazz lead, succumb to the pressures of conformity, and produce a fusion that is palatable but without substance? Or will it be the jazz that Wynton Marsalis (cited in Ward & Burns, 2000) recognizes?

That's the thing in jazz that got Bix Beiderbecke up out of his bed at two o'clock in the morning to pick that cornet up and practice with it into the pillow for another two or three hours. Or that would make Louis Armstrong travel around the world for fifty years non-stop, just get up out of his sickbed, crawl up on the bandstand, and play. The thing that would make Duke Ellington, Thelonius Monk, Miles Davis, Charlie Parker—any of these people that we've heard about—all these wonderful people—give their lives. And they did give their lives for it, because it gives us a glimpse into what America is going to be when it becomes itself. And this music tells you that it *will* become itself. (p. 460)

SUMMARY COMMENTS AND FUTURE QUESTIONS

This chapter began by highlighting the growing presence of multicultural forms in the society. It points out that the current popularity of multiculturalism and multicultural education does not necessarily speak to the complexity and dissonance that is occurring within the field. The chapter uses work by McLaren (1994) and King (2001) as rubrics for rethinking and rearticulating what we mean by multiculturalism and multicultural education. Rather than one multiculturalism, both theorists offer multiple representations of multiculturalism that are aimed at decidedly different agendas. The chapter endorses McLaren's critical resistant multiculturalism and King's deciphering knowledge as a form of emancipatory practice.

Next, the chapter discusses some of the tensions that exist within the field. It points out that some traditional issues of multiculturalism began to bump up against each other around race, class, gender, language, immigrant status, ability, and sexuality. Uneasy alliances seem to find multiculturalism an uncomfortable space, and several movements for social justice and equity actually worked against each other. Out of this discussion flows an explanation and analysis of Critical Race Theory (CRT) as a heuristic for multiculturalism and multicultural education. The chapter explains CRT as a strategy for reinventing legal scholarship in civil rights and then explores ways it might apply to education. Finally, the chapter points out the ongoing challenges multiculturalism and multicultural education face with increasing demands by diverse groups, the growing complexities of the human condition, and expanding methodologies. The chapter concludes by recognizing globalization as an ever-present force in our thinking about multiculturalism and multicultural education.

In the midst of the complexity and seeming confusion, what, then, are the research and scholarship agendas for multiculturalism and multicultural education? How will academics take on the challenge of writing and researching in a rapidly changing sociocultural reality? Where do the concerns of schoolchildren (no matter where they are in the world) who are left behind in the information age surface as we attempt to unravel and unpack our projects? What, if anything, is to be done about the fissures and fractures? What will constitute the next generation of new scholarship for even newer directions in multicultural education?

These are important questions as we move into a world where globalization defines the economy, culture, and politics of people everywhere (Suárez-Orozco, 2001). The fact of a worldwide media that transports not only news and information but also cultural images of how to be and act in the world means that our conceptions of culture can no longer be simplistic, one-dimensional, and essentialized. The hegemony of world English rein-scribes the power of the West—particularly the United States and its allies—at the same moment the West itself is being contested. The United States and the Western European nations are undergoing demographic changes that challenge perceptions of them as White, Christian nations.

Scholars will need to respond to the postcolonial and multiple discourses that worldwide change demands. Their work will have to incorporate het-erogeneity, hybridity, and multiplicity and be more tentative in its asser-tions. Scholarship will be more like everyday life: less certain, less definitive, and less prescriptive. In K–12 classrooms, teachers will have to work back and forth between individual and group identities, while at the same mo-ment taking principled stands on behalf of students who, because of some perceived difference or sense of otherness, are left behind. The new work of multicultural education must be more generative. Both scholars and class-room teachers must look for opportunities, new ways to think and learn about human diversity and social justice. They must be willing to push inno-vation in multicultural education. Multicultural education must be open to conflict and change, as is true of any culture and cultural form if it is to sur-vive. Multicultural education, like jazz, must remain "gloriously inclusive" (Ward & Burns, 2000, p. 460). Each epoch must offer us a new direction in multicultural education.

REFERENCES

Afsaruddin, A. (Ed.). (1999). *Hermeneutics and honor: Negotiating female public space in Islamic/ate societies*. Boston: Harvard University Press.

Aleinikoff, T. A. (1991). A case for race-consciousness. *Columbia Law Review, 91,* 1060–1125.

Anzaldúa, G. (1987). *Borderlands/la frontera: The new mestiza*. San Francisco: Aunt Lute Press.

Apple, M. W. (1993). Official knowledge: *Democratic education in a conservative age*. New York: Routledge.

Banks, J. A., & Banks, C.A.M. (Eds.). (2001). *Multicultural education: Issues and perspectives* (4th ed.). New York: Wiley.

Bell, D. (1980). *Brown v. Board of Education* and the interest convergence dilemma. *Harvard Law Review, 93,* 518–533.

Bell, D. (1987). *And we are not saved: The elusive quest for racial justice*. New York: Basic Books.

Bell, D. (1998). *Afrolantic legacies*. Chicago: Third World Press.

Bennett, T. (1992). Putting policy into cultural studies. In L. Grossbert, C. Nelson, & P. Treichler (Eds.), *Cultural Studies* (pp. 23–27). London: Routledge.

Bourdieu, P. (1977). Cultural reproduction and social reproduction. In J. Karabel & F. Halsey (Eds.), *Power and ideology in education* (pp. 487–511). New York: Oxford University Press.

Code, L. (1991). *What can she know? Feminist theory and the construction of knowledge*. Ithaca, NY: Cornell University Press.

Coffey, M. (2000). What puts the "culture" in "multiculturalism"? An analysis of culture, government, and the politics of Mexican identity. In R. Mahalingam & C. McCarthy (Eds.), *Multicultural curriculum: New directions for social theory, practice, and policy* (pp. 37–55). New York: Routledge.

Collins, C., & Yeskel, F. (2000). Economic apartheid: A primer on economic inequality and security. New York: New Press.

Conley, D. (2000). *Honky*. New York: Vintage Books.

Crenshaw, K. (1988). Race, reform, and retrenchment: Transformation and legitimation in antidiscrimination law. *Harvard Law Review, 101*, 1331–1387.

Davis, F. (1985). Ornette's permanent revolution. Available: www.theatlantic.com/unbound/jazz/dornette.htm

Delgado, R. (1992). Rodrigo's chronicle. *Yale Law Journal, 101*, 1357–1383.

Delgado, R. (Ed.). (1995). *Critical race theory: The cutting edge*. Philadelphia: Temple University Press.

Delgado, R. (2000). Derrick Bell's toolkit—Fit to dismantle that famous house? *New York University Law Review, 75*, 283–307.

Du Bois, W. E. B. (1953/1989). *The souls of Black folk*. New York: Bantam Books. (Originally published in 1953)

Dyson, M. E. (1994). Essentialism and the complexities of racial identity. In D. T. Goldberg (Ed.), *Multiculturalism: A critical reader* (pp. 218–229). Cambridge, MA: Blackwell Press.

Dyson, M. E. (2000). *I may not get there with you: The true Martin Luther King, Jr.* New York: Free Press.

Eck, D. (2001). *A new religious America: How a "Christian country" has become the world's most religiously diverse nation*. San Francisco: Harper.

Engel, C. (1922). Jazz: A musical discussion. [On-line]. Available: www.theatlantic.com/unbound/jazz/cengel.htm

Fanon, F. (1963). *The wretched of the earth*. New York: Grove Press.

Fanon, F. (1967). *Black skins, White masks*. New York: Grove Press.

Foucault, M. (1972). *The archaeology of knowledge* (A. M. Sheridan-Smith, Trans.). London: Tavistock.

Foucault, M. (1991). Governmentality. In G. Burchell, C. Gordon, & P. Miller (Eds.), *The Foucault effect: Studies in governmentality* (pp. 87–104). Chicago: University of Chicago Press.

Frankenberg, R. (1993). *White women, race matters: The social construction of whiteness*. Minneapolis: University of Minnesota Press.

Fuss, D. (Ed.). (1991). *Inside/out: Lesbian theories, gay theories*. New York: Routledge.

Gay, G. (2001). Curriculum theory and multicultural education. In J. A. Banks & C.A.M. Banks (Eds.), *Handbook of research on multicultural education* (pp. 25–43). San Francisco: Jossey-Bass.

Gilligan, C. (1977). In a different voice: Women's conceptions of self and of morality. *Harvard Educational Review, 47*, 481–517.

Gilroy, P. (1993). *The Black Atlantic: Modernity and double consciousness*. Cambridge, MA: Harvard University Press.

Glazer, N. (1997). *We are all multiculturalists now.* Cambridge, MA: Harvard University Press.

Goldman, S. (Ed.). (1953). *The words of Justice Brandeis.* New York: Schuman.

Gordon, E. W. (1997). Task force on the role and future of minorities: American Educational Research Association. *Educational Researcher, 26*(3), 44–52.

Gould, S. J. (1981). *The mismeasure of man.* New York: Norton.

Grant, C. A., & Sleeter, C. E. (1997). Turning on learning: Five approaches for multicultural teaching plans for race, class, gender, and disability (2nd ed.). Upper Saddle River, NJ: Merrill/Prentice Hall.

Grillo, T., & Wildman, S. M. (1995). Obscuring the importance of race: The implication of making comparisons between racism and sexism (or other-isms). In R. Delgado (Ed.), *Critical Race Theory: The cutting edge* (pp. 564–572). Philadelphia: Temple University Press.

Haberman, M. (1991). The pedagogy of poverty versus good teaching. *Phi Delta Kappan, 73,* 290–294.

Hacker, A. (1992). *Two nations: Black and White, separate, hostile, unequal.* New York: Basic Books.

Haney López, I. (1995). White by law. In R. Delgado (Ed.), *Critical Race Theory: The cutting edge* (pp. 542–550). Philadelphia: Temple University Press.

Harris, C. (1993). Whiteness as property. *Harvard Law Review, 106,* 1707–1791.

Heble, A. (2000). *Landing on the wrong note: Jazz, dissonance and critical practice.* New York: Routledge.

Hollinger, D. (1995). *Postethnic America: Beyond multiculturalism.* New York: Basic Books.

hooks, b. (1989). *Talking back: Thinking feminist, thinking Black.* Boston: South End Press.

Huntington, S. (1997). *The clash of civilization and the remaking of world order.* New York: Touchstone.

Jaimes, M. A., & Halsey, T. (1992). American Indian women at the center of indigenous resistance in contemporary North America. In M. A. Jaimes (Ed.), *The state of Native America: Genocide, colonization, and resistance* (pp. 311–344). Boston: South End Press.

James, S., & Busia, A. (Eds.). (1993). *Theorizing Black feminisms: The visionary pragmatism of Black women.* New York: Routledge.

King, J. E. (1992). Diaspora literacy and consciousness in the struggle against miseducation in the Black community. *Journal of Negro Education, 61,* 317–340.

King, J. E. (2001). Culture-centered knowledge: Black studies, curriculum transformation, and social action. In J. A. Banks & C.A.M. Banks (Eds.), *Handbook of research on multicultural education* (pp. 265–290). San Francisco: Jossey-Bass.

Kohn, A. (1998). Only for *my* kid: How privileged parents undermine school reform. *Phi Delta Kappan, 79,* 568–577.

Kozol, J. (1991). *Savage inequalities: Children in America's schools.* New York: HarperCollins.

Kymlicka, W. (Ed.).(1995). *The rights of minority cultures.* New York: Oxford University Press.

Ladson-Billings, G. (1994). *The dreamkeepers: Successful teachers of African American children.* San Francisco: Jossey-Bass.

Ladson-Billings, G. (1998). Just what is critical race theory and what's it doing in a nice field like education? *International Journal of Qualitative Studies in Education, 11*(1), 7–24.

Ladson-Billings, G., & Tate, W. F. (1995). Toward a critical race theory of education. *Teachers College Record, 97*(1), 47–68.

Lather, P. (1991). *Getting smart: Feminist research and pedagogy with/in the postmodern.* New York: Routledge.

Lawrence-Lightfoot, S., & Davis, J. H. (1997). *The art and science of portraiture.* San Francisco: Jossey-Bass.

Linton, S. (1998). *Claiming disability: Knowledge and identity.* New York: New York University Press.

Lowe, L. (1996). *Immigrant acts.* Durham, NC: Duke University Press.

McCarthy, C. (1988). Reconsidering liberal and radical perspectives on racial inequality in schooling: Making the case for nonsynchrony. *Harvard Educational Review, 58,* 265–279.

McCarthy, C. (1993). After the canon: knowledge and ideological representation in the multicultural discourse on curriculum reform. In C. McCarthy & W. Crichlow (Eds.), *Race, identity and representation in education* (pp. 289–305). New York: Routledge.

McKay, S., & Wong, S. (1996). Multiple discourses, multiple identities: Investment and agency in second-language learning among Chinese adolescent immigrant students. *Harvard Educational Review, 66,* 577–608.

McLaren, P. (1994). White terror and oppositional agency: Towards a critical multiculturalism. In D. T. Goldberg (Ed.), *Multiculturalism: A critical reader* (pp. 45–74). Cambridge, MA: Blackwell.

McLaren, P. (2000). *Che Guevara, Paulo Freire, and the pedagogy of revolution.* Lanham, MD: Rowman & Littlefield.

McNeil, L. (2000). *Contradictions of school reform: Educational costs of standardized testing.* New York: Routledge.

McWhorter, J. (2001). *Losing the race: Self-sabotage in Black America.* New York: HarperPerennial Library.

Minh-ha, T. T. (1989). *Woman, native, other: Writing postcolonially and feminism.* Bloomington: Indiana University Press.

Moodley, K. A. (1983). Canadian multiculturalism as ideology. *Ethnic and racial studies, 6,* 320–331.

Morrison, T. (1989). Unspeakable things unspoken: The Afro-American presence in American literature. *Michigan Quarterly Review, 28*(1), 1–34.

Morrison, T. (1991). *Playing in the dark: Whiteness in the literary imagination.* Cambridge, MA: Harvard University Press.

Morrison, T., & Lacour, C. B. (Eds.). (1997). *Birth of a nation'hood: Gaze, script, and spectacle in the O. J. Simpson case.* New York: Pantheon Books.

National Council for Accreditation of Teacher Education. (2002). *Professional standards for the accreditation of schools, colleges, and departments of education.* Washington, DC: Author.

Noddings, N. (1984). *Caring: A feminine approach to ethics and moral education.* Berkeley: University of California Press.

Okin, S., Cohen, J., Howard, M., & Nussbaum, M. (Eds.). (1999). *Is multiculturalism bad for women?* Princeton, NJ: Princeton University Press.

Olivas, M. (1995). The chronicles, my grandfather's stories, and immigration law: The slave traders chronicle as racial history. In R. Delgado (Ed.), *Critical Race Theory: The cutting edge* (pp. 9–20). Philadelphia: Temple University Press.

Olneck, M. (1990). The recurring dream: Symbolism and ideology in intercultural and multicultural education. *American Journal of Education, 98*(2), 147–174.

Palumbo-Liu, D. (Ed.). (1995). *The ethnic canon: Histories, institutions and interventions*. Minneapolis: University of Minnesota Press.

Parker, L., Deyhle, D., & Villenas, S. (Eds.). (1999). *Race is . . . race isn't: Critical race theory and qualitative studies in education*. Boulder, CO: Westview Press.

Ravitch, D. (1990). Multiculturalism: E pluribus plures. *American Scholar, 59*(3), 337–354.

Reed, I. (Ed.). (1997). *Multi-America: Essays on cultural wars and cultural peace*. New York: Viking Press.

Schlesinger, A. (1991). *The disuniting of America: Reflections of a multicultural society*. Knoxville, TN: Whittle Direct Books.

Schmitz, B., Butler, J., Rosenfelt, D., & Guy-Sheftall, B. (2001). Women's studies and curriculum transformation. In J. A. Banks & C.A.M. Banks (Eds.), *Handbook of research on multicultural education* (pp. 708–728). San Francisco: Jossey-Bass.

Sedgwick, E. (1990). *Epistemology of the closet*. Berkeley: University of California Press.

Sen, A. (1995). *Inequality reexamined*. Cambridge, MA: Harvard University Press.

Shakespeare, T. (Ed.). (1998). *Disability reader: Social sciences perspectives*. London: Cassell.

Shujaa, M. (Ed.). (1996). *Beyond desegregation*. Thousand Oaks, CA: Corwin Press.

Siddle Walker, E. V. (1996). *Their highest potential: An African American school community in the segregated south*. Chapel Hill: University of North Carolina Press.

Sims, R. (1982). *Shadow and substance: Afro-American experience in contemporary children's fiction*. Urbana, IL: National Council of Teachers of English.

Sleeter, C. E., & Grant, C. A. (1987). An analysis of multicultural education in the United States. *Harvard Educational Review, 7*, 421–444.

Smith, L. T. (1999). *Decolonizing methodologies: Research and indigenous peoples*. London: Zed Books.

Sowell, T. (1984). *Civil rights: Rhetoric or reality?* New York: Morrow.

Steele, S. (1990). *The content of our character: A new vision of race in America*. New York: St. Martin's Press.

Strickland, E. (1987). What Coltrane wanted. [On-line]. Available: www.theatlantic.com/unbound/jazz/strickla.htm

Suárez-Orozco, M. (2001). Globalization, immigration, and education: The research agenda. *Harvard Educational Review, 71*, 345–365.

Sundgaard, A. (1955). Jazz, hot and cold. [On-line]. Available: www.theatlantic.com/unbound/jazz/sungaar.htm

Swartz, E. (1992). Emancipatory narratives: Rewriting the master script in the school curriculum. *Journal of Negro Education, 61*, 341–355.

Tate, W. F. (1997). Critical race theory and education: History, theory, and implications. In M. W. Apple (Ed.), *Review of Research in Education* (vol. 22, pp. 195–247). Washington, DC: American Educational Research Association.

Taylor, E. (1998, Spring). A primer on CRT. *Journal of Blacks in Higher Education, 19,* 122–124.

Tierney, W. (1995). (Re)presentation and voice. *Qualitative Inquiry, 1,* 379–390.

Troyna, B., & Williams, J. (1986). *Racism, education, and the state: The racialisation of education policy.* London: Croom Helm.

U.S. Census Bureau. (2000). *Report of the Population.* [On-line]. Available: www.census.gov

U.S. Department of Education. (2001, August). *Back to school, moving forward.* Washington, DC: Educational Publications Center.

U.S. Department of State. (2001). [On-line]. Available: http://usinfo/state/gov/products/pubs/muslimlife

Verma, G., & Bagley, C. (Eds.). (1982). *Self-concept, achievement and multicultural education.* London: Macmillan.

Wa Thiong'o, N. (1986). *Decolonizing the mind: The politics of language in African literature.* London: Currey.

Ward, G. C., & Burns, K. (2000). *Jazz: A history of America's music.* New York: Knopf.

Warrior, R. A. (1995). *Tribal secrets: Recovering American Indian intellectual traditions.* Minneapolis: University of Minnesota Press.

West, C. (1993). *Keeping faith: Philosophy and race in America.* New York: Routledge.

West, C. (1995). Foreword. In K. Crenshaw, N. Gotanda, G. Peller, & K. Thomas (Eds.), *Critical race theory: The key writings that formed the movement* (pp. xi–xii). New York: New Press.

White, J. E. (1996, November 25). Texaco's high-octane racism problems. *Time, 148,* pp. 33–34.

Williams, R. (1976). *Keywords.* London: Fontana.

Wynter, S. (1989). Beyond the word of man: Glissant and the new discourse of the Antilles. *World Literature Today, 63,* 637–648.

Wynter, S. (1992). *Do not call us "Negroes": How "multicultural" textbooks perpetuate racism.* San Francisco: Aspire Books.

CHAPTER 6

Landing on the Wrong Note
The Price We Paid for *Brown*

The first part of the title of this talk[1] is taken from Ajay Heble's (2000) book *Landing on the Wrong Note: Jazz, Dissonance, and Critical Practice*. I have chosen this musical image to convey the problem of good intentions gone awry. No musician plans to play the wrong note. The plaintiffs, litigators, Supreme Court Justices, and civil rights advocates all expressed good intentions regarding *Brown*, and although playing one wrong note does not destroy or invalidate an entire performance, it does create a kind of dissonance that is more or less evident depending on one's vantage point. I am suggesting that the results of the *Brown v. Board of Education* decision of 1954 represent a kind of landing on the wrong note. *Brown's* intentions were good and honorable. Its fight was just, but from a 2004 perspective, one might argue that we have landed on a wrong note. I am also using this jazz metaphor as a way to conceive a new vision of America that is more complex and multifaceted than the prevailing cultural narrative.

This article addresses what I have identified as the price we paid for *Brown*. I want to deal with my concerns by providing a justification for discussing *Brown*, exploring the historical context in which *Brown* was conceived, detailing what I see as the specific limitations of the ruling, and considering where we might go from here.

WHY *BROWN*? WHY NOW?

The obvious reason for this particular discussion is to fulfill the specifics of the DeWitt-Wallace–Reader's Digest Lecture to address issues of concern for education. A more relevant reason is that this year marks the 50th anniversary of the decision, and half a century gives us ample time to look back on it soberly and critically. Another reason for considering *Brown* is the degree to which school desegregation has become an international issue. Schools in South Africa, Eastern Europe, the Middle East, Russia, and China are dealing with the dismantling of separate and unequal school systems to better integrate subordinate populations into the mainstream (Greenburg, 2003). I have also chosen *Brown* as a topic for discussion because of its central role in the U.S. school curriculum. Diana Hess (2003) refers to the "classroom iconization of *Brown*," pointing out that this one Supreme Court case is listed in more state curriculum standards documents than any other. She also points out that when queried, law professors, high school teachers, judges, and two Supreme Court Justices (Ginsburg and O'Connor) all include *Brown* in the list of cases that students should learn in school.

Finally, I have settled on *Brown* because this past fall I was called upon to be an expert witness in a school funding adequacy case in South Carolina (*Abbeville et al. v. the State of South Carolina, et al.*). The case involves eight rural school districts that assert that their property values cannot generate enough tax money for their children to have "an opportunity . . . to acquire . . . a minimally adequate education" (*Abbeville et al. v. South Carolina*, 24939, April 1999). The amazing irony of this case is that it is being heard in the very same Manning, SC, Clarendon County courthouse as *Briggs v. Elliott*, a case that began in South Carolina on May 17, 1950, and was later folded into *Brown* along with three other cases.

HISTORICAL CONTEXT OF *BROWN*

Hess (2003) has argued the *Brown* decision is reified in the classroom. I contend that it also is reified in U.S. legal, political, and popular culture. On October 26, 1992, the U.S. Congress passed Public Law 102-525, establishing the Monroe Elementary School and its adjacent grounds in Topeka, KS, as a National Historic Site (the school was one of the segregated schools to which African American students were assigned). The National Archives and Records Administration (NARA) includes documents related to the case in its digital classroom, and the decision is a linchpin of much civil rights argumentation.

Brown has taken on a mythic quality that actually distorts the way many Americans have come to understand its genesis and function in the society. Our tendency is to view *Brown* as a "natural" occurrence in the nation's steady march toward race relations progress (Crenshaw, 1988). This notion of progress is coupled with a view of America as a nation endowed with inherent "goodness" and exceptionality. Historians like Joyce Appleby challenge our view of this exceptionalism:

> Exceptionalism . . . is America's peculiar form of Eurocentrism. In the nation's critical first decades, it provided a way to explain the connection of the United States to Europe within a story about its geographic and political disconnection. But today, exceptionalism raises formidable obstacles to appreciating America's original and authentic diversity. . . . [O]ur peculiar form of Eurocentrism . . . created a national identity for the revolutionary generation . . . [and] foreclosed other ways of interpreting the meaning of the United States. It is to that

foreclosure two centuries ago that we should now look to diagnose our present discomfort with calls for a multicultural understanding of the United States. (Appleby, 1992, p. 420)

I want to suggest that the *Brown* decision is not the result of America as a good and altruistic nation but rather the result of the decision's particular historical and political context. This argument is not new, particularly to legal scholars, political scientists, and historians. Nevertheless, it has gained little or no currency in the education community, as evidenced by the way *Brown* is taught in the nation's schools.

Again, I refer to Hess who states, "an object of uncritical devotion, *Brown* is most likely to be taught not simply as a correctly decided court case, but as an important symbol that continues to shape contemporary ideas about justice, equality, and the power of the Supreme Court" (Hess, 2003, p. 6). In an earlier article (Tate, Ladson-Billings, & Grant, 1993) colleagues and I raised questions about the Supreme Court's attempt to propose a mathematical solution (i.e. determine what constitutes segregation and desegregation by strict numbers) to complex social problems.

My argument here is that the case came at a time when the Court had almost no other choice but to rule in favor of the plaintiffs. *Brown* is not just one case, but rather the accumulation of a series of cases over a more than 100-year period.[2] In 1849, Benjamin F. Roberts sued the city of Boston on behalf of his five-year-old daughter, Sarah (Cushing, 1883). Sarah Roberts walked past five White elementary schools to a dilapidated elementary school for Black children. Initially Benjamin Roberts attempted to enroll his daughter in one of the White schools. Failing this, he enlisted the legal support of Robert Morris, an African American attorney who recruited well-known White abolitionist Charles Sumner to join him on the case. Despite Sumner's attempt to leverage the Massachusetts Constitution by arguing that school segregation was discriminatory and harmful to *all* children, the court ruled in favor of the school committee.

Of course, the primary legal referent for *Brown* is the 1896 *Plessy v. Ferguson* case that *Brown* reversed. Homer Plessy was an African American who tested the Louisiana segregation law by riding in a train car reserved for Whites. The law stated that segregation was legal as long as the facilities maintained for Blacks were equal to those established for Whites. Plessy argued his case on the basis of the 14th Amendment and its guarantee of equal protection. But, the U.S. Supreme Court upheld Judge Ferguson's ruling and in so doing, validated segregation throughout the nation. A number of subsequent challenges to the ruling failed to sway the court.

Although *Plessy* was concerned with a public accommodation, specifically transportation, later the NAACP would see equal education as the bigger, more significant prize. Two cases in Delaware, *Belton v. Gebhart* and *Bulah v. Gebhart* (1952) started out as school transportation cases that the

NAACP encouraged the plaintiffs to turn into school integration cases. The plaintiffs won limited local victories that did not have national impact. But, their cases would become a part of the larger *Brown* plea along with *Briggs v. Elliott*,[3] *Bolling v. Sharpe*,[4] and *Davis v. County School Board of Prince Edward County*.[5]

At the same time that parents were fighting for desegregated K–12 schools, activity at the college and professional school level was also heating up. In *McLaurin v. Oklahoma State Regents* (1950) the Supreme Court struck down University of Oklahoma rules that allowed a Black man to attend classes but fenced him off from the other students. On that same day, the Court ruled in *Sweatt v. Painter* (1950) that a makeshift law school that the state of Texas had created to avoid admitting Black students to the University of Texas Law School did not represent an equal facility as called for in *Plessy*.

One might think that the sheer volume of cases that the Court was hearing during this time made the reversal of *Plessy* seem inevitable. Instead, I want to suggest that the real catalyst for *Brown* is the larger socio-political context of the post-war era. There is no indication that the Eisenhower Administration was enthusiastic about the ruling; the President wrote in a letter to his friend, retired Navy Captain Swede Hazlett (October, 1954), "The segregation issue will, I think, become acute or tend to die out according to the character of the procedure orders that the Court will probably issue this winter. My own guess is that they will be very moderate and accord a maximum of initiative to the local courts."[6] Eisenhower was counting on the power of states' rights to hold school segregation in check while the federal government could point to the ruling as an example of its commitment to equality.

Bell (1980) points out that with the Cold War struggle to prevent the Soviets from spreading communism among emerging Third-World peoples, the United States was compelled to confront its own credibility issue concerning Black people and their civil liberties. The amicus brief filed in *Brown* by the U.S. Justice Department argued that desegregation was in the national interest in part because of foreign policy issues (Dudziak, 1995). The Justice Department said (1954), "The United States is trying to prove to the people of the world, of every nationality, race and color, that a free democracy is the most civilized and secure form of government yet devised by man." The brief also quoted Secretary of State Dean Acheson's letter to the attorney general, in which Acheson wrote:

> During the past six years, the damage to our foreign relations attributable to [race discrimination] has become progressively greater. The United States is under constant attack in the foreign press, over foreign radio, and in such international bodies as the United Nations because of various practices of discrimination against minority groups in this country. . . . Soviet spokesmen

regularly exploit this situation in propaganda against the United States. . . . Some of these attacks against us are based on falsehoods or distortion; but the undeniable existence of racial discrimination gives unfriendly governments the most effective kind of ammunition for their propaganda warfare. (cited by Layton, 2000, p. 116)

Dudziak points out that the continued legal segregation and racism that pervaded U.S. society created an embarrassing reality for U.S. foreign policy. "Newspapers throughout the world carried stories about discrimination against non-white visiting foreign dignitaries, as well as against American Blacks. At a time when the U.S. hoped to reshape the postwar world in its own image, the international attention given to racial segregation was troublesome and embarrassing" (Dudziak, 1995, p. 110). After all, Adolf Hitler had used the racial superiority argument to spread his Nazi ideology, and the United States, through both Jesse Owens's brilliant athletic demonstration in the 1938 Olympics and its triumph in World War II, resolutely repudiated such thinking.

What we have in the *Brown* decision is a prime example of what Derrick Bell calls "interest convergence." In addition to the international embarrassment, Bell suggests that *Brown* provided "much needed assurance to American Blacks that the precepts of equality and freedom so heralded during World War II might yet be given meaning at home" (Bell, 1980, p. 96). Nevertheless, dissident voices such as Paul Robeson's asserted, "It is unthinkable . . . that American Negroes would go to war on behalf of those who have oppressed us for generations . . . against a country [the Soviet Union] which in one generation has raised our people to the full human dignity of mankind" (Bell, 1980, p. 96).

Bell also suggests that *Brown* was championed by Whites who understood that the South could never make the economic transition from a "rural, plantation society to the sunbelt with all its potential and profit" (Bell, 1980, p. 96) unless it eradicated state-sponsored segregation. Thus the *Brown* case could be positioned as serving White interests—improving the national image, quelling racial unrest, and stimulating the economy—as well as Black interests—improving the educational condition of Black children and promoting social mobility. It is this convergence of interests that made *Brown* feasible. Now the focus of the discussion is to begin to understand the social and cultural costs that were incurred as a result of *Brown*.

UNDERSTANDING THE LIMITATIONS OF *BROWN*

First, it is important to acknowledge that the attorneys, scholars, educators, and community members who worked tirelessly on behalf of school desegregation were working for the right cause. And I affirm the principle that separate is inherently unequal. My issue is with *Brown* as the remedy, or more specifically, with the *implementation* of *Brown* as endorsed by the Court.

Despite making the right decision, the justices and the plaintiffs and other champions of social justice and equality did not (and indeed, could not) anticipate the depth of White fear and resentment toward the decision and the limitations such a decision would have in a racist context. In a recent lecture, Jack Greenburg (2003), one of the NAACP Legal Defense Fund lawyers who argued the *Brown* case, said, "We knew there would be resistance, but we were unprepared for the depth of the hatred and violence aimed at Black people in the South." Tate, Grant, and Ladson-Billings (1993) argued that the Court allowed for a "mathematical" solution to a social problem, particularly in the *Brown II* decision, where the local school districts were left with the responsibility to desegregate "with all deliberate speed." What the decision and its supporters could not account for was the degree to which White supremacy and racism were instantiated in the U.S. cultural model.

Issues of race and racism permeate U.S. culture—through law, language, politics, economics, symbols, art, public policy—and the prevalence of race is not merely in those spaces seen as racially defined spaces. For example, in the case of law, "race suffuses all bodies of law, not only obvious one like civil rights, immigration law, and federal Indian law, but also property law, contracts law, criminal law, federal courts, family law and even . . . corporate law" (Haney López, 1995, p. 192). The Warren court was making a decision about race *in* the context of racism. According to Mark Tushnet, former law clerk for Justice Thurgood Marshall, civil rights litigants attempted to "work within a racist system to combat racism" (Tushnet, 1944, p. 3).

One example of that context is the way the plaintiff attorneys used a discourse of Black inferiority to bolster their case. Prendergast states, "the arguments of psychological harm, as construed in *Brown I*, provided the grounds for overturning separate but equal without challenging White supremacy" (Prendergast, 2003, p. 24). Thus the experts for the plaintiffs argued that Black inferiority that was exacerbated by segregation was the reason to overturn the separate but equal principle. Citing Whitman, Prendergast shares a portion of the expert testimony of David Krech, professor of psychology from the University of California:

> I would say that most white people have cause to be prejudiced against the Negro, because the Negro in most cases is indeed inferior to the white man, because the white man has made him [that] through the practice of legal segregation. . . . [A]s a consequence of inadequate education we build into the Negro the very characteristic, not only intellectual, but also personality characteristics, which we then use to justify prejudice. (Prendergast, 2003, p. 25)

The ability to pathologize the plaintiff instead of addressing the underlying pathology—White supremacy—of the defendant severely limited the ruling and its implementation throughout the land.

In a different, but strangely related case, Latino families in the Lemon Grove School District experienced White supremacist attitudes firsthand more than two decades before *Brown* (Espinosa & Christopher, 1985; Alvarez, 1986). In 1930, the Lemon Grove, CA, school board attempted to create a segregated school for Mexican American children of the district. This small district, comprising 95 Anglos and 75 Latinos, was persuaded by the PTA and local Chamber of Commerce to send its Mexican American children to another school, without prior notice to the Latino families, because it claimed that the children did not speak English and were unsanitary. The Latino families went to court and the judge ruled against the school district, but the basis of his ruling was that the Mexican Americans were "officially" White and not Black, Asian, or Indian—groups that the law permitted districts to place in segregated schools. Thus again the ability to leverage non-White inferiority became a way to access social, economic, and political privileges.

Legal scholar Charles Lawrence asserts that the flaw in *Brown* comes as a result of the Court's fostering of "a way of thinking about segregation that has allowed both the judiciary and society at large to deny the reality of race in America" (Lawrence, 1980, p. 50). More important, Lawrence points out that if we are to have a real and meaningful remedy we have to recognize that racial reality in order to reframe *Brown* and "make it stand for what it should have stood for in 1954." Lawrence offers three underlying characteristics of segregation:

1. Its only purpose is to "label or define Blacks as inferior and thus exclude them from full and equal participation in the society."
2. The injury of segregation comes from its "system" or "institution" rather than from "particular segregating acts."
3. This institution of segregation is "organic" and "self-perpetuating" and cannot be dismantled via public sanction. It "must be affirmatively destroyed." (Lawrence, 1980, p. 50)

Lawrence points out that Black children suffered injury not because they were sitting in classrooms with other Black children, but rather because they were in those classrooms within a larger system that defined them and their schools as inferior. Indeed, as Siddle-Walker (1996) documents, some of the all-Black schools were superior to their White counterparts. But in a segregated system it is difficult to make their excellence evident.

The system of segregation was so comprehensive that African American teachers regardless of their qualifications were relegated to all Black schools. Their professional development options in the South were limited because of segregation, and the paradox was that many southern Black teachers received advanced training in some of the best northern institutions, including Teachers College, University of Wisconsin-Madison, and University of Chicago making them better qualified than White southern teachers, but still legally prohibited from teaching White children. Further, Lawrence argues, it will never be enough to try to punish segregationist behavior; rather it is necessary to work toward deliberate dismantling of segregation as an institution. Desegregating schools is a limited way of dealing with segregation as an institution. We need to think about ways to desegregate the society.

If we consider *Brown* as a ruling designed to eliminate school segregation, we know that, for the most part, it has been a failure. Orfield and Eaton (1996) show that after the ruling Southern school segregation continued almost undisturbed well into the 1960s. Northern schools remained segregated until the mid-1970s. Segregation actually grew in the 1990s. Of course one of the major problems that we have in understanding *Brown* is that we conflate two incompatible decisions—*Brown I* and *Brown II*. *Brown I*, the May 1954 decision, is the right decision, the one that pronounces the principle of separate as inherently unequal. *Brown I* is totally congruent with the principles of democracy and what the nation claims to stand for. *Brown II*, on the other hand, is the implementation phase of the decision. It effectively serves to undo any of the promise of the original decision. According to Orfield and Eaton, "the statement of principle was separated from the commitment to implementation, and the implementation procedures turned out not to work. For this reason, *Brown* and its implementation decision, *Brown II*, might most accurately be viewed as flawed compromises that combined a soaring repudiation of segregation with an unworkable remedy" (1996, p. 7).

It would be wrong to suggest that desegregation was never implemented. By the mid-1960s when the Civil Rights Movement was exploding across the nation and Congress passed the 1964 Civil Rights Act, southern schools felt the full enforcement of the law at the behest of a more aggressive Johnson Administration. But shortly after Richard Nixon's election, the Republican Party's Southern strategy emerged and enforcement of school desegregation waned. In his memoir, Nixon chief of staff H.R. Haldeman wrote in 1970:

> Feb. 4 . . . he plans to take on the integration problem directly. Is really concerned about situation in Southern schools and feels we have to take some leadership to try to reverse Court decisions that have forced integration too far, too fast. Has told Mitchell [Attorney General] to file another case, and keep filing until we get a reversal. (Haldeman, 1994, p. 126/ Orfield & Eaton, 1996, p. 9)

Over the next 20 years, several legal cases functioned effectively to roll back the principle of *Brown*. Among the cases were *Milliken v.*

Bradley (1974), *San Antonio School District v. Rodriguez* (1973), *Board of Education of Oklahoma v. Dowell* (1991), and *Freeman v. Pitts* (1992). Briefly, *Milliken* closed off the opportunity for racially isolated communities of color to draw from White suburbs in order to desegregate; in *Rodriguez* the Court ruled that children had no constitutional right to equal school expenditures; *Dowell* and *Pitts* allowed formerly desegregated school districts to return to neighborhood schools because they were determined to be "unitary," there was no separate school district for children of color. The power and impact of *Brown* on school desegregation had become substantially diluted. But even when *Brown* represented a hope for change in the nation's schools, that hope came at a cost.

One of the costs of *Brown* was the job loss and demotions for Black teachers and administrators. Epps (1999) puts the number of jobs lost at about 38,000 in 17 states in the South between 1954 and 1965. Hudson and Holmes (1994) concur with Epps and go on to document the steady decline of African Americans in the teaching profession. They assert that before 1954, "approximately 82,000 African American teachers were responsible for educating the nation's two million African American public school students" (Hudson & Holmes, 1994, p. 388). Fultz (2004) refers to the "displacement of Black educators" that includes both job loss and demotions. Haney (1978) states that as desegregation began to be implemented some state legislatures and school boards throughout the South began a campaign of "economic reprisal and intimidation against Black educators" (Haney, 1978, p. 90). The Alabama legislature introduced a bill in 1956 that would have given school boards the right to dismiss Black educators "with or without cause, and with or without a hearing and right to appeal." Haney further states that in North Carolina, "128 out of 131 white superintendents believed that it would be 'impracticable to use Negro teachers' in schools under their jurisdiction" (Haney, 1978, p. 90). Despite job losses and demotions, Black teachers and administrators generally supported school desegregation even though it meant likely displacement for them.

Detweiler (1967) has suggested that Black teachers in the South shouldered a special burden during school desegregation. While the *Brown* ruling defined the rights of Black students, the Black teacher's position became much less secure. In the 1965–66 school year the U.S. Department of Health, Education, and Welfare reported that only 1.8% of the Black teachers in the eleven states of the former Confederacy taught on a desegregated faculty. Not a single Black teacher in Alabama, Louisiana, or Mississippi had been assigned to a school where there were White teachers. The paradox of this failure to hire Black teachers is that approximately 85 percent of the Black teachers in the nation were located in the South. If the school districts were going to pair school desegregation with the reduction of the number of Black teachers they would actually be accelerating school desegregation and increasing the teaching load of White teachers.

If we consider the big picture we might argue that the loss of jobs was relatively insignificant and served the greater good. But like general unemployment figures, these numbers are not insignificant if you, or a member of your family, are among the unemployed. Some scholars (e.g., Orfield & Eaton, 1996) argue that the continued problem of recruiting Black teachers and other teachers of color is a result of the increased opportunities in other fields such as medicine, law, and business. I do not dispute this shift in the job market and career aspirations of young people, but I cannot help wondering why, if the emerging middle class in the Black community chose other job opportunities, working class Blacks weren't recruited to fill the void in the teaching ranks. Could it be that the loss of Black teachers in the early post-*Brown* years created what Randall Robinson (2000) identifies as the ongoing cumulative effects of discrimination? Since African American students saw fewer African American teachers, might they have surmised that the profession was not fully available to them?

Another consequence of the *Brown* decision was the emergence of "segregation academies" as a form of White resistance to desegregation. In 1971 about a half million White children attended segregated private schools in the South. Despite the threat these schools posed to the court decision, only a limited number of legal challenges were mounted to combat them, because they did not receive direct public support in the form of tuition grants. In the case of Smallville, Louisiana, when White parents failed to comply with court-ordered school desegregation their private academy was supplemented by a "donation" of all the school's desks and a library from the public school board. The state of Louisiana provided the textbooks. The local sheriff's department provided security for the academy because of White fears that some Blacks would violently oppose the school. In addition, the academy's costs were lessened with a supplementary payment by the state of Louisiana to private school teachers. When the State Supreme Court found such payments to be unconstitutional the teachers who had formerly been public school teachers were determined to be old enough to retire from the school system and received a pension that acted as a salary supplement (Champagne, 1973).

The long-term legacy of the academy as resistance strategy is another interesting phenomenon. For instance, in South Carolina White citizens developed academies as a way to avoid school desegregation. South Carolina delayed desegregation until 1963, when Clemson University was the first school in the state to desegregate. Some two years later on August 10, 1965, the South Carolina Independent School Association (SCIA) was founded with 7 schools. Today, SCIA comprises 90 schools with 28,000 students. South Carolina is also home to a private Christian school association that includes more than 100 schools.

Just a cursory look at some of the current Web sites of private academies in South Carolina is revealing.[7] Andrew Jackson Academy, "Home of the Confederates," was established in 1971; Jefferson Davis Academy, "Home of the Raiders," was established in 1965 along with Robert E. Lee Academy, "Home of the Cavaliers." Although most of the Web sites include the federal nondiscrimination language, the student photographs generally show all White student bodies in a state with an almost 30% Black population. Tuition at the schools I looked at ranges from $277.50 per month at Patrick Henry Academy (est. 1965) to $7,400 per year for the high school program at Beaufort Academy (est. 1965). This wide disparity in costs suggests that the ability to opt out of the public schools was one of the prime considerations for the establishment of such schools, not merely creating elite, college preparatory environments.

Another of the costs of *Brown*, to which I alluded earlier, is the way the legal strategy exploited notions of Black inferiority to ask for benevolence on the part of Whites. I would argue that a significant (and overlooked) issue is what school segregation does to White students. What if *Brown* had asked what disadvantage do Whites experience as a result of attending racially isolated, White monocultural schools? This might be the question posed by a critical race theorist searching for the possible interest-convergence that the decision could promote. I ask this question after examining Klarman's backlash thesis which argues that Brown's *direct* impact on school desegregation was limited and its *indirect* contribution to racial change is "more generally assumed than demonstrated" (Klarman, 1994, p. 81). For example, Klarman refers to opinion surveys that suggest that in 1955 few Northern Whites discussed the Supreme Court decision and print media coverage of civil rights events did not pay significant attention to the court decisions, including *Brown* as compared to events involving confrontation and violence, such as the 1955–1956 Montgomery Bus Boycott. Indeed "the percentage of respondents identifying civil rights as the nation's most urgent problem surged after the Montgomery bus boycott, not after *Brown*, and even that increase was dwarfed by the explosion in public attention to civil rights after the Birmingham demonstrations in the spring of 1963."

More dramatic than its indirect impact on civil rights, says Klarman was the catalytic effect that *Brown* had on Southern Whites. He suggests that "*Brown* crystallized southern resistance to racial change, which . . . had been scattered and episodic. . . . *Brown* temporarily destroyed racial moderation" (Klarman, p. 81). Klarman's argument is that the civil rights movement did not need *Brown* as a catalyst, but the massive White resistance movement did. Although any number of civil rights activists pointed to *Brown* in hindsight as inspiration for the struggle, the record suggests that in the case of the Montgomery Bus Boycott the leaders had been challenging seating practices on city buses well before *Brown*, and the boycott itself was patterned on a similar boycott in Baton Rouge, Louisiana. In addition, the Montgomery Bus Boycott was not specifically to end segregation but rather for a less degrading form of segregation (Klarman, 1994).

Although it is clear that antagonism toward Blacks was already present in the South and throughout the nation, Klarman's backlash thesis argues that "southern resistance to racial change was of different orders of magnitude before and after *Brown*" (Klarman, 1994, p. 92). Before *Brown* there were of course some hard-line southern Whites who reacted violently to changes such as the returning Black World War II veterans' claims on equal citizenship and President Truman's 1948 civil rights proposals. But the scope of that resistance was limited. *Brown* elevated race over class for the working-class and poor Whites who were the main constituency of the rising populist coalitions in the southern states during this period. *Brown* incited rural Whites to "exert their disproportionate power in state politics to exact racial conformity from Whites less preoccupied with race" (Klarman, 1994, p. 98) and Whites who were less compelled by race were forced to coalesce with White supremacists in an effort to assert states' rights over federal intervention. Essentially, Klarman's argument is that *Brown* forced a polarization of White politics and moderation became untenable.

Although I do not dispute Klarman's assertions that *Brown* was limited in both its direct impact on school desegregation and its indirect impact on the overall civil rights movement, I think in terms of cost to African Americans, the backlash thesis is not particularly significant. True, there was the increased threat posed by a mobilized White resistance, but the African American community had lived with virulent White anger and violence for centuries. By allowing race to trump class, the real cost, as I see it, is the missed opportunity to build a coalition between African Americans and poor Whites, both of whom were receiving an inferior education.

By framing the debate as solely racial, the remedy offered relief in the form of balancing racial numbers with no regard to educational quality. In a case like the Boston, MA, school desegregation plan, poor African American students from Roxbury were sent to desegregate White working class schools in South Boston (Hochschild, 1984). Articulated by Roediger (1991), and previously by W. E. B. Du Bois (1935/1995), we see in its reaction to *Brown* a White working class that again trades a class identity to maintain solidarity with whiteness. Du Bois asserted:

> The South, after the [Civil] war presented the greatest opportunity for a real national labor movement which the nation ever saw or is likely to see for many decades. Yet the [white] labor movement, with but few exceptions, never realized the situation. It never had the intelligence or knowledge, as a whole, to see in black slavery and Reconstruction, the kernel and the meaning of the labor movement in the United States. (Du Bois, 1935/1995, p. 353)

Had the Supreme Court's remedy focused on the quality of education students received, White working class and poor students could have been folded into the decision in a way that might benefit them rather than underscore the adversarial relationship between Blacks and Whites. Instead, the focus on school desegregation obscured the more pressing need for quality education. Actually, the focus on school desegregation obscured the need for school *integration* and the myriad ways that local K–12 schools would thwart the full inclusion of Black children into the school community. Unlike college and university education, where the possibility to create separate and distinct learning tracks does not exist, pre-collegiate education has devised many ways to re-segregate students by race.

One of the popular desegregation solutions that emerged in the North was the magnet school (Winston, 1996). School districts can designate certain schools (particularly those located in Black communities) as specialty schools (e.g., math and technology, fine arts, science) to attract White students from other neighborhoods to them. On paper this seems like a reasonable desegregation solution. But, in many cases the magnet programs became two schools or a school within a school with White students attending the magnet program and Black and/or Latino students attending the "regular" school. In one school in San Jose, CA, located in a Latino community there was a fine arts magnet. White students did come from throughout the city to attend the magnet program. Inside the school, however, the top two floors that housed the fine arts magnet were almost exclusively White while the lower two floors were filled with Latino neighborhood students. In another California example students were enticed to attend high school in a predominantly Black community with offers of free camping trips and ski trips. Although the school offered the trips to all students, both the nature and the equipment needs of the activities limited the participation of the Black students. Ultimately, the incentives were not enough to convince White families to send their children to the school, and the high school eventually closed.[8] With no high school available in their community, the Black and (later Latino) students were dispersed across the four White schools where they began dropping out at a rate of 65%–70%.

The re-segregation of students is prevalent in our current post-*Brown* era. Of course, schools alone cannot take responsibility for the increasing re-segregation. Housing, immigration, and employment patterns guarantee that urban communities will reflect a higher proportion of Black, Latino, and poor students. Several studies (Orfield & Yun, 1999; Frankenberg & Lee, 2002) indicate that the nation's schools are rapidly re-segregating. We see a nation where public school enrollment reflects the country's growing diversity but Blacks and Latinos are more likely to attend racially isolated schools. This isolation is related in part to the differential birth rates in the White, Black, and Latino communities. But when we look at the actual numbers, we see that fewer Whites live in major urban centers, whereas Blacks and Latinos are concentrated in these areas. Even so, urban schools reflect a hyper-segregation beyond that of their cities' overall population.

Lomotey & Staley (1990) argued that school desegregation programs are said to be successful when White parents are satisfied. Therefore school districts incorporate a variety of perks to attract them. Free or low-cost after-school care, magnet programs, and extracurricular opportunities are paid for with federal "desegregation" monies but Black and Latino children rarely benefit from such programs. When Lomotey and Staley looked more carefully at what was occurring in the schools in the district they studied they learned that African American and Latino students continued to have high school suspension, drop out, and failure rates but school desegregation in the district was considered a "model" program.

In yet another example, an elementary school located in a historically Black community in San Francisco was ordered to desegregate because no schools in the district were permitted to have a population of more than 47% of any one "designated" minority. For years the school was dilapidated and lacked the necessary technology and supplies to support a quality education. Once the district announced that White students would be assigned to the school, repairs began. The building was repainted, the floors were stripped and waxed, broken windows were replaced, a new computer lab was constructed and equipped with state-of-the-art computers, and books and other supplies were plentiful. When I asked the school principal about the school demographics, she responded, "Do you want to know what it is on paper or what it is in reality?" I was surprised to learn that when African American parents saw that the school district was willing to improve the school once White children were coming in and their children were being

Table 6.1. Enrollment of the 12 Largest City School Districts by Race and Ethnicity

City	Enrollment	% White	% Black	% Latino	% Asian
New York	1,091,717	16.1	36.1	37.3	10.0
Los Angeles	735,000	9.6	12.9	71.4	6.0
Chicago	438,589	9.2	50.9	36.4	3.3
Miami	374,806	10.6	30.1	57.2	>2.0
Houston	212,099	9.3	30.5	57.1	3.0
Philadelphia	204,851	16.4	65.3	13.1	4.9
Detroit	187,590	5.2	90.1	2.8	1.0
Dallas	163,327	6.7	32.9	58.9	1.2
San Diego	141,171	26.6	15.6	39.7	17.2
Memphis	118,000	9.0	87.0	0.7	1.4
Milwaukee	105,000	22.2	58.96	12.5	3.6
Baltimore	95,875	10.4	87.7	0.4	0.5

Note. These figures come from current school district websites.

sent out of the community, a large contingent of them re-enrolled their children in the neighborhood school with the racial/ethnic designation "Native American." The principal told me, "I have the largest concentration of "Native American" students in the city!" Because the United States allows people to self-designate their racial/ethnic identity, the school officials were in no position to reject the formerly identified African Americans, who reconstituted themselves as Native Americans. This strategy underscores the ongoing discussion in many communities of color that ask why is it that money and resources follow White middle class children?

WHERE WE GO FROM HERE

Bell (1983) suggests that despite the inclusion of social scientists and the enthusiasm of community and civil rights activists, the *Brown* decision omitted the perspectives and insights of educators, particularly teachers. Without these perspectives, it was difficult to arrive at a decision that focused on the quality of the education Black children were to receive. The overriding logic was not only one of Black inferiority, but the concomitant one of White superiority and the idea that placing Blacks in the midst of that superiority would be sufficient to create equal education opportunities. There is no provision in *Brown* for equality of outcomes. As long as Blacks and other children of color were given the *opportunity* to attend the same schools that Whites did, the state had met its legal and civic obligations. Communities of color, desperate to receive a better education, were satisfied with the terms of the decision.

So my discussion has offered a rather pessimistic picture of the possibilities of school desegregation via the *Brown* decision. Indeed, some of the most vocal proponents of the decision have expressed similar pessimism. Linda Brown-Thompson, whose father filed the Topeka claim, lamented, "Sometimes I wonder if we really did the children and the nation a favor by taking this case to the Supreme Court. I know it was the right thing for my father and others to do then. But after nearly forty years we find the Court's ruling unfulfilled" (Patterson, 2001, p. 207). Robert Carter, a former aide of Thurgood Marshall, wrote that "for most black children, *Brown's* constitutional guarantee of equal education opportunity has been an arid abstraction, having no effect whatever on the educational offerings black children are given or the deteriorating schools they attend" (Patterson, 2001, p. 210). And, psychologist Kenneth Clark, whose work on Black self-concept was used as testimony in the case, when asked in 1995, "What is the best thing for blacks to call themselves?" answered, "White" (Patterson, 2001, p. 210).

The costs that I outlined—job loss and displacement over time, the re-inscription of Black inferiority, the rise of the segregation academies, the missed opportunity for working-class White and Black coalitions to work together for quality education, and the focus on race over quality education—all point to the high price that was paid in the name of getting the Supreme Court and the nation to acknowledge a principle it already understood to be important to democracy. Still, I want to suggest that not all was lost on behalf of the principle. *Brown* created some important space for new kinds of discursive and critical moves that marginalized communities might make. The legal foundation of *Brown* made possible some important legislative, educational, and social changes—for example, the passage of the Civil Rights Act of 1964 and the enforcement of co-education and gender equity at a number of schools through Title IX.

It is important to remember that as far as one might argue the *Brown* decision went in eradicating the notion of "separate but equal", nevertheless it has minimal power to limit or constrain private behaviors that maintain and support separate institutions.[9] Therefore, the Court's ruling could not affect the growing number of segregation academies or the "White flight" to suburban communities. Communities of color also have the ability to create separate institutions. Efforts by individuals (e.g., Marva Collins' Westside Preparatory in Chicago, William Green's Ivy Leaf School in Philadelphia, Chris Bischof's Eastside Preparatory in East Palo Alto, CA) and groups (e.g., Council of Independent Black Institutions) have served as small(er)-scale exemplars of academic excellence in segregated African American settings.

Although White southerners organized segregation academies, some 100 historically Black boarding schools existed prior to 1960 (Roach, 2003). These schools, primarily based in the South, came about, in general, because Black parents were searching for alternatives to the substandard, inadequate segregated systems that Jim Crow laws produced. The promise of *Brown* caused significant enrollment declines and financial hardship to these boarding schools. Today, only four Black boarding schools remain—Laurinburg Institute, North Carolina; Pine Forge Academy, Pennsylvania; Piney Woods, Mississippi; and Redemption Christian Academy, New York. But small boutique programs like Westside Prep, Eastside Prep, and the boarding schools are not realistic options for the millions of students in the public schools. What other options exist?

Critical race theorists might argue that the way to deal with persistent school segregation would be to allow White middle-income schools to remain segregated if they choose but to attach exorbitant monetary fines to such behavior. These monies would be directed into low-income communities' schools to improve the quality of their education. Such a proposal has no chance of being taken seriously in the United States. Therefore we will continue to permit such segregation without acknowledgment or sanction. What then can be done both to combat the hyper-segregation we find in our urban centers and elite suburbs and to improve the education that all students receive?

Brown is more accurately characterized as a *first* step in a long, arduous process to rid the nation of its most pernicious demons—racism and White supremacy. While we celebrate its potential, we must be clear about its limitations. The nation has never fully and honestly dealt with its "race" problem. Our lack of historical understanding seems to obliterate some rather daunting facts. For example, slavery existed legally in North America for almost 250 years. An apartheid-like social segregation was legally sanctioned for another hundred years. The United States as a nation is but 228 years old and existed as a slave nation longer than it has existed as a free one. The norms, customs, mores, and folkways that surround our racial ecology are not easily cast aside. Our attempt to deal with racial problems through our schools is an incomplete strategy.

In its volume on housing and school segregation, the Institute on Race and Poverty (Powell, Kearney, & Kay, 2001) points out that by tackling school segregation and leaving neighborhood segregation intact, the Court's virtually guaranteed the maintenance of a separate and unequal society. Nancy Denton (2001), identifies three persistent myths about residential segregation: (a) segregation has always been with us, (b) residential segregation in cities is natural, and (c) because housing discrimination is illegal it must not be a problem. In confronting the first myth Denton points out that housing patterns at the beginning of the 20th century were nowhere near as segregated as they are now.[10] In addressing the second myth, Denton argues, "persisting residential segregation is not a normal part of the development of cities" (Denton, 2001, p. 94). Rather, a combination of public and private actors—the real estate industry, appraisers, banks, and insurance agencies—played on private prejudices that were ultimately translated into public policy through the Federal Housing Authority.[11] It is striking that the implementation of *Brown* coincided with the building of highways and suburban developments. Denton says that the assumption that the 1968 Fair Housing Act ended housing discrimination is false. The empirical data detail widespread discrimination in the sale and rental of housing to Blacks and Latinos (Fix & Struyk, 1993).

As long as residential segregation remains an issue, school segregation will be a partial and difficult reality. Increasingly, communities endorse "neighborhood schools" and reject busing to achieve desegregation. Currently, Chinese-American parents in San Francisco are fighting to avoid sending their children to schools in African American and Latino neighborhoods (Knight, 2003). Today, the language of "choice" is recruited to help middle-income parents maintain segregated schools. While in principle many states and school districts offer school choice, this choice is possible on a space-available basis. The best schools and school districts rarely have space for any students outside their neighborhood boundaries.[12] The issue of public school charters, private school choice, and vouchers is beyond the scope of this discussion, but my position is they do not represent a practical alternative to the massive numbers of students locked in segregated, sub-standard urban and rural schools.

If school desegregation has been severely eroded and racial segregation has become more solidified, what hope remains for a diverse, racially inte-grated educational experience for students—particularly those students who are least well-served by schools? Charles Willie offers a bit of light on the very dark road we have been traveling. Instead of focusing on the school as the sole site of racial integration and democracy, he offers a "theory of complementarity" (Willie, 2000, p. 197) that weds individual needs and de-sires to group responsibility. This means that while individuals may want to attend particular schools the group must address its responsibility to great-er social goals. Willie (2000) believes in a system of "controlled choice" (Willie, 2000, p. 198) that focuses on upgrading the worst schools as well as promoting the best. He points to work in Cambridge, MA, where controlled choice made desegregation workable.

Willie's (2000) work shows some promise, but I am less persuad-ed that such a plan is feasible outside of college communities that draw high-income, high-achieving students to local public schools. As always, I am drawn to critical race theory analyses and solutions. I would argue for the need to show Whites how they are disadvantaged by racial segregation as a catalyst for change. For example, in a number of large cities such as New York, Chicago, Philadelphia, Baltimore, and San Francisco, there exist high schools like Bronx Science, Whitney Young, Central, Polytechnic, and Lowell where parents seem not at all concerned about the racial make-up or location of the school because they believe that what the school offers overrides their personal prejudices and racial discomforts.

Until K–12 parents have what I would call the "Bear Bryant/Adolph Rupp epiphany"[13] they will continue to seek schooling in racially, eco-nomically, and culturally homogeneous communities. Currently, there is no compelling reason for people to leave the safe and comfortable confines of neighborhood schools where they wield influence and can demand priv-ileges. The only way to ensure more school desegregation is to disconnect schools altogether from local property taxes and reconstitute students as citizens of states, not merely residents of particular communities. Some of the most egregious school funding disparities occur *within* states (Kozol, 1991). Students in Newark, NJ, fare much worse than their Princeton and Toms River counterparts; students in Chicago fair much worse than their New Trier and Palatine counterparts; students in Detroit fair much worse than their Grosse Pointe counterparts. But all are citizens of their respec-tive states. Here I invoke not states' rights but states' responsibilities to ensure their entire citizenry a quality education. Rather than allow the tre-mendous variability that emerges when property taxes determine school district resources and expenditures, the state must be proactive in the fight for equity and excellence in public schooling. Such a proposal will not sit well with wealthier citizens who have grown accustomed to wielding broad decision-making power at the local school level. But consider the facts: the state serves as the credentialing agency for teachers and administrators, it typically oversees curriculum standards and requirements, two major sources of school revenue (state and federal) are administered at the state level, the state often determines exit or completion criteria, and nation-wide performance data (e.g. NAEP, ACT, SAT) are reported by states. The state is the logical (and sufficiently distant) entity to equalize education.

Of course I am not naïve enough to believe that the state-as-equalizer solution will be embraced. There are certain to be critics who will rightly point to the extant interstate disparities. Southern states do worse educationally than those in the Northeast and Midwest. Structural issues of differential economic bases and population demographics disadvantage some states, but at least my solution might begin to correct the intrastate disparities. Outside of education, more comprehensive systems—the military, hospitals, and the postal service—have made significant strides in racial desegregation.

I would be less than honest if I said that creating statewide school systems represented the full answer to our school desegregation and equity problems. The truth is that these issues emerge from a much higher level of abstraction. We have the schools we have because of the culture we have. The real answer resides in cultural transformation, a much more difficult and unpopular solution.

The United States originally conceived itself as a nation of pilgrims (small 'p'). The Mayflower became history's largest boat, which inscribed on us an identity as pure, persecuted, and preordained. In time, the pilgrim metaphor failed to capture the American reality, and we substituted the immigrant metaphor: the United States as a nation of immigrants.[14] Europeans were said to have an Ellis Island immigrant experience, Asians were said to have an Angel Island immigrant experience. American Indians were described as the "first immigrants." African Americans were "forced immigrants," and I presume Latinos are "synthetic immigrants"—something new created in the Americas. Once again, the metaphor, though popular, is problematic.

I want to propose a new metaphor that I believe better describes the dynamic and conflicting cultural narrative that is the United States of America. That metaphor is America as jazz (Ladson-Billings, 2003). I choose this art form because of its flexibility and versatility. Jazz does not lend itself easily to definition and prescription and, like jazz, America has conceived itself as an expression of freedom. Such notions of freedom and liberation themselves involve contestation. Carl Engel said that, "good jazz is a composite, the happy union of seemingly incompatible elements . . . It is the upshot of a transformation . . . and culminates in something unique, unmatched in any other part of the world" (Engel, 1922, p. 6).

With jazz as America's metaphor we can begin to see how, through different eras, the nation created and re-created itself—from blues and ragtime to swing and be-bop to cool jazz, avant garde, and free jazz there are tensions and struggles to be a new thing. This new thing pulls on the traditions of the old while pushing toward new forms and expression. If jazz is a metaphor for America, then I would argue that the *Brown v. Board of Education* decision represents an Ornette Coleman–like rupture from the preceding legal decisions. When alto saxophonist Coleman began playing his new music he created what Davis called, "a permanent revolution" in the field (Davis, 1985, p. 1). In 1959 Coleman's quartet appeared at New York's Five Spot jazz club about the same time as the release of Coleman's album, *The Shape of Jazz to Come*. Reportedly, be-bop drummer Max Roach punched Coleman in the mouth on the bandstand and later showed up at his apartment threatening to do him more harm (Ake, 2002). On the other hand, Modern Jazz Quartet leader John Lewis referred to Coleman's sound as "exciting and different . . . the only really new thing in jazz since the innovations in the mid-forties of Dizzy Gillespie, Charlie Parker, and those of Thelonius Monk" (Ake, 2002, p. 63).

And so it must be with *Brown*. The decision provoked strong negative and positive reactions, primarily because it represented a social and cultural break with the past. It was so radical a departure from what had gone before that almost every civil rights challenge that came after it found itself trying to limit and contain its potentially far-reaching and life-changing impact. And, just as Ornette Coleman may have cost jazz some of its mainstream audience, so did *Brown* force moderate Whites who claimed to advocate a gradual approach to desegregation into a defensive posture and alignment with more reactionary and racist communities. But the role of *Brown*, like that of jazz, was to serve as a re-articulation of freedom. Duke Ellington said:

> Jazz is a good barometer of freedom . . . In its beginnings, the United States of America spawned certain ideals of freedom and independence through which eventually jazz evolved, and the music is so free that many people say it is the only unhampered, unhindered expression of complete freedom yet produced in this country. (quoted in Ward & Burns, 2000, p. vii)

But even as *Brown I* attempted to rend us from a racially troubled past, *Brown II* worked to suture us to that history. By allowing school districts to use delaying tactics and endorsing their legal challenges the federal government effectively backed away from a new vision of the United States. But such a new vision is not easily quashed. I would argue like LeRoi Jones (Amiri Baraka) in 1961 in his comparison of Ornette Coleman to Charlie Parker that *Brown I* was only a "hypothesis" and our "conclusions [will be] quite separate and unique" (cited by Ake, 2002, p. 69).

The real challenge before us is not to enact *Brown* as a solution to seg-regated schools but rather to use *Brown* as a hypothesis for a new future. Might it be a place to argue that real education is impossible in isolation from diverse and critical perspectives? Might it be a place to begin to exam-ine not just the mis-education of children of color and the poor but also that of White, middle-class children whose limited perspectives severely hamper their ability to function effectively in the global community? *Brown* is nei-ther the panacea that we imagined, nor the problem that we experience. Rather, it is the hope that landing on a wrong note does not signal the end of the music.

NOTES

1. This article was presented as the DeWitt Wallace–Reader's Digest Lecture of the American Education Research Association Annual Meeting, San Diego, CA April, 2004. I would like to thank Doug McAdam and Fellows at the Center for Advanced Study in the Behavioral Sciences for their thoughtful comments and ques-tions on this paper. I would also like to thank James Anderson from the University of Illinois and Michael Fultz from the University of Wisconsin for help with historical resources.

2. The original Civil Rights Act of 1875 contained a school desegregation pro-vision that was struck down before its passage. The Supreme Court later declared the act with its prohibition against discrimination in public accommodations uncon-stitutional.

3. This case was argued by Thurgood Marshall in South Carolina on May 17, 1950.

4. This case was filed in Washington, DC, by James Nabrit Jr. on September 11, 1950.

5. This case was filed in Virginia by the NAACP on May 23, 1951.

6. See www.archives.gov/digital_classroom/lessons/brown_v_board_documents/images/letter_3.gif (retrieved 02/11/04).

7. I specifically looked at some of the academies in the counties where the plain-tiff districts from the school funding adequacy case are located.

8. See http://belmont.gov/orgs/alumni/ravenswood/about_rhs.htm. Retrieved 12/03/03.

9. The federal government can exercise financial sanctions over schools that receive federal monies and practice racial, gender, ability, national origin, and other forms of discrimination.

10. Henry Louis Taylor Jr. notes, "The structure of the commercial city kept black ghettoes from forming. The population had no choice but to mix. Lack of adequate transportation systems, mixed patterns of land use, and the ubiqui-ty of cheap housing led to the dispersal of both the immigrant and black popula-tions. . . . Throughout the nineteenth century in both the North and South, blacks lived in biracial residential areas; even in the most segregated locations blacks and whites lived adjacent to one another or shared the same dwellings" (Taylor, 1993, p. 159).

11. The Federal Housing Administration (FHA) fostered loan policies and high-way programs that supported racial segregation and encouraged White suburban growth.

12. During my own school district's "open enrollment period" I was unable to enroll my child in a school across town because it was "over-enrolled."

13. On September 17, 1970, a Black football player, Sam "Bam" Cunningham of the University of Southern California, scored 3 touchdowns against Bear Bryant's all-White University of Alabama defense. In 1966 the University of Texas-El Paso (formerly Texas Western) started five Black players against Adolph Rupp's all-White University of Kentucky team in the NCAA championship game. Both USC and UTEP won their respective contests and made clear to big-time college athletics that winning required recruiting players from beyond all-White prep fields.

14. See popular social studies textbooks at the fifth and eighth grade level.

REFERENCES

Ake, D. (2002). *Jazz cultures*. Berkeley, CA: University of California Press.

Alvarez, R. (1986). The Lemon Grove incident: The nation's first successful desegregation court case. *The Journal of San Diego History, 32*(2), 116–135.

Appleby, J. (1992). Rediscovering America's historic diversity: Beyond exceptionalism. *The Journal of American History, 79*, 419–431.

Bell, D. (1980). Brown and the interest-convergence dilemma. In D. Bell (Ed.), *Shades of Brown: New perspectives on school desegregation* (pp. 90–106). New York: Teachers College Press.

Bell, D. (1983). Time for the teachers: Putting educators back into the Brown remedy. *The Journal of Negro Education, 52*(3), 290–301.

Champagne, A. (1973). The segregation academy and the law. *The Journal of Negro Education, 42*(1), 58–66.

Crenshaw, K. (1988). Race, reform, and retrenchment: Transformation and legitimation in antidiscrimination law. *Harvard Law Review, 101*, 1331–1387.

Cushing, L. (1883). *Reports of cases argued and determined in the Supreme Judicial Court of Massachusetts*, vol. 5. Boston, MA: Little, Brown & Co.

Davis, F. (1985). *Ornette's permanent revolution*. Retrieved December 12, 2003 from www.theatlantic.com/unbound/jazz/dornette.htm

Denton, N. (2001). The persistence of segregation: Links between residential segregation and school segregation. In J. Powell, G. Kearney & V. Kay (Eds.), *In pursuit of a dream deferred: Linking housing and education policy* (pp. 89–119). New York: Peter Lang.

Detweiler, J. (1967). The Negro teacher and the Fourteenth Amendment. *The Journal of Negro Education, 36*(4), 403–409.

Du Bois, W. E. B. (1935/1995). *Black reconstruction*. New York: Atheneum.

Dudziak, M. (1995). Desegregation as a cold war imperative. In R. Delgado (Ed.), *Critical race theory: The cutting edge* (pp. 110–121). Philadelphia, PA: Temple University Press.

Engel, C. (1922, August). *Jazz: A musical discussion*. Retrieved December 12, 2003 from www.theatlantic.com/unbound/jazz/cengel.htm

Epps, E. (1999). *Race and school desegregation: Contemporary legal and education-al issues.* Retrieved November 12, 2003 from http://www.urbanedjournal.org /articles/article0003.pdf

Espinosa, P. (Producer) & Christopher, F. (Director) (1985). *The Lemon Grove Incident* [motion picture], San Diego, CA: KPBS.

Fix, M., & Struyk, R. (Eds.) (1993). *Clear and convincing evidence: Measurement of discrimination in America.* Washington, DC: Urban Institute Press.

Frankenberg, E., & Lee, C. (2002). *Race in American public schools: Rapidly reseg-regating school districts.* Cambridge, MA: The Civil Rights Project, Harvard University.

Fultz, M. (2004). The displacement of Black educators post-*Brown*: An overview and analysis. *History of Education Quarterly, 44*(1), 11–45.

Greenburg, J. (2003, Dec. 5). *Brown plus 50.* Public lecture, Stanford University Law School, Stanford, CA.

Haldeman, H. R. (1994). *The Haldeman Diaries: Inside the Nixon White House.* New York: G. P. Putman's Sons.

Haney, J. (1978). The effects of the *Brown* decision on Black educators. *The Journal of Negro Education, 47,* 88–95.

Haney López, I. (1995). The social construction of race. In R. Delgado (Ed.), *Critical race theory: The cutting edge* (pp. 191–203). Philadelphia, PA: Temple University Press.

Heble, A. (2000). *Landing on the wrong note: Jazz, dissonance, and critical practice.* New York: Routledge.

Hess, D. (2003). *The classroom iconization of Brown.* Unpublished paper. University of Wisconsin, Madison.

Hochschild, J. (1984). *The new American dilemma: Liberal democracy and school desegregation.* New Haven, CT: Yale University Press.

Hudson, M., & Holmes, B. (1994). Missing teachers, impaired communities: The unanticipated consequences of *Brown v. Board of Education* on the African American teaching force at the precollegiate level. *The Journal of Negro Education, 63*(3), 388–393.

Klarman, M. (1994). How *Brown* changed race relations: The backlash thesis. *The Journal of American History, 81*(1), 81–118.

Knight, H. (2003, October 7). S.F. Parents rekindle desegregation debate. *San Francisco Chronicle,* pp. A1, A5.

Kozol, J. (1991). *Savage inequalities: Children in America's schools.* New York: Crown.

Ladson-Billings, G. (2003). New directions in multicultural education: Complexities, boundaries, and critical race theory. In J. A. Banks & C. M. Banks (Eds.), *Handbook of research in multicultural education,* 2nd ed. (pp. 50–65). San Francisco, CA: Jossey-Bass.

Lawrence, C. (1980). One more river to cross—Recognizing the real injury in *Brown*: A prerequisite to shaping new remedies. In D. Bell (Ed.), *Shades of Brown: New perspectives on school desegregation* (pp. 48–68). New York: Teachers College Press.

Layton, A. S. (2000). *International politics and civil rights policy in the United States, 1941–1960.* Cambridge, UK: Cambridge University Press.

Lomotey, K., & Staley, J. (1990, April). *The education of African Americans in the Buffalo Public Schools: An exploratory study.* Paper presented at the annual meeting of the American Educational Research Association, Boston, MA.

Orfield, G., & Eaton, S. (1996). *Dismantling desegregation.* New York: The Free Press.

Orfield, G., & Yun, J. (1999). *Resegregation in American schools.* Cambridge, MA: The Civil Rights Project, Harvard University.

Patterson, J. T. (2001). *Brown v. Board of Education: A civil rights milestone and its troubled legacy.* New York: Oxford University Press.

Powell, J., Kearney, G., & Kay, V. (Eds.) (2001). *In pursuit of a dream deferred: Linking housing and education policy.* New York: Peter Lang.

Prendergast, C. (2003). *Literacy and racial justice: The politics of learning after Brown v. Board of Education.* Carbondale, IL: Southern Illinois University Press.

Roach, R. (2003, Aug. 14). A rich but disappearing legacy: Remembering Black boarding schools: A tradition obscured by desegregation impact. *Black Issues in Higher Education.* Retrieved December 12, 2003 from https://diverseeducation.com/article/3117

Robinson, R. (2000). *The debt: What America owes to Blacks.* New York: E. P. Dutton.

Roediger, D. (1991). *The wages of whiteness: Race and the making of the American working class.* London: Verso Books.

Siddle-Walker, V. (1996). *Their highest potential: An African American school community in the segregated South.* Chapel Hill, NC: University of North Carolina Press.

Tate, W. F., Ladson-Billings, G., & Grant, C.A. (1993). The *Brown* decision revisited: Mathematizing social problems. *Educational Policy, 7,* 255–275.

Taylor, H. L., Jr. (Ed.). (1993). *Race and the city: Work, community, and protests in Cincinnati, 1820–1970.* Urbana, IL: University of Illinois Press.

Tushnet, M. (1994). *Making civil rights law: Thurgood Marshall and the Supreme Court, 1936–1961.* New York: Oxford University Press.

Ward, G., & Burns, K. (2000). *Jazz: A history of American music.* New York: Knopf.

Willie, C. V. (2000). The evolution of community education: Content and mission. *Harvard Educational Review, 70*(2), 191–210.

Winston, J. (1996). Fulfilling the promise of Brown. In E. C. Lagemann & L. P. Miller (Eds.), *Brown v. Board of Education: The challenge for today's schools* (pp. 157–166). New York: Teachers College Press.

COURT CASES CITED

Abbeville et al. v. State of South Carolina, et al. SC 24939 (1999).
Belton v. Gebhart, et al. 152, nos. 12–18, 33 Del. Chapt. 144; 91A, 2nd 137.
Board of Education of Oklahoma v. Dowell (1991) 498 U.S. 237.
Bolling v. Sharpe (1954) 347 US 497.
Briggs v. Elliott, 132 F. Supp. 776, 777 (E.D.S.C. 1955).
Brown v. Board of Education, 347 U.S. 483 (1954).
Brown v. Board of Education II, 349 U.S. 294 (1955).

Bulah v. Gebhart, et al. 152, nos. 12–18, 33 Del. Chapt. 144; 91A, 2nd 137.

Davis v. County School Board of Prince Edward County (1951), No. 191, 103 F Supp. 337.

Freeman v. Pitts (1992), 503 U.S. 467.

McLaurin v. Oklahoma State Regents (1950), 339 U.S. 637.

Milliken v. Bradley (1974), 418 U.S. 717.

Plessy v. Ferguson (1896), 163 U.S. 537.

San Antonio Independent School District v. Rodriguez (1973), 541 U.S. 1.

Sweatt v. Painter (1950), 339 U.S. 629.

United States Department of Justice (1954), *Brief for the U.S. as Amicus Curiae at 6, Brown v. Board of Education*, 347 U.S. 483.

Part III

EPISTEMOLOGY AND METHODOLOGIES

CHAPTER 7

Racialized Discourses and Ethnic Epistemologies

I think, therefore I am.

—René Descartes, *Le Discours de la Méthode*, 1637

Ubuntu [I am because we are].

—African saying

When René Descartes proclaimed that he thought himself into being, he articulated a central premise upon which European (and Euro-American) worldviews and epistemology rest—that the individual mind is the source of knowledge and existence. In contrast, the African saying "*Ubuntu*," translated "I am because we are," asserts that the individual's existence (and knowledge) is contingent upon relationships with others. These two divergent perspectives represent two distinct and often conflicting epistemological stances with which the academy has grappled since the mid- to late 1960s. The two traditions are not merely matters of "alternatives" or "preferences," but rather represent a deliberate choice between hegemony (Gramsci, 1971) and liberation. This strongly worded statement is not meant to be polemical; it is meant to be urgent. I have chosen to explore this dichotomy to demonstrate the "effectively aggressive manner" (Ani, 1994) of the Euro-American epistemological tradition. And I will trace how different discourses and epistemologies serve as both counterknowledge and liberating tools for people who have suffered (and continue to suffer) from the Euro-American "regime of truth" (Foucault, 1973).

It is important to reinforce that the concept of epistemology is more than a "way of knowing." An epistemology is a "system of knowing" that has both an internal logic and external validity. This distinction between an epistemology and "ways of knowing" is not a trivial one. For example, literary scholars have created distinctions between literary genres such that some works are called *literature* whereas other works are termed *folklore*.

Not surprisingly, the literature of peoples of color is more likely to fall into the folklore category. As a consequence, folklore is seen as less rigorous, less scholarly, and, perhaps, less culturally valuable than literature. The claim of an epistemological ground is a crucial legitimating force.

Epistemology is linked intimately to worldview. Shujaa (1997) argues that worldviews and systems of knowledge are symbiotic—that is, how one views the world is influenced by what knowledge one possesses, and what knowledge one is capable of possessing is influenced deeply by one's worldview. Thus the conditions under which people live and learn shape both their knowledge and their worldviews. The process of developing a worldview that differs from the dominant worldview requires active intellectual work on the part of the knower, because schools, society, and the structure and production of knowledge are designed to create individuals who internalize the dominant worldview and knowledge production and acquisition processes. The hegemony of the dominant paradigm makes it more than just another way to view the world—it claims to be the only legitimate way to view the world. In this chapter I argue that there are well-developed systems of knowledge, or epistemologies, that stand in contrast to the dominant Euro-American epistemology.

I look briefly at the ideological underpinnings of the Euro-American epistemological tradition through its construction of race, and then describe how the Euro-American tradition conflicts with those traditions established by people who have been subordinated in U.S. society and the world. Next, I investigate the notions of double consciousness (Du Bois, 1903/1953), *mestiza* consciousness (Anzaldúa, 1987), and "tribal secrets" (Warrior, 1995) discovered and uncovered by scholars of color to explicate the ways that discursive, social, and institutional structures have created a sense of "otherness" for those who are outside of the dominant culture· paradigm. Then I explore two theoretical notions, "alterity" (Wynter, 1992) and "critical race theory" (Delgado, 1995a), as rubrics for considering the scholarship of racial and ethnic "others." Finally, I conclude the chapter with an examination of what these alternate paradigms mean for qualitative research methods.

THE CULTURAL LOGIC OF THE EUROCENTRIC PARADIGM

Traditional scientific method can't tell you where you ought to go, unless where you ought to go is a continuation of where you were going in the past.

—Robert M. Pirsig, *Zen and the Art of Motorcycle Maintenance,* 1972

Ani (1994) says, "Rob the universe of its richness, deny the significance of the symbolic, simplify phenomena until it becomes mere object, and you have a knowable quantity. Here begins and ends the European episte-mological mode" (p. 29). One such example of this epistemological stance is the way the construct of race has been formulated in the West (Omi & Winant, 1994). New languages and a new regime of truth (Foucault, 1973) were constituted around race: These new languages became "pub-lic" languages that are systems of knowledge whose object of inquiry is the social order in which the knower and inquirer are always already subjects.

Wynter (1992) argues that "such systems of knowledge, as 'acts of com-munication' which influence the behaviors of those being studied, are al-ways generated from the 'paradigm of value and authority' on whose basis the order is instituted" (p. 21). The idea that "there exist three races, and that these races are 'Caucasoid,' 'Negroid,' and 'Mongoloid' is rooted in the European imagination of the Middle Ages, which encompassed only Europe, Africa, and the Near East" (Haney López, 1995, p. 194). The cod-ification of this three-races theory occurred in the treatise of Count Arthur de Gobineau's *Essays on the Inequality of Races*, published in France in 1853–1855. That Gobineau excluded the peoples of the Americas, the Indian subcontinent, East and Southeast Asia, and Oceania (those living outside of the European imagination) reflects social and political decisions, not scientific ones.

Appleby, Hunt, and Jacob (1994) argue that by the 18th century, a small group of reformers established science as the "new foundation for truth" (p. 15). This new truth was much like the older truth established by the Christian church in that it transferred "a habit of mind associated with religiosity—the conviction that transcendent and absolute truth could be known—to the new mechanical understanding of the natural world" (p. 15). Eventually, this mode of thought and conviction was taken up by other forms of inquiry.

This new mode of thought, coming out of a period termed the Enlightenment, suggested that scientific knowledge was pure, elegant, and simple. Natural science could be summarized by its laws and employed an experimental method to seek truth. This mode of thought reasoned that everything from human biology to the art of governing could and should imitate science. Appleby et al. (1994) call this model of science heroic, "because it made scientific geniuses into cultural heroes" (p. 15). They note:

> Until quite recently, heroic science reigned supreme. The heroic model equated science with reason: disinterested, impartial, and, if followed closely, a guar-antee of progress in this world. Science took its character from nature itself, which was presumed to be composed solely of matter in motion and hence to be "neutral." . . . The neutral, value-free, objective image of science inherited

from the Enlightenment had wide influence in every discipline until well into the postwar era. (pp. 15–16)

This Enlightenment thinking permeated the thinking of the leaders of the American Revolution. However, these men—Washington, Jefferson, Madison, and others—had to rationalize their commitment to liberty, justice, and equality with the fact that they endorsed slavery (Zinn, 1980). Rather than being bound by a religious code that insisted on the dignity and worth of all people (however, a case for master–servant relationships was often made about Christianity), these leaders of the revolution relied on science to justify the injustice of slavery. Jefferson, in his *Notes on the State of Virginia* (1784/1954), insisted that Blacks and Whites could never live together because there were "real distinctions" that "nature" had made between the two races. But we know that there is no biological basis to this concept of race. There are no genetic characteristics possessed by all the members of any group (Lewontin, Rose, & Kamin, 1984). Indeed, even the Enlightenment science demonstrates that there are more intragroup differences than intergroup ones. Current thinking about race argues that it is a social construction, and the process by which racial meanings arise is termed *racial formation* (Haney López, 1995).

Consider how this racial formation operates. According to Haney López (1995), "In the early 1800s, people in the United States ascribed to Latin American nationalities and, separate from these, races. Thus, a Mexican might also be White, Indian, Black, or Asian" (pp. 196–197). However, by the mid-1800s, when animosity developed in the U.S. Southwest between Anglos and Mexicans, social prejudices developed. These social prejudices soon became legal ones, with laws designed to reflect and reify racial prejudices. Enlightenment notions of science (and later, law) did not work independent of prevailing discourses of racial and class superiority. This discourse of Enlightenment science allowed the dominant culture to define, distance, and objectify the other.

Scheurich and Young (1997) identify epistemological racism that exists in the research paradigms that dominate academic and scholarly products. The epistemological challenge that is being mounted by some scholars of color is not solely about racism, however; it is also about the nature of truth and reality. Rosaldo (1993) argues that, in what he terms the classic period (from about 1921 to 1971), "norms of distanced normalizing description gained a monopoly on objectivity. Their authority appeared so self-evident that they became the one and only legitimate form for telling the literal truth about other cultures. . . . All other modes of composition were marginalized or suppressed altogether" (p.106). As classic norms gain exclusive rights to objective truth, ethnography (as well as other social science methods) becomes "as likely to reveal where objectivity lies as where it tells the truth" (p. 115).

MULTIPLE CONSCIOUSNESS, MULTIPLE JEOPARDY

The Idea of a single civilization for everyone, implicit in the cult of progress
and technique, impoverishes and mutilates us.

—Octavio Paz, *The Labyrinth of Solitude,* 1961

Although some scholars of color have attempted to find legitimacy in the
dominant paradigm (see, e.g., Williams, 1882–1883) other scholars have
looked to a different epistemological frame to describe the experiences and
knowledge systems of peoples outside of the dominant paradigm.[1] In 1903,
W. E. B. Du Bois wrote in *The Souls of Black Folk* that the African American
"ever feels his two-ness . . . two souls, two thoughts, two unreconciled strivings" (1903/1953, p. 5). Historian David Levering Lewis (1993) lauds this
conception, stating:

> It was a revolutionary concept. It was not just revolutionary; the concept of
> the divided self was profoundly mystical, for Du Bois invested this double con-
> sciousness with a capacity to see incomparably farther and deeper. The African
> American . . . possessed the gift of "second sight in this American world," an
> intuitive faculty enabling him/her to see and say things about American society
> that possessed heightened moral validity. (p. 281)

Du Bois's notion of double consciousness is being read here not as a pathetic
state of marginalization and exclusion, but rather as a transcendent position
allowing one to see and understand positions of inclusion and exclusion—
margins and mainstreams.

An important synchronic aspect of Du Bois's work is that both he and
African American scholar Carter G. Woodson (1933) mounted challenges
to the dominant Euro-American scholarly paradigm at about the same
time as the formation of the Frankfurt school, out of which critical theories emerged. Max Horkheimer, Theodor Adorno, and Herbert Marcuse
were the three primary scholars known for their engagement with the theoretical perspectives of Marx, Hegel, Kant, and Weber and their challenge
to the "taken-for-granted empirical practices of American social science
researchers" (Kincheloe & McLaren, 1998, p. 261). However, Du Bois
and Woodson remain invisible in the scholarly canon except as "Negro"
intellectuals concerned with the "Negro" problem. Their forthright and
insightful critique of Euro-American scholarship was every bit as "critical" as that of the members of the Frankfurt school, but they would never be mentioned in the same breath as Horkheimer, Weber, Adorno, and
Marcuse.

Du Bois's notion of double consciousness applies not only to African
Americans but to any people who are constructed outside of the dominant

paradigm. It is important to read this entire discussion of multiple consciousness as a description of complex phenomena. It is not an attempt to impose essentialized concepts of "Blackness," "Latina/oness," "Asian American-ness" or "Native Americanness" onto specific individuals or groups.[2] Rather, this discussion is about the multiple ways in which epistemological perspectives are developed. Indeed, the authors cited are not placed here to operate as proxies for what it means to be of a particular race, ethnicity, or cultural group. They are a few examples of the ways *particular* scholars have developed *specific* epistemological stances informed by their own cultural and identity positions.

Anzaldúa describes identities fractured not only by her gender, class, race, religion, and sexuality, but also by the reality of life along the U.S.-Mexico border. In one chapter of *Borderlands/La Frontera,* Anzaldúa (1987) explains the complexity of her life as a Mexican American living along the border:

> My "home" tongues are the languages I speak with my sister and brothers, with my friends. They are [*Pachuco* (called *calo*), Tex-Mex, Chicano Spanish, North Mexican Spanish dialect, and Standard Mexican Spanish, with Chicano Spanish] being closest to my heart. From school, the media and job situations, I've picked up standard and working class English. From Mamagrande Locha and from reading Spanish and Mexican literature, I've picked up Standard Spanish and Standard Mexican Spanish. From *los recien llegados*, Mexican immigrants and *braceros*, I learned Northern Mexican dialect. (pp. 55–56)

Anzaldúa's work, which reflects a long intellectual history of Chicanas/os (see Acuña, 1972; Almaguer, 1974; Balderrama, 1982; GomezQuinones, 1977; Mirande & Enriquez, 1979; Padilla, 1987; Paz, 1961), has become a part of what Delgado Bernal (1998) calls a Chicana feminist epistemology. Chicana writers such as Alarcón (1990), Castillo (1995), and the contributors to de la Torre and Pesquera's (1993) edited collection exemplify these intersections of race, class, and gender.

But it is important not to assume a unified Latino/a (or even Chicano/a) subject. Oboler (1995) challenges the amalgamation of Spanish speakers in the Western Hemisphere under the rubric *Hispanic:* The Hispanic label belies the problematic inherent in attempts to create a unitary consciousness from one that is much more complex and multiple than imagined or constructed. According to Oboler:

> Insofar as the ethnic label Hispanic homogenizes the varied social and political experiences of 23 million people of different races, classes, languages, and national origins, genders, and religions, it is perhaps not so surprising that the meanings and uses of the term have become the subject of debate in the social sciences, government agencies, and much of the society at large. (p. 3)

Similarly, American Indians have had to grapple with what it means to be Indian. Despite a movement toward "Pan-Indianism" (Hertzberg, 1971), the cultures of American Indians are very diverse. Broad generalizations about American Indians can be essentializing. However, the U.S. federal government movement to "civilize" and detribalize Indian children through boarding schools helped various groups of Indians realize that the experiences of their tribes were not unique and that American Indians share any number of common problems and experiences (Snipp, 1995). Lomawaima (1995) argues that "since the federal government turned its attention to the 'problem' of civilizing Indians, its overt goal has been to educate Indians to be non-Indians" (p. 332). Much of the "double consciousness" Indians face revolves around issues of tribal sovereignty. A loss of sovereignty is amplified by four methods of disenfranchisement experienced by many American Indians (Lomawaima, 1995): relocation by colonial authorities (e.g., mission, reservations), systematic eradication of the native language, religious conversion (to Christianity), and restructured economies toward sedentary agriculture, small-scale craft industry, and gendered labor.

Warrior (1995) asks whether or not an investigation of early American Indian writers can have a significant impact on the way contemporary Native American intellectuals develop critical studies. He urges caution in understanding the scholarship of Fourth World formulations such as that of Ward Churchill and M. Annette Jaimes because it tends to be essentializing in its call for understanding American Indian culture as part of a global consciousness shared by all indigenous peoples in all periods of history. Warrior's work is a call for "intellectual sovereignty" (p. 87)—a position free from the tyranny and oppression of the dominant discourse.

Among Asian Pacific Islanders there are notions of multiple consciousness. Lowe (1996) expresses this in terms of "heterogeneity, hybridity, and multiplicity" (p. 60). She points out:

> The articulation of an "Asian American identity" as an organizing tool has provided unity that enables diverse Asian groups to understand unequal circumstances and histories as being related. The building of "Asian American culture" is crucial to this effort, for it articulates and empowers the diverse Asian-origin community vis-à-vis the institutions and apparatuses that exclude and marginalize it. Yet to the extent that Asian American culture fixes Asian American identity and suppresses differences—of national origin, generation, gender, sexuality, class—it risks particular dangers: not only does it underestimate the differences and hybridities among Asians, but it may inadvertently support the racist discourse that constructs Asians as a homogeneous group. (pp. 70–71)

Espiritu (1992) also reminds us that "Asian American" as an identity category came into being within the past 30 years. Prior to that time, most members of the Asian-descent immigrant population "considered them-selves culturally and politically distinct" from other Asian-descent groups (p. 19). Indeed, the historical enmity that existed between and among vari-ous Asian groups made it difficult for them to transcend their national alle-giances to see themselves as one unified group. And the growing anti-Asian sentiments with which the various Asian immigrant groups were faced in the United States caused specific groups to "disassociate themselves from the targeted group so as not to be mistaken for members of it and suffer any possible negative consequences" (p. 20).

Trinh (1989) and Mohanty (1991) offer postmodern analyses of Asian Americanness that challenge any unitary definitions of *Asian American*. Rather than construct a mythical solidarity, these authors examine the ways that Asianness is represented in the dominant imagination. One of the most vivid examples of the distorted, imagined Asian shows up in the work of David Henry Hwang, whose play *M. Butterfly* demonstrates how a con-stellation of characteristics—size, temperament, submissiveness—allowed a French armed services officer to mistake a man for a woman even in intimate situations. Lowe (1996) reminds us that "the grouping 'Asian American' is not a natural or static category; it is a socially constructed unity, a situa-tionally specific position assumed for political reasons" (p. 82), but it co-exists with the "dynamic fluctuation and heterogeneity of Asian American culture" (p. 68).

What all of these groups (i.e., African Americans, Native Americans, Latino/as, and Asian Americans) have in common is the experience of a racialized identity. Each group is constituted of myriad national and ances-tral origins, but the dominant ideology of the Euro-American epistemology has forced each into an essentialized and totalized unit that is perceived to have little or no internal variation. However, at the same moment, members of these groups have used these unitary racialized labels for political and cultural purposes. Identification with the racialized labels means acknowl-edgment of some of the common experiences group members have had as outsiders and others.

LIFE ON THE MARGINS

Anthropologist Jacob Pandian (1985) points out that in the Judeo-Christian local culture of the West (Geertz, 1983), the *True Christian* was the medie-val metaphor of the *Self*. *Alterity* refers to the alter ego category of otherness that is specific to each culture's "metaphor of the self." Wynter (1992) ar-gues that those constructed as other have a perspective advantage. This ad-vantage does not speak to the economic, social, and political disadvantage that subordinated groups may experience, but rather to the way that not be-ing positioned in the center allows for "wide-angle" vision. This advantage is not due to an inherent racial/cultural difference but is the result of the dialectical nature of constructed otherness that prescribes the liminal status of people of color as beyond the normative boundary of the conception of Self/Other (King, 1995).

King (1995) further argues that this epistemic project is more than simply adding on multiple perspectives or "pivoting" the center. Rather, this liminal position or point of alterity attempts to transcend an "either/or" epistemology. Alterity is not a dualistic position that there are multiple and equally partial standpoints that are either valid or inexorably ranked hierarchically. Recognizing the alterity perspective does not essentialize other perspectives, such as Blackness, Indianness, Asianness, Latino/aness, as homogenizing reverse epistemics (West, 1990).

Those occupying the liminal position do not seek to move from the margins to the mainstream because they understand the corrupting influences of the mainstream—its pull to maintain status quo relations of power and inequities. This liminal view is not unlike the view from the bottom that poor and working-class people have on the middle class. The poor and working classes have a perspective on their own experiences while simultaneously grasping the fundamentals of the workings of the dominant class. Because most poor and working-class people rely on the dominant class for food, clothing, shelter, and work, they are forced to learn dominant practices, at least minimally. The undocumented child-care workers or African American domestics find themselves inside the homes of dominant group members. There they have intimate access to sanctioned beliefs and patterns of behavior.[3]

Legesse (1973) suggests that the liminal group is that which is forcibly constrained to play the role of alter ego to the ideal self prescribed by the dominant cultural model. This dominant cultural model sets up prescriptive rules and canons for regulating thought and action in the society. Thus the "issue is about the 'nature of human knowing' of the social reality in a model of which the knower is already a socialized subject" (Wynter, 1992, p. 26).

> The system-conserving mainstream perspectives of each order (or well-established scholarship) therefore clash with the challenges made from the perspectives of alterity. . . . For it is the task of established scholarship to rigorously maintain those prescriptions which are critical to the order's existence. (Wynter, 1992, p. 27)

Thus the work of the liminal perspective is to reveal the ways that dominant perspectives distort the realities of the other in an effort to maintain power relations that continue to disadvantage those who are locked out of the mainstream. This liminal perspective is the condition of the dominant order's self-definition that "can empower us to free ourselves from the 'categories and prescriptions' of our specific order and from its 'generalized horizon of understanding'" (Wynter, 1992, p. 27).

CRITICAL RACE THEORY: CHALLENGING MAINSTREAM ORTHODOXY

One research paradigm in which racialized discourses and ethnic epistemologies or the liminal perspective may be deployed is critical race theory (CRT).[4] According to Delgado (1995b):

> Critical Race Theory sprang up in the mid-1970s with the early work of Derrick Bell and Alan Freeman, both of whom were deeply concerned over the slow pace of racial reform in the U.S. They argued that traditional approaches of filing *amicus* briefs, conducting protests and marches, and appealing to moral sensibilities of decent citizens produced smaller and fewer gains than in previous times. Before long, Bell and Freeman were joined by other legal scholars who shared their frustration with traditional civil rights strategies. (p. xiii)

Critical race theory is both an outgrowth of and a separate entity from an earlier legal movement called critical legal studies (CLS). Critical legal studies is a leftist legal movement that challenges the traditional legal scholarship that focuses on doctrinal and policy analysis (Gordon, 1990) in favor of a form of law that speaks to the specificity of individuals and groups in social and cultural contexts. CLS scholars also challenge the notion that "the civil rights struggle represents a long, steady march toward social transformation" (Crenshaw, 1988, p. 1334).

According to Crenshaw (1988), "Critical [legal] scholars have attempted to analyze legal ideology and discourse as a social artifact which operates to recreate and legitimate American society" (p. 1350). Scholars in the CLS movement decipher legal doctrine to expose both its internal and external inconsistencies and reveal the ways that "legal ideology has helped create, support, and legitimate America's present class structure" (p. 1350). The contribution of CLS to legal discourse is in its analysis of legitimating structures in society. Much of the CLS ideology emanates from the work of Gramsci (1971) and depends on the Gramscian notion of "hegemony" to describe the continued legitimacy of oppressive structures in American society (Unger, 1983). However, CLS fails to provide pragmatic strategies for material and social transformation. Cornel West (1993) asserts:

> Critical legal theorists fundamentally question the dominant liberal paradigms prevalent and pervasive in American culture and society. This thorough questioning is not primarily a constructive attempt to put forward a conception of a new legal and social order. Rather, it is a pronounced disclosure of inconsistencies, incoherences, silences, and blindness of legal formalists, legal positivists,

and legal realists in the liberal tradition. Critical legal studies is more a concerted attack and assault on the legitimacy and authority of pedagogical strategies in law school than a comprehensive announcement of what a credible and realizable new society and legal system would look like. (p. 196)

CLS scholars have critiqued mainstream legal ideology for its portrayal of the United States as a meritocracy, but they have failed to include racism in their critique. Thus CRT became a logical outgrowth of the discontent of legal scholars of color.

CRT begins with the notion that racism is "normal, not aberrant, in American society" (Delgado, 1995b, p. xiv), and because it is so enmeshed in the fabric of the U.S. social order, it appears both normal and natural to people in this society. Indeed, Derrick Bell's major premise in *Faces at the Bottom of the Well* (1992) is that racism is a permanent fixture of American life. Therefore, the strategy of those who fight for racial social justice is to unmask and expose racism in all of its various permutations.

Second, CRT departs from mainstream legal scholarship by sometimes employing storytelling to "analyze the myths, presuppositions, and received wisdoms that make up the common culture about race and that invariably render blacks and other minorities one-down" (Delgado, 1995b, p. xiv). According to Barnes (1990), "Critical race theorists . . . integrate their *experiential knowledge*, drawn from a shared history as 'other,' with their ongoing struggles to transform a world deteriorating under the albatross of racial hegemony" (pp. 1864–1865; emphasis added). Thus the experience of oppressions such as racism and sexism has important components for the development of a CRT perspective.

A third feature of CRT is its insistence on a critique of liberalism. Crenshaw (1988) argues that the liberal perspective of the "civil rights crusade as a long, slow, but always upward pull" (p. 1334) is flawed because it fails to understand the limits of the current legal paradigm to serve as a catalyst for social change because of its emphasis on incrementalism. CRT argues that racism requires sweeping changes, but liberalism has no mechanism for such change. Instead, liberal legal practices support the painstakingly slow process of arguing legal precedents to gain citizen rights for people of color.

Fourth, CRT argues that Whites have been the primary beneficiaries of civil rights legislation. For example, although the policy of affirmative action is under attack throughout the nation, it is a policy that also has benefited Whites. A close look at the numbers reveals that the major beneficiaries of affirmative action hiring policies have been White women (Guy-Sheftall, 1993). The logic of this argument is that many of these women earn incomes that support households in which other Whites live—men, women, and children. Thus White women's ability to secure employment ultimately benefits Whites in general.

In a recent compilation of key writings in critical race theory, the editors point out that there is no "canonical set of doctrines or methodologies to which [CRT scholars] all subscribe" (Crenshaw, Gotanda, Peller, & Thomas, 1995, p. xiii). But these scholars are unified by two common interests—understanding how a "regime of white supremacy and its subordination of people of color have been created and maintained in America" (p. xiii) and changing the bond that exists between law and racial power.

In the pursuit of these interests, legal scholars such as Patricia Williams (1991) and Derrick Bell (1980, 1992) were among the early critical race theorists whose ideas reached the general public. Some might argue that their wide appeal was the result of their abilities to tell compelling stories into which they embedded legal issues. This use of story is of particular interest to social science scholars because of the growing popularity of narrative inquiry (Connelly & Clandinin, 1990). But merely because the research community is more receptive to story as a part of scholarly inquiry does not mean that all stories are judged as legitimate in knowledge construction and the advancement of a discipline.

Lawrence (1995) asserts that there is a tradition of storytelling in law and that litigation is highly formalized storytelling, although the stories of ordinary people, in general, have not been told or recorded in the literature of law (or any other discipline). But this failure to make it into the canons of literature or research does not make stories of ordinary people less important. The ahistorical and acontextual nature of much law and other "science" renders the voices of the dispossessed and marginalized group members mute. In response, much of the scholarship of CRT focuses on the role of "voice" in bringing additional power to the legal discourses of racial justice. Critical race theorists attempt to inject the cultural viewpoints of people of color, derived from a common history of oppression, into their efforts to reconstruct a society crumbling under the burden of racial hegemony (Barnes, 1990).

Until recently, little of CRT found its way into the literature outside of law. In my own work with Tate, we broached the subject as a challenge to traditional multicultural education paradigms (Ladson-Billings & Tate, 1995). We argued that race continues to be salient in U.S. society; that the nation was premised on property rights, not human rights; and that the intersection of race and property could serve as a powerful analytic tool for explaining social and educational inequities. Later, Tate (1997) provided a comprehensive description of critical race theory and its antecedents as a way to inform the educational research community more fully of CRT's meanings and possible uses in education. In his discussion he cites Calmore (1992), who identified CRT as

> a form of opposition scholarship . . . that challenges the universality of white experience/judgement as the authoritative standard that binds people of color

and normatively measures, directs, controls, and regulates the terms of proper thought, expression, presentation, and behavior. As represented by legal scholars, critical race theory challenges the dominant discourses on race and racism as they relate to law. The task is to identify values and norms that have been disguised and subordinated in the law. . . . [C]ritical race scholars . . . seek to demonstrate that [their] experiences as people of color are legitimate, appropriate, and effective bases for analyzing the legal system and racial subordination. This process is vital to . . . transformative vision. This theory-practice approach, a praxis, if you will, finds a variety of emphases among those who follow it. . . . From this vantage, consider for a moment how law, society, and culture are texts—not so much like a literary work, but rather like a traditional black minister's citation of a text as a verse or scripture that would lend authoritative support to the sermon he is about to deliver. Here, texts are not merely random stories; like scripture, they are expressions of authority, preemption, and sanction. People of color increasingly claim that these large texts of law, society, and culture must be subjected to fundamental criticisms and reinterpretation. (pp. 2161–2162)

Although CRT has been used as an analytic tool for understanding the law (particularly civil rights law), as previously noted, it has not been deployed successfully in the practical world of courts and legal cases or schools. In fact, the first public exposure CRT received proved disastrous for presidential civil rights commission nominee Lani Guinier. CRT's radical theoretical arguments were seen as a challenge to "the American way." Guinier's (1994) writings about proportional representation were seen as antithetical to the U.S. constitutional notion of one "man," one vote. She had argued that in a postapartheid South Africa it would be necessary to ensure that the White minority had a political voice despite the fact that they were grossly outnumbered within the electorate. Similarly, she argued, people of color in the United States might have to seek new ways to be represented beyond that of majority rule through one person, one vote. Guinier's ideas meant that she could not be confirmed, and the president did nothing to support her nomination.

CRT, THE KNOWER, AND THE KNOWN

The power and pull of a paradigm is more than simply a methodological orientation. It is a means by which to grasp reality and give it meaning and predictability.

—Ray Rist, "On the Relations Among Educational Research Paradigms," 1990

What are the relationships among liminality, alterity, CRT, and new forms of qualitative research that incorporate racialized discourses and ethnic epistemologies? To answer this question we need to examine the relationship between the knower (the researcher) and the known (the subject, participant, informant, collaborator). Lorraine Code (1991) poses the question, Does the gender of the knower matter in the construction of knowledge? She contends that it does. I assert that along with the gender of the knower, the race, ethnicity, language, class, sexuality, and other forms of difference work to inform his or her relationship to knowledge and its production. However, Narayan (1993) argues that it is dangerous to presume that because the researcher (in her case as an anthropologist) is a member of a particular racial or ethnic group, she or he has emic knowledge of that particular group or community:

> "Native" anthropologists, then, are perceived as insiders regardless of their complex backgrounds. The differences between kinds of "native" anthropologists are also obviously passed over. Can a person from an impoverished American minority background who, despite all prejudices, manages to get an education and study her own community be equated with a member of a Third World elite group who, backed by excellent schooling and parental funds, studies anthropology abroad yet returns home for fieldwork among the less privileged? Is it not insensitive to suppress the issue of location, acknowledging that a scholar who chooses an institutional base in the Third World might have a different engagement with Western-based theories, books, political stances, and technologies of written production? Is a middle-class white professional researching aspects of his own society also a "native" anthropologist? (p. 677)

Narayan's points are well-taken if we accept an essentialized view of what group membership means. We know that the categories we use to describe also delimit. Who and what constitutes group membership is always at play. However, the search for an approach to research that better represents indigenous and community knowledge remains a worthwhile one.

Asante (1987) builds upon the work of Woodson and Du Bois to craft an Afrocentric or "African-centered" approach to education. Although some other Black scholars have challenged his approach as essentialist and a form of ethnic "cheerleading" (e.g., Appiah, 1992), Asante's (1991) own words suggest that his search for an alternate paradigm is more directed at getting out from under the oppression of dominant perspectives:

> Afrocentricity is *not* a black version of Eurocentricity. Eurocentricity is based on white-supremacist notions whose purposes are to protect white privilege and advantage in education, economics, politics, and so forth. Unlike Eurocentricity, Afrocentricity does not condone ethnocentric valorization at the expense of degrading other groups' perspectives. Moreover, Eurocentricity presents the particular historical reality of Europeans as the sum total of the human experience. It imposes Eurocentric realities as universal; i.e., that which is white is presented

as applying to the human condition in general, while that which is nonwhite is viewed as group-specific and therefore not human. (p. 172)

Asante's (1987) major argument, as I see it, is that scholars of color have been searching for a "place to stand . . . in relation to Western standards, imposed as interpretative measures on other cultures" (p. 11). He argues for a "flexible frame of reference" (p. 11) that will allow a more dynamic and transformational interaction between the knower and the known.

Similarly, Anzaldúa (1987) reminds us that dominant culture is defined by the powerful and often operates as a kind of tyranny against those defined as other. Her response against the inequitable relationship between the knower and the known is to press toward a new *mestiza* consciousness that is a consciousness of the borderlands. Her work represents the complexity of identity, representation, and scholarship in the more dynamic way proposed by Asante. Her work moves in a fluid yet exciting way between exposition and art, prose and poetry, Spanish and English, displaying the borders in multiple ways. For instance, she writes in *"Una Lucha de Fronteras*/A Struggle of Borders" (p. 77):

> Because I, a *mestiza*,
> continually walk out of one culture, and into another,
> because I am in all cultures at the same time,
> *alma entre dos mundos, tres, cuatro, me zumba la cabeza con lo*
> *contradictorio.*
> *Estoy norteada por todas las voces que me hablan*
> *simultaneamente.*

She writes in an unapologetic, multivocal style to reinforce the multiple epistemological positions in which all human beings find themselves, even those who have assumed unitary voices.

Highwater (1981) raises similar issues when he argues that "the greatest distance between people is not space, but culture" (p. 3). He further asserts the importance of representation as a "complex and infinitely varied relationship between reality and the symbols used to depict it" (p. 70). The concept of representation can (and should) be extended to scholarship. Scholars must be challenged to ask not only *about* whom is the research, but also *for* whom is the research. The question of *for whom* is not merely about advocacy, but rather about who is capable to act and demonstrate agency. This agency is enacted through both epistemological and discursive forms.

Fanon (1968) argues that although the oppressed resort to the language of the oppressor for their liberation, ultimately liberation will come from a new person with a new discourse. This new discourse represents the primary argument of Black feminist Audre Lorde (1984), who notes in her oft-quoted essay that "the master's tools will never dismantle the master's house." However, other scholars suggest that "the master's house will only be dismantled with the master's tools."[5] This epistemological limbo—between the old discourse and the new—is the place where many scholars of color find themselves. The mechanisms for scholarly recognition, promotion, tenure, and publication are controlled primarily by the dominant ideology. Scholars of color find themselves simultaneously having been trained in this dominant tradition and needing to break free of it.

This ambivalence about the research that scholars of color are trained to do and the research they ultimately do creates the condition that Delgado-Gaitan (1993) describes as "insider/outsider status." One initially begins as an outsider and gradually gains enough trust to be granted insider status. But the move from "outside" to "inside" can be a form of oppression and colonization. As Villenas (1966) notes, "By objectifying the subjectivities of the researched, by assuming authority, and by not questioning their own privileged positions, ethnographers have participated as colonizers of the researched" (p. 713). Rosaldo (1989) has also warned of the dangers the dominant discourse may have for ethnographers by describing the "Lone Ethnographer," who "rode off into the sunset in search of his 'natives'" (p. 30). After spending time among these "natives," this same Lone Ethnographer returned to the comfort and convenience of his (or her) office to write a "true" account of the culture. But scholars born of "new studies" have begun to ask different questions of themselves and their research.[6] Siddle-Walker (1996) raises the question of data versus "real" data. The insider status that scholars of color may have can alert them to the way oppressed peoples both protect themselves and subvert the dominant paradigm by withholding and "distorting" data. These actions may reflect the suspicions of the researched community rather than malice.

In my own research I have attempted to tell a story about myself as well as about my work (Ladson-Billings, 1997). This discursive turn is not merely a new narcissism; rather, it is a concern for situating myself as a researcher—who I am, what I believe, what experiences I have had—because it affects what, how, and why I research. My decision to research the exemplary practices of teachers who are successful with African American children was a decidedly political (not partisan) decision (Ladson-Billings, 1994). It also was a decision to demystify the research process in communities of color, the members of which are often the objects but rarely the beneficiaries of research.[7]

In my work I broke several canons of traditional research. I relied on low-income African American parents to help me locate excellent teachers. I allowed the teachers to assume responsibility for the theoretical leadership of the project, and I created a research collaborative in which I served as one of nine members along with the teachers, not as the expert/researcher. This changed relationship between researcher and researched forced me to participate in a more self-revealing, vulnerable way. Throughout the process, I sent the other members of the study copies of everything I wrote. They scolded me when I misrepresented their thoughts and ideas, and they affirmed me when I got it right. Over the course of 3 years we became a group of friends with a common concern about the education of African American children. This long-term, intensive form of research made it difficult for members to lie or hide their feelings. It also meant that the end of the funding could not mean the end of the relationship. So, 7 years later, we continue to consult each other and send each other greeting cards. I know who has suffered bereavement, who has coped with illness, whose children have entered college, who has become a grandparent. My research is a part of my life and my life is a part of my research.

The needs to know and to be known are powerful aspects of the human condition. Unfortunately, knowledge of and by people of color has been repressed, distorted, and denied by a Euro-American cultural logic that represents an "aggressive seizure of intellectual space [that,] like the seizure of land, amounts to the aggressor occupying someone else's territory while claiming it as his own" (Asante, 1987, p. 9).

Critical race theory offers the researcher an opportunity to stand in a different relationship to the research (and researched). Some of the key features of CRT are storytelling, counter-storytelling, and "naming one's own reality" (see Delgado, 1995a). The value of storytelling in qualitative research is that it can be used to demonstrate how the same phenomenon can be told in different and multiple ways depending on the storytellers. For instance, where an anthropologist might describe the ritual scarification of a male infant's genitalia, Bertha Rosenfeld may tell of the wonderful bris performed on her new nephew as a part of her family's Jewish religious tradition (Ladson-Billings, 1993). Which story is true? Whose story is deemed legitimate? Who has the power to shape the public perception about the logic and worth of the event? One might argue that the example presented here is an exaggeration, much like that of Horace Miner's classic, "Body Ritual Among the Nacirema" (*Nacirema* is *American* spelled backward), but it is representative of the power of different storytellers. As Robert Williams (1995) notes:

> To be a Storyteller . . . is to assume the awesome burden of remembrance for a people, and to perform this paramount role with laughter and tears, joy and sadness, melancholy and passion, as the occasion demands. The Storyteller never wholly belongs to himself or herself. The Storyteller is the one who sacrifices everything in the tellings and retellings of the stories belonging to the tribe.
>
> . . . Whether the story gets the "facts" right is really not all that important. An Indian Storyteller is much more interested in the "truth" contained in a story. And a great Storyteller always makes that "truth" in the story fit the needs of the moment. (pp. xi–xii)[8]

No story was so widely disputed as that told at the murder trial of O.J. Simpson. The prosecutors told a story of a crazed and controlling man who after years of battering his ex-wife snapped when he learned of her romantic interests. They presented it as an open-and-shut case. They asserted that Simpson had motive and they had evidence of opportunity. But the defense attorneys told a different story. They talked about the implausibility of the prosecution's scenario and the deep-seated racism that is a part of the Los Angeles Police Department. They changed the focus of the case from one murder case to the general experiences of men of color (particularly Black and Latino men) with police departments in the United States. Although the telling of vastly differing stories is part of most legal cases, criminal or civil, the response of the jury to these two stories stunned White and/or middle-class Americans.

The posttrial analysis suggested that a "Black" jury failed to convict a Black celebrity defendant, even though the jury had at least one White and one Latino juror. Other analyses asserted that the jury was not intelligent enough to make the "right" decision. The O.J. Simpson murder trial came on the heels of the trials of four Los Angeles police officers for the beating of Rodney King. A predominantly White jury in the suburb of Simi Valley had acquitted the officers of a beating that the entire nation (including the jurors) had witnessed via videotape. In that trial, the defense attorneys told a story of how frame-by-frame analysis of the videotape could lead to an interpretation different from that evoked by real-time viewing. In the context of King's background and driving record, the defense's story was credible to the jurors.

Similarly, "stories" told in the research literature are received differently by different people. In the educational and social science research literature of the 1960s, the stories about children of color were stories of "cultural deprivation" and "cultural disadvantage" (see, e.g., Bettelheim, 1965; Bloom, Davis, & Hess, 1965; Ornstein & Vairo, 1968; Riessman, 1962). These were stories of the substandard, abnormal child of color and poverty, and they positioned White middle-class cultural expression as the normative and correct way of being in school and society. Policy at federal and local levels flowed out of these stories in an attempt to "compensate" for the perceived inadequacies of children of color and their families.

Siddle-Walker's (1996) counterstory of the "good" segregated school presents a decidedly different picture of a working-class community of color. Indeed, throughout the southern United States there are counterstories of poor people working together to secure a better education for their children despite the neglect and antipathy of the dominant culture. The Historically Black Colleges and Universities, tribal colleges, and early ethnic studies programs are examples of some of the ways in which people of color have attempted to create educational structures and discourses that challenge the notion of exclusivity as the only route to excellence.

In 1969, the Asian American Studies Program at San Francisco State College (now San Francisco State University) operated an independent program of study that was conceived on democratic and inclusive principles (Hirabayashi & Alquizola, 1994). The program (in concert with the college's Ethnic Studies Program) grew out of the demands from a student strike staged by the Third World Liberation Front. The program goals were open admissions and the immediate admission of all "non-White" applicants, community control of the curriculum and hiring practices, and self-governance. This model of education represented a radical departure from the top-down, hierarchical, and bureaucratic forms that characterize much of higher education. The Asian American Studies Program dared to tell a counterstory, and it proved to be disruptive and destabilizing to the dominant paradigm.

THE CHILDREN OF FIELD HANDS RETURN TO DO FIELDWORK

My master used to read prayers in public to the ship's crew every Sabbath day; and when I first saw him read, I was never so surprised in my life, as when I saw the book talk to my master, for I thought it did, as I observed him to look upon it, and move his lips. I wished it would do so with me. As soon as my master had done reading, I followed him to the place where he put the book . . . and when nobody saw me, I opened it, and put my ear down close upon it, in great hope that it would say something to me.

—James Gronniosaw, *A Narrative of the Most Remarkable Particulars in the Life of James Albert Ukawsaw Gronniosaw*, 1770

When I was a young child growing up in Philadelphia, there were groups of African American men (some from my family) who waited on street corners during the summer months for the farm labor bus. This broken-down yellow school bus arrived in the Black community looking for willing workers to go to the fields to do the harsh stoop labor of picking tomatoes, strawberries, or any other fruit or vegetable that was in season. Anyone who did not have a steady job could hope to be among those selected to go to the fields. This backbreaking labor did not yield much financial reward, but it was an honest day's work available to people who rarely could find work.

When I moved to California, I saw people with brown faces standing on street corners. This time, instead of a school bus, open-bed trucks would pull up to the curb and the men inside would select a few of those waiting on the corner to do a day's labor at a construction site. Not far from one of the nation's most prestigious universities was a strawberry ranch owned by the university, where a group of itinerant farmworkers lived and worked in inhumane and squalid conditions. Within a few years I began to see people with yellow faces scrubbing dishes and mopping floors in the kitchens of a growing number of restaurants in a community that boasted of a median home price of almost $300,000. The "real" fieldwork being done by people of color and poor people is rarely represented fully in the literature of the academy.

Today, as I attempt to do my own work I am struck by the growing number of scholars of color who have chosen to go back into those fields, construction sites, and kitchens to give voices to their own people—their perspectives, worldviews, and epistemologies. These scholars, like James Gronniosaw (quoted above), are attempting to have the lives of subordinated people "talk to them." Tired of bending their ears to hear the master's book talk, scholars of color are writing new texts from the lives and experiences of people much like themselves. The work of scholars such as Gwaltney (1980), Torres Guzman (1992), Nieto (1992), Takaki (1989, 1993), Ellison (1986), Churchill (1992, 1993), Silko (1977, 1981), Spivak (1988), hooks (1984, 1989, 1992), and countless others has begun to reshape the contours of scholarly research about communities of color. Perhaps even more important is the work of scholars of color who have taken on the task of turning a critical gaze on the dominant paradigms. Scholars such as Said (1979), Ani (1994), Morrison (1992), and Hwang (1994) use deciphering knowledge to change "consciousness and [develop] cognitive autonomy . . . [in an] 'archaeology of knowledge' (Foucault, 1972) to expose the belief structures of race . . . and other discursive practices" (King, 1995, p. 276).

For example, although Collins (1990) has developed a theoretical rubric for explicating a Black feminist standpoint, this rubric also represents a framework for critique of Euro-American paradigms. Collins argues for concrete experiences as a criterion of meaning, the use of dialogue in the assessment of knowledge claims, an ethic of caring, and an ethic of personal accountability. In the vernacular, Collins asks, What have you been through? What are you talkin' about? How do I know you care and, by the way, who *are* you? Scrutiny about subjectivities generally is absent in positivist paradigms that rely on a notion of objectivity, even when it cannot be attained.

The return of researchers of color to communities of color and the casting of a critical eye on the Euro-American paradigm are not calls to a romantic, "noble savage" notion of otherness. Rather, this work is about uncovering the complexities of difference—race, class, and gender. Work such as Gilroy's (1993) makes a compelling case for complex and multiple readings of race, ethnicity, and gender:

> The themes of nationality, exile, and cultural affiliation accentuate the inescapable fragmentation and differentiation of the [racialized] subject. This fragmentation has recently been compounded further by the questions of gender, sexuality, and male domination which have been made unavoidable by the

struggles of [racial and ethnic minority] women. . . . As indices of differentiation, they are especially important because of the intracommunal antagonisms
which appear between the local and immediate levels of our struggles and their
hemispheric and global dynamics can only grow. (p. 35)

The point of working in racialized discourses and ethnic epistemologies
is not merely to "color" the scholarship. It is to challenge the hegemonic structures (and symbols) that keep injustice and inequity in place. The
work also is not about dismissing the work of European and Euro-American
scholars. Rather, it is about defining the limits of such scholarship. The push
from scholars of color is to raise the bar or up the ante of qualitative inquiry.

Perhaps a crude but relevant analogue for what racialized discourses
and ethnic epistemologies can do for scholarship can be found in the world
of sports. Prior to 1947, "America's favorite pastime"—professional baseball—was a game for White men. No players of color were considered
"qualified" to play in the big leagues. Once a Black player was selected to
play in the league, there was talk of "lowered standards." However, no such
downward slide happened in professional baseball. Inclusion of players of
color—African Americans, Latinos, Asians—has made for a more competi-
tive game and a game more widely played throughout the world.

Similarly, scholars of color remain woefully underrepresented in the
academy. Too often, concern is voiced that scholars of color will not be
able to meet certain standards and that hiring such scholars will lower the
prestige and status of the institution. But how can the full range of scholarship be explored if whole groups of people are systematically excluded from
participating in the process of knowledge production? Some might argue
that scholars of color who subscribe to these racialized discourses and ethnic epistemologies are "biased" in their approach to scholarly inquiry. But
the point of the multiple consciousness perspective and the view from the
liminal is that scholars of color who have experienced racism and ethnic discrimination (yet survived the rigors of the degree credentialing process) have
a perspective advantage. As Delgado (1995c) argues: "Many members of
minority groups speak two languages, grow up in two cultures. . . . And so,
. . . who has the advantage in mastering and applying critical social thought?
Who tends to think of everything in two or more ways at the same time?
Who is a postmodernist virtually as a condition of his or her being?" (p. 8).

The paradigm shifts that are occurring in qualitative research are both
about representation and beyond representation. They are about developing
a "tolerance for ambiguity" (Anzaldúa, 1987). Indeed, Anzaldúa (1987) has
uttered prophetically:

[La mestiza] has discovered that she can't hold concepts or ideas in rigid boundaries. The borders and walls that are supposed to keep the undesirable ideas out
are entrenched habits and patterns of behavior; these habits and patterns are

the enemy within. Rigidity means death. Only by remaining flexible is she able to stretch the psyche horizontally and vertically. *La mestiza* constantly has to shift out of habitual formations; from convergent thinking, analytical reasoning that tends to use rationality to move toward a single goal, to divergent thinking, characterized by movement away from set patterns and goals and toward a more whole perspective, one that includes rather than excludes. The new *mestiza* copes by developing a tolerance for contradictions, a tolerance for ambiguity. (p. 79)

The "gift" of the new *mestiza* is a new vision of scholarship. To be able to accept that gift, scholars must shed the bonds of rigid paradigms and stand in new relationship to knowledge, the knower, and the known. The position of alterity—the liminal—is not a privileged position, but it is an advantaged one. It offers an opportunity to create a "public scholarship" (J. E. King, personal communication, April 1998) that prompts social action and transformation.

WHAT DIFFERENCE CAN CRT MAKE
FOR THE CRITICAL QUALITATIVE RESEARCHER?

Collins (1998) points out that rather than allow her language to "masquerade as seeming objectivity and apolitical authority," she chooses language through "both an intellectual and a political decision" (p. xxi). She cites legal scholar Patricia Williams, who asks, "What is 'impersonal' writing but denial of self?" (p. xxi). Thus CRT asks the critical qualitative researcher to operate in a self-revelatory mode, to acknowledge the double (or multiple) consciousness in which she or he is operating. My *decision* to deploy a critical race theoretical framework in my scholarship is intimately linked to my understanding of the political and personal stake I have in the education of Black children. All of my "selves" are invested in this work—the self that is a researcher, the self that is a parent, the self that is a community member, the self that is a Black woman. No technical-rational approach to this work would yield the deeply textured, multifaceted work I attempt to do. Nor would a technical-rational approach allow for the "archaeology of knowledge" (Foucault, 1972) that is necessary to challenge the inequitable social, economic, and political positions that exist between the mainstream and the margins.

The "gift" of CRT is that it unapologetically challenges the scholarship that would dehumanize and depersonalize us. The question we confront is not merely one of the difference between "quantitative" and "qualitative" scholarship. More than two decades ago, Cronbach (1975) tried to put to rest the false dichotomy of quantity versus quality. The significant issues with which we grapple are paradigmatic and epistemological. Out of those paradigms grow particular methodologies. Frankenstein (1990), Nettles and Perna (1997), and Wilson (1987) have all used quantitative methods to turn a critical gaze on social inequity. The sheer volume and disparity of the numbers they present underscore the ways in which people are systematically subordinated and excluded from the society. Thus there is no magic in employing participant observation, narrative inquiry, or interviews. Indeed, the qualitative researcher must guard against the connotation that qualitative work represents some more "authentic" form of research. As we consider various examples of qualitative research we must be mindful of the ways "the research" may render the researcher invisible. The ethnographer stands as a kind of *deus ex machina* who tells a tightly organized and neatly contrived story. Unlike the television journalist who conducts an interview in plain sight of a huge audience, no critique of the questions, the format, or the tone of voice is offered to the researcher.[9]

In CRT the researcher makes a deliberate appearance in his or her work or, like Bell (1987, 1992, 1998) and Delgado (1992, 1993), may create an alter ego who can speak directly to power. For Bell, Geneva Crenshaw, a Black woman, served this purpose. Delgado created Rodrigo, Crenshaw's half brother, to argue against mainstream legal scholarship. The deeply personal rendering of social science that CRT scholars bring to their work helps break open the mythical hold that traditional work has on knowledge. When Williams (1991) presented the bill of sale of her enslaved great-great-grandmother in her law school contracts course, she destabilized the students' notions of contracts as documents devoid of human emotion and personal consequences.

CRT helps to raise some important questions about the control and production of knowledge—particularly knowledge about people and communities of color. Where is "race" in the discourse of critical qualitative researchers? To what degree have critical qualitative researchers reinscribed liberalism in their work? How has the quest to embrace the postmodern perspectives on human agency obscured the need for collective effort? In what ways will critical qualitative research be forced to "work the hyphens" or "probe how we are in relation with the contexts we study and with our informants, understanding that we are all multiple in those relations" (Fine, 1988, p. 135)?

EPILOGUE

As I reflect back on what I have written in this chapter, I am reminded that the nagging questions about the "mixing" of race and ethnicity with "scholarship" persist. The claims of lack of objectivity and politicized inquiry nip at my heels. For me, Lucius Outlaw (1995) offers a fitting last word:

Why race and ethnicity in relation to philosophy? In short because I am convinced that we are living through a period in which race and ethnicity are so challenging to the prospect of our enjoying a future in which we can and will flourish that we are compelled to undertake a fundamental revision of some of our basic convictions regarding who we are, what our lives should be about, and how we will achieve our goals, both individually and collectively. Since such concerns have provided the motivating core for much of Western philosophy (and its sibling fields of inquiry) for more than two thousand years. . . . Finally, there is the deeply personal dimension to . . . focusing on these issues, for they come together in a poignant way to constitute my very being and to inform my daily life, and thereby to condition the lives of all who interact with me: I am a philosopher; I teach portions of the history of the discipline; but I do so as a person of a racial/ethnic group whose existence in America . . . is marked by the holocaust of enslavement and other forms of oppression which have been rationalized by some of the "best" minds in the pantheon of Western philosophers. Thus, not only in practical living must I contend with constricting factors having to do with the politics of race and ethnicity, I must do battle as well, inside the very citadel of reason where enlightenment leading to enhanced living is supposed to have its wellspring. . . . I have committed myself to confronting this seedy aspect of its underside and to the clearing of intellectual and social spaces in which we might come together to work and dwell in peace and harmony with justice. (pp. 305–306)

NOTES

1. The heading on this section is a reversal of Deborah King's (1988) "Multiple Jeopardy, Multiple Consciousness."

2. Although I refer to African Americans, Latinas/os, Asian Americans, Native Americans, and Whites throughout this essay, it is important not to reify what Hollinger (1995) terms the "ethnic pentagon." The boundaries separating various racial, ethnic, and cultural groups have become much more permeable and have created more complex and multifaceted identities in the late years of the 20th century.

3. Members of my own family made their livings by working as domestics in the homes of wealthy White people. From their jobs they learned about middle-class notions of etiquette, fashion, and financial sense.

4. Portions of this section are adapted from Ladson-Billings (1998).

5. This statement was made by Henry Louis Gates, Jr., in 1997 at a conference presenting the *Norton Anthology of African American Literature* at the University of Wisconsin-Madison.

6. Sylvia Wynter (1992) has referred to the ethnic studies of the 1960s—African American, American Indian, Asian American, Chicano, Puerto Rican, and Latino studies—as "New Studies" to represent their break from old paradigms and orthodoxy.

7. At a professional meeting, one of my colleagues, an African American woman, suggested that African American communities had become "data plantations" where researchers reap benefits without contributing much of substance.

8. This stance is particularly interesting in light of current controversies over the life story of Rigoberta Menchú (1984), titled *I, Rigoberta Menchú*. A Dartmouth researcher who visited Menchú's Guatemalan village discovered "inconsistencies" and "fabrications" in her autobiography (Stoll, 1999).

9. I am completing this chapter just after the airing of television journalist Barbara Walters's interview with the infamous Monica Lewinsky. I am struck by how many people commented after the interview on the types of questions Walters asked, the way she asked them, and the kinds of questions she omitted.

REFERENCES

Acuña, R. (1972). *Occupied America: The Chicano struggle toward liberation*. New York: Canfield.

Alarcón, N. (1990). Chicana feminism: In the tracks of "the" native woman. *Cultural Studies, 4*, 248–256.

Almaguer, T. (1974). Historical notes on Chicano oppression: The dialectics of racial and class domination in North America. *Aztlan, 5*(1-2), 27–56.

Ani, M. (1994). *Yurugu: An African-centered critique of European cultural thought and behavior*. Trenton, NJ: Africa World Press.

Anzaldúa, G. (1987). *Borderlands/la frontera: The new mestiza*. San Francisco: Aunt Lute.

Appiah, K. A. (1992). *In my father's house: Africa in the philosophy of culture*. New York: Oxford University Press.

Appleby, J., Hunt, L., & Jacob, M. (1994). *Telling the truth about history*. New York: W. W. Norton.

Asante, M. K. (1987). *The Afrocentric idea*. Philadelphia: Temple University Press.

Asante, M. K. (1991). The Afrocentric idea in education. *Journal of Negro Education, 60*, 170–180.

Balderrama, F. E. (1982). *In defense of la raza: The Los Angeles Mexican consulate and the Mexican community, 1929 to 1936*. Tucson: University of Arizona Press.

Barnes, R. (1990). Race consciousness: The thematic content of racial distinctiveness in critical race legal scholarship. *Harvard Law Review, 103*, 1864–1871.

Bell, D. (1980). *Brown v. Board of Education* and the interest convergence dilemma. *Harvard Law Review, 93*, 518–533.

Bell, D. (1987). *And we are not saved: The elusive quest for racial justice*. New York: Basic Books.

Bell, D. (1992). *Faces at the bottom of the well*. New York: Basic Books.

Bell, D. (1998). *Afrolantic legacies*. Chicago: Third World Press.

Bettelheim, B. (1965). Teaching the disadvantaged. *National Education Association Journal, 54*, 8–12.

Bloom, B., Davis, A., & Hess, R. (1965). *Comprehensive education for cultural deprivations*. Troy, MO: Holt, Rinehart & Winston.

Calmore, J. O. (1992). Critical race theory, Archie Shepp and fire music: Securing an authentic intellectual life in a multicultural world. *Southern California Law Review, 65*, 2129–2230.

Castillo, A. (1995). *Massacre of the dreamers: Essays on Xicanisma.* New York: Plume.

Churchill, W. (1992). *Fantasies of the master race: Literature, cinema, and the colonization of American Indians.* Monroe, ME: Common Courage.

Churchill, W. (1993). I am indigenist. In W. Churchill, *Struggle for the land: A land rights reader.* Monroe, ME: Common Courage.

Code, L. (1991). *What can she know? Feminist theory and the construction of knowledge.* Ithaca, NY: Cornell University Press.

Collins, P. H. (1990). *Black feminist thought: Knowledge, consciousness, and the politics of empowerment.* New York: Routledge, Chapman & Hall.

Collins, P. H. (1998). *Fighting words: Black women and the search for justice.* Minneapolis: University of Minnesota Press.

Connelly, F. M., & Clandinin, D. J. (1990). Stories of experience and narrative inquiry. *Educational Researcher, 19*(5), 2–14.

Crenshaw, K. (1988). Race, reform and retrenchment: Transformation and legitimation in anti-discrimination law. *Harvard Law Review, 101,* 1331–1387.

Crenshaw, K., Gotanda, N., Peller, G., & Thomas, K. (1995). Introduction. In K. Crenshaw, N. Gotanda, G. Peller, & K. Thomas (Eds.), *Critical race theory: The key writings that formed the movement.* New York: Free Press.

Cronbach, L. (1975). Beyond the two disciplines of scientific psychology. *American Psychologist, 30,* 116–127.

de la Torre, A., & Pesquera, B. (Eds.). (1993). *Building with our hands: New directions in Chicano studies.* Berkeley: University of California Press.

Delgado, R. (1992). Rodrigo's chronicle. *Yale Law Journal, 101,* 1357–1383.

Delgado, R. (1993). Rodrigo's sixth chronicle: Intersections, essences, and the dilemma of social reform. *New York University Law Review, 68,* 639–674.

Delgado, R. (Ed.). (1995a). *Critical race theory: The cutting edge.* Philadelphia: Temple University Press.

Delgado, R. (1995b). Introduction. In R. Delgado (Ed.), *Critical race theory: The cutting edge.* Philadelphia: Temple University Press.

Delgado, R. (1995c). Racial realism—after we're gone: Prudent speculations on America in a post-racial epoch. In R. Delgado (Ed.), *Critical race theory: The cutting edge.* Philadelphia: Temple University Press.

Delgado Bernal, D. (1998). Using a Chicana feminist epistemology in educational research. *Harvard Educational Review, 68,* 555–582.

Delgado-Gaitan, C. (1993). Researching change and changing the researcher. *Harvard Educational Review, 63,* 389–411.

Du Bois, W. E. B. (1953). *The souls of Black folk.* New York: Fawcett. (Original work published 1903)

Ellison, R. (1986). What America would be like without Blacks. In R. Ellison, *Going to the territory* (pp. 104–112). New York: Random House.

Espiritu, Y. L. (1992). *Asian American panethnicity: Bridging institutions and identities.* Philadelphia: Temple University Press.

Fanon, F. (1968). *The wretched of the earth.* New York: Grove.

Fine, M. (1998). Working the hyphens: Reinventing self and other in qualitative research. In N. K. Denzin & Y. S. Lincoln (Eds.), *The landscape of qualitative research: Theories and issues* (pp. 130–155). Thousand Oaks, CA: Sage.

Foucault, M. (1972). *The archaeology of knowledge* (A. M. Sheridan Smith, Trans.). New York: Harper & Row.

Foucault, M. (1973). *The order of things: An archaeology of the human sciences.* New York: Random House.

Frankenstein, M. (1990). Incorporating race, gender, and class issues into a critical mathematics literacy curriculum. *Journal of Negro Education, 59,* 336–351.

Geertz, C. (1983). *Local knowledge: Further essays in interpretive anthropology.* New York: Basic Books.

Gilroy, P. (1993). *Black Atlantic: Modernity and double consciousness.* Cambridge, MA: Harvard University Press.

Gomez-Quinones, J. (1977). On culture. *Revista Chicano-Riqueiia, 5*(2), 35–53.

Gordon, R. (1990). New developments in legal theory. In D. Kairys (Ed.), *The politics of law: A progressive critique* (pp. 413–325). New York: Pantheon.

Gramsci, A. (1971). *Selections from the prison notebooks* (Q. Hoare & G. N. Smith, Eds. & Trans.). New York: International.

Guinier, L. (1994). *The tyranny of the majority: Fundamental fairness in representative democracy.* New York: Free Press.

Guy-Sheftall, B. (1993, April). *Black feminist perspectives on the academy.* Paper presented at the annual meeting of the American Educational Research Association, Atlanta.

Gwaltney, J. L. (1980). *Drylongso: A self-portrait of Black America.* New York: Random House.

Haney López, I. F. (1995). The social construction of race. In R. Delgado (Ed.), *Critical race theory: The cutting edge* (pp. 191–203). Philadelphia: Temple University Press.

Hertzberg, H. W. (1971). *The search for an American Indian identity.* Syracuse, NY: Syracuse University Press.

Highwater, J. (1981). *The primal mind: Vision and reality in Indian America.* New York: Meridian.

Hirabayashi, L. R., & Alquizola, M. C. (1994). Asian American studies: Re-evaluating for the 1990s. In K. Aguilar-San Juan (Ed.), *The state of Asian America: Activism and resistance in the 1990s* (pp. 351–364). Boston: South End.

Hollinger, P. (1995). *Postethnic America: Beyond multiculturalism.* New York: Basic Books.

hooks, b. (1984). *Feminist theory: From margin to center.* Boston: South End.

hooks, b. (1989). *Talking back: Thinking feminist, thinking Black.* Boston: South End.

hooks, b. (1992). *Black looks: Race and representation.* Boston: South End.

Hwang, D. H. (1994). Foreword: Facing the mirror. In K. Aguilar-San Juan (Ed.), *The state of Asian America: Activism and resistance in the 1990s* (pp. ix–xii). Boston: South End.

Jefferson, T. (1954). *Notes on the state of Virginia.* New York: W. W. Norton. (Original work published 1784)

Kincheloe, J. L., & McLaren, P. L. (1998). Re-thinking critical theory and qualitative research. In N. K. Denzin & Y. S. Lincoln (Eds.), *The landscape of qualitative research: Theories and issues* (pp. 260–299). Thousand Oaks, CA: Sage.

King, D. K. (1988). Multiple jeopardy, multiple consciousness: The context of a Black feminist ideology. *Signs, 14,* 42–72.

King, J. E. (1995). Culture centered knowledge: Black studies, curriculum transformation, and social action. In J. A. Banks & C. M. Banks (Eds.), *Handbook of research on multicultural education* (pp. 265–290). New York: Macmillan.

Ladson-Billings, G. (1993). Through a looking glass: Politics and the history curriculum. *Theory and Research in Social Education, 21,* 84–92.

Ladson-Billings, G. (1994). *The dreamkeepers: Successful teachers of African American children.* San Francisco: Jossey-Bass.

Ladson-Billings, G. (1997). For colored girls who have considered suicide when the academy isn't enough: Reflections of an African American woman scholar. In A. Neumann & P. Peterson (Eds.), *Learning from our lives: Women, research and autobiography in education* (pp. 52–70). New York: Teachers College Press.

Ladson-Billings, G. (1998). Just what is critical race theory and what is it doing in a "nice" field like education? *International Journal of Qualitative Studies in Education, 11,* 7–24.

Ladson-Billings, G., & Tate, W. F. (1995). Toward a critical race theory of education. *Teachers College Record, 97,* 47–68.

Lawrence, C. (1995). The word and the river: Pedagogy as scholarship and struggle. In K. Crenshaw, N. Gotanda, G. Peller, & K. Thomas (Eds.), *Critical race theory: The writings that formed the movement* (pp. 336–351). New York: Free Press.

Legesse, A. (1973). *Three approaches to the study of an African society.* New York: Free Press.

Lewis, D. L. (1993). *W. E. B. Du Bois: Biography of a race 1868–1919.* New York: Henry Holt.

Lewontin, R. C., Rose, S., & Kamin, L. (1984). *Not in our genes: Biology, ideology and human nature.* New York: Pantheon.

Lomawaima, K. T. (1995). Educating Native Americans. In J. A. Banks & C. M. Banks (Eds.), *Handbook of research on multicultural education* (pp. 331–347). New York: Macmillan.

Lorde, A. (1984). *Sister outsider: Essays and speeches.* New York: Crossing.

Lowe, L. (1996). *Immigrant acts: On Asian American cultural politics.* Durham, NC: Duke University Press.

Menchú, R. (1984). *I, Rigoberta Menchú: An Indian woman in Guatemala* (E. Burgos Debray, Ed.; A. Wright, Trans.). London: Verso.

Mirande, A., & Enriquez, E. (1979). *La Chicana: The Mexican American woman.* Chicago: University of Chicago Press.

Mohanty, C. T. (1991). Under Western eyes: Feminist scholarship and colonial discourses. In C. T. Mohanty, A. Russo, & L. Torres (Eds.), *Third World women and the politics of feminism* (pp. 50–80). Bloomington: Indiana University Press.

Morrison, T. (1992). *Playing in the dark: Whiteness and the literary imagination.* Cambridge, MA: Harvard University Press.

Narayan, K. (1993). How native is a "native" anthropologist? *American Anthropologist, 95,* 671–686.

Nettles, M., & Perna, L. (1997). *The African American education data book.* Fairfax, VA: Frederick D. Patterson Research Institute.

Nieto, S. (1992). We have stories to tell: A case study of Puerto Ricans in children's books. In V. A. Harris (Ed.), *Teaching multicultural literature in grades K-8* (pp. 171–201). Northwood, MA: Christopher-Gordon.

Oboler, S. (1995). *Ethnic labels, Latino lives: Identity and the politics of (re)presentation in the United States.* Minneapolis: University of Minnesota Press.

Omi, M., & Winant, H. (1994). *Racial formation in the United States: 1960-1990* (2nd ed.). New York: Routledge.

Ornstein, A., & Vairo, P. (1968). *How to teach disadvantaged youth.* New York: McKay.

Outlaw, L. (1995). Philosophy, ethnicity, and race. In F. L. Hord & J. S. Lee (Eds.), *I am because we are: Readings in Black philosophy* (pp. 304–328). Amherst: University of Massachusetts Press.

Padilla, F. (1987). *Latino ethnic consciousness.* Notre Dame, IN: Notre Dame University Press.

Pandian, J. (1985). *Anthropology and the Western tradition: Towards an authentic anthropology.* Prospects Heights, IL: Waveland.

Paz, O. (1961). *The labyrinth of solitude: Life and thought in Mexico.* New York: Random House.

Pirsig, R. M. (1972). *Zen and the art of motorcycle maintenance.* New York: Bantam.

Riessman, F. (1962). *The culturally deprived child.* New York: Harper & Row.

Rist, R. (1990). On the relations among educational research paradigms: From disdain to detentes. In K. Dougherty & F. Hammack (Eds.), *Education and society: A reader* (pp. 81–95). New York: Harcourt Brace Jovanovich.

Rosaldo, R. (1989). *Culture and truth: The remaking of social analysis.* Boston: Beacon.

Rosaldo, R. (1993). After objectivism. In S. During (Ed.), *The cultural studies reader* (pp. 104–117). New York: Routledge.

Said, E. W. (1979). *Orientalism.* New York: Vintage.

Scheurich, J. J., & Young, M. (1997). Coloring epistemologies: Are our research epistemologies racially biased? *Educational Researcher, 26*(4), 4–16.

Shujaa, M. (1997, April). *Transformation of the researcher working toward liberation.* Paper presented at the annual meeting of the American Educational Research Association, San Diego, CA.

Siddle-Walker, V. (1996). *Their highest potential: An African American school community in the segregated South.* Chapel Hill: University of North Carolina Press.

Silko, L. M. (1977). *Ceremony.* New York: Viking.

Silko, L. M. (1981). *Storyteller.* New York: Seaver.

Snipp, C. M. (1995). American Indian studies. In J. A. Banks & C. M. Banks (Eds.). *Handbook of research on multicultural education* (pp. 245–258). New York: Macmillan.

Spivak, G. C. (1988). *In other worlds: Essays in cultural politics.* New York: Routledge.

Stoll, D. (1999). *Rigoberta Menchú and the story of all poor Guatemalans.* Boulder, CO: Westview.

Takaki, R. (1989). *Strangers from a different shore: A history of Asian Americans.* Boston: Little, Brown.

Takaki, R. (1993). *A different mirror: A multicultural history of America.* Boston: Little, Brown.

Tate, W. F. (1997). Critical race theory and education: History, theory, and implications. In M. W. Apple (Ed.), *Review of research in education* (Vol. 22, pp. 191–243). Washington, DC: American Educational Research Association.

Torres-Guzman, M. E. (1992). Stories of hope in the midst of despair: Culturally responsive education for Latino students in an alternative high school in New York City. In M. Saravia-Shore & S. F. Arvizu (Eds.), *Cross cultural literacy: Ethnographies of communication in multiethnic classrooms* (pp. 477–490). New York: Garland.

Trinh T. M. (1909). *Woman, native, other: Writing postcoloniality and feminism.* Bloomington: Indiana University Press.

Unger, R. M. (1983). The critical legal studies movement. *Harvard Law Review, 96,* 561–675.

Villenas, S. (1966). The colonizer/colonized Chicana ethnographer: Identity, marginalization, and co-optation in the field. *Harvard Educational Review, 66,* 711–731.

Warrior, R. A. (1995). *Tribal secrets: Recovering American Indian intellectual traditions.* Minneapolis: University of Minnesota Press.

West, C. (1990). The new cultural politics of difference. In R. Ferguson, M. Gever, T. M. Trinh, & C. West (Eds.), *Out there: Marginalization and contemporary cultures* (pp. 19–36). Cambridge: MIT Press.

West, C. (1993). *Keeping faith: Philosophy and race in America.* New York: Routledge.

Williams, G. W. (1882–1883). *History of the Negro race in America from 1619 to 1880: Negroes as slaves, as soldiers, as citizens* (2 vols.). New York: G. P. Putnam's Sons.

Williams, P. (1991). *The alchemy of race and rights: Diary of a law professor.* Cambridge, MA: Harvard University Press.

Williams, R. (1995). Foreword. In R. Delgado, *The Rodrigo chronicles: Conversations about America and race* (pp. xi–xv). New York: New York University Press.

Wilson, W. J. (1987). *The truly disadvantaged: The inner city, the underclass, and public policy.* Chicago: University of Chicago Press.

Woodson, C. G. (1933). *The mis-education of the Negro.* Washington, DC: Association Press.

Wynter, S. (1992). Do *not call us "Negroes": How "multicultural" textbooks perpetuate racism.* San Francisco: Aspire.

Zinn, H. (1980). *A people's history of the United States.* New York: HarperCollins.

CHAPTER 8

Critical Race Theory and the Postracial Imaginary

With Jamel K. Donnor

How can we be racist, we have a Black president?

—Overheard on college campus

This trial is not about race.

—George Zimmerman trial prosecutor

Given our once-bright expectations for racial progress, it follows that an honest assessment of our current status is cause for despair as the necessary price of much needed enlightenment. Facing up to the real world is the essential prerequisite for a renewed vision, and for a renewed commitment to struggle based on that vision.

—Derrick Bell, *Faces at the Bottom of the Well*, p. xi

INTRODUCTION: KEEPING IT REAL

Posited by the late constitutional scholar Derrick Bell to describe the initial hopes and subsequent disappointments regarding the collective social and economic status of African Americans since the civil rights movement of the mid-20th century, we contend that his epigraph is especially relevant to the present sociopolitical context.[1] Despite the two-term presidency of Barack Obama, the United States has *not* entered into a "postracial" epoch whereby race no longer functions as the primary determinant in shaping the life fortunes of people of color. To the contrary, the life experiences and life opportunities for people of color continue to be qualitatively distinct. For example, despite comprising only 13% of the U.S. population (U.S. Department of Justice, 2007), African Americans "had higher rates of violent victimization than Whites, Hispanics, and Asians" (U.S. Department of Justice, 2007, p. 3). In fact, "only American Indians had a higher rate" (U.S. Department of Justice, 2007, p. 3) of violent crimes than African Americans. In education, African American and Latino/a students are more likely to be taught by unqualified or "ineffective" teachers, have higher rates of in-school-related arrests and law enforcement referrals despite respectively constituting 16% and 24% of the total number of students enrolled in public schools (Center for American Progress, 2014; U.S. Department of Education and U.S. Department of Justice, 2014).

The foregoing examples are illustrative of the complex ways the lives of people of color remain disproportionately less promising, and how race is central to their existence. Unfortunately, however, much of the contemporary social and political discourse in the United States continues to advance the idea that colorblindness is the most effective approach for solving the country's racial problems (Lopez, 2014). According to this conservative perspective on race and social inequality, racial equality is best achieved through the "formal removal of race" (Crenshaw, 1997, p. 103) as a social category. Discursively and cognitively appealing, the public removal of race according to the colorblind perspective is the most legitimate method for ensuring that all citizens are treated equally. The reality, however, is that colorblindness (and the "leftist" companion term, postracialism) decontextualizes the symbiotic relationship between race, opportunity, exclusion, marginalization, and exploitation (Donnor, 2011b; Lopez, 2014). Indeed, outside of acknowledging and condemning the most vile instances of racial animus, such as NBA team owner Donald Sterling's recorded remarks regarding African Americans, the colorblind and postracial paradigms contend that efforts to explicitly redress racial inequality are a form of racism or, at the least, privileging race (Black, 2002; Freeman, 1978; Lawrence, 1976; McCristal Culp, 1994; Donnor, 2011a, 2001b). We fundamentally disagree with the colorblind and postracial points of view.

The purpose of this chapter is to speak back to the postracial and colorblind narratives by discussing what critical race theory (CRT) teaches researchers and scholars about qualitative research, and the lives of people of color. Moreover, we contend that race is the most viable and reliable analytical tool for holistically understanding and improving the collective fortunes of people of color in the United States (and globally).

Before we begin, however, we believe it is necessary to provide the reader with a working understanding of our positionality on race and inequity. To assist, we synthesize our chapter "Waiting for the Call: The Moral Activist Role of Critical Race Theory Scholarship" (Ladson-Billings & Donnor, 2005), which appeared in the third edition of *The Sage Handbook of Qualitative Research* (Denzin & Lincoln, 2005). Next, we discuss how race influences social science and education research. Highlighting education's interdisciplinarity, we demonstrate how fields such as psychology, sociology, and anthropology rely heavily on race as a meaning-making category that directly informs education research. Third, we respond to the critique that CRT scholars are simply "telling stories" by describing how counter-narratives and critical race chronicles have a long history/tradition in law, social science research, and public policy. Despite the form offered by more traditional versions of social science research we contend that *all* scholars are "telling a story." Fourth, we address the proliferation of CRT scholarship in education and issues regarding rigor (or lack thereof), conceptual weakness, and methodological misappropriation. While we recognize the allure of critical race theory as the next "new thing," much of work under this designation does not incorporate the legal scholarship, which is a foundational component. Finally, we conclude this chapter by examining critical theory across education areas (e.g., administration, leadership, curriculum and instruction, special education, policy, and special education), as well as its internationalization and iterations among various racial/ethnic groups (e.g., LatCrit, Tribal Crit, etc.) to illustrate the theory's richness and complexity.

THE MORAL CLARION CALL

In our first iteration of this chapter we pointed out the liminal space (Wynter, 1992) that people of color, particularly Black people, occupy in the U.S. society. We detailed the transposition from hero to brute that former NFL player O.J. Simpson experienced when he was accused of murdering his ex-wife and her male friend. We also shared our own personal stories of racist and discriminatory acts we have experienced regardless of our positions as academics. Recently, Donnor and another colleague (who was driving a high-end, late model sedan) dropped Ladson-Billings off at her hotel while attending a conference. After Ladson-Billings stepped out of the car, the hotel bellman asked of the two African American[2] scholars, "What Company do you fellas drive for?" One might argue that this response is an "honest mistake." However, we assert that such incidents reflect the regular and predictable occurrence of what critical race theorists call "microaggressions" (Davis, 1989).

However, in addition to the experiences of everyday racism we also identified what might be termed epistemological (and methodological) racism because of our positions as "intellectual marginals" (Ladson-Billings & Donnor, 2005). The work of researching race from the margins demands new paradigmatic and methodological tools to deconstruct what Wynter (1992) calls the "system conserving model" (p. 27) of the society. Our previous chapter identifies other scholars of color whose work attempts to forge epistemological freedom from this system-conserving model (see, e.g., Acuna, 1972; Alarcon, 1993; Espiritu, 1992; Lowe, 1996; Minh-Ha, 1989; Warrior, 1994). But, we claim that it is not enough to recognize the counternarratives of scholars not included in the mainstream. It is also important to look at the ways that mainstream liberal ideologies are limited in their ability to seek just remedies for social inequities. In this section of the chapter we identified what we term "the limits of liberal ideology" (Ladson-Billings & Donnor, 2005, p. 285) to point out the inability of the mainstream to develop an epistemological turn being deployed by scholars of color. Ikemoto (1995) states, "To the extent that we interpret our experience from within the master narrative, we reinforce our own subordination. Whether [people of color] can counter racism may depend, finally, on our ability to claim identities outside the master narrative" (pp. 312–313).

We began our previous chapter during the 2004 U.S. presidential race between George W. Bush and John Kerry, and we revised this chapter during the second term of Barack H. Obama. Some might ask how the election of the first president of color impacts the position we take on race and scholarship. We observed a curious phenomenon with the election of President Obama that allows mainstream members of both the left and right ideological spectrum to declare that race no longer matters in the same ways. On the right there is an insistence that we were now a "colorblind" society. On the left we were told we are "postracial." Both perspectives are dangerously naïve and can have a pernicious effect on that part of the democratic project aimed at ensuring equity for racially subordinate groups. News magazines and papers ran stories with headlines like, "Does race still matter?" (Tolson, 2008), "Is Obama the end of Black politics?" (Bai, 2008), and "The end of White America?" (Hsu, 2009).

The notion of colorblindness seems a laudable goal for a nation to aspire to. It presumes that individuals and institutions discount race when making decisions related to educational, employment, and housing opportunities, as well as public policy decisions. People holding this view readily reference Martin Luther King, Jr.'s statement about having his children one day be judged by the "content of their character" and not the color of their skin. King's vision is indeed emblematic of an ideal state but should not be taken out of the context of his time. King was operating in the midst of state-sanctioned apartheid. There were schools, housing, and other public accommodations that were legally unavailable to African Americans. He was calling for equal protection under the law or the true enforcement of the 14th Amendment.

White America embraces the notion of colorblindness because it absolves them of the nation's deepest sin—racism in the context of White supremacy. To be White is to not think about race, but rather to worry about other daily concerns—money, children, health, or whatever challenges life brings. Being White means not having to figure race into one's daily calculus. To be White is to reference the terms *man*, *woman*, *child*, and *American* and always be prefiguring a White subject. Colorblindness is the way Whites have always already lived their lives except when non-Whites have advocated for similar opportunities or privileges.

Proponents of colorblindness believe that Blacks, Latinas/os, and other people of color have not taken advantage of the opportunities the government has generously "given" them; thus their inability to progress represents their own individual failures. Colorblind advocates believe that African Americans, Latinas/os, American Indians, and other non-White groups should "get over" the past and relinquish group identities and allow the "meritocracy" to function. But how does "meritocracy" actually work in the United States?

According to sociologist David Wellman (2002), in the 1980s unemployment for all Black men rose relative to White men. However, it rose especially for Black college-educated men. In the late 1960s when the civil rights movement was ending, the unemployment rate for Black and White men was equal. This was a major improvement from the disparities that existed in the 1950s and early 1960s. However, by the 1980s educated Black men were three times more likely to be unemployed than their White peers. This employment disparity is greater than that of Black high school dropouts and their White counterparts. So, if the system is meritocratic what explains the employment disparities for *college-educated* Black men?

For the colorblind advocate, race is no longer the site of social inequality. In this discourse people of color are *using* race to get an advantage. By ticking off "minority race" on job, college, or housing applications, they reason, they are accorded more consideration for social benefits. This, according to the colorblind perspective, is undemocratic and thus it becomes necessary to rid all aspects of public policy of "race-based" remedies. California's Proposition 209 and initiatives in the states of Washington and Michigan have passed and spelled the end of race consideration in public policy. These same measures do not speak to our consideration of gender when the data show that White women have been the greatest beneficiaries of affirmative action.

While the colorblind advocates see Barack Obama's presidential victory as proof positive that we are a colorblind society, the postracial advocates, many of whom identify with left-leaning perspectives, assert that we have moved beyond race. They still see diversity and difference, but race just doesn't mean the same thing in a technologically sophisticated, global, "flat world" (Friedman, 2007). Postracial discourse attempts to complicate difference and subjectivities to suggest that race is but one among many. The postracialists suggest that talk about race as a category is essentializing and simplistic so we have to look toward our postracial future toward a more hybrid existence. What Michael Lind (1996) refers to as the "beiging" of America references the reality of demographics in the United States. What the postracialists do not recognize is the way race has always been deployed in American to mean what the more powerful group wants it to mean.

In 1923, the U.S. Supreme Court ruled that despite recent anthropological studies that expanded the definition of Caucasian to include those from India the justices argued that despite the presence of "Aryan blood" in the veins of World War I veteran Bhagat Singh Thind, Mr. Thind was not White. The Court determined that Thind was not white "in accordance with the understanding of the common man." We suspect that since race is such an arbitrary concept, powerful interests can rearrange and coalesce around "shades and degrees" of Blackness. Tiger Woods, Barack Obama, Mariah Carey, and Halle Berry could easily fit into this new category of acceptability. Others of darker hues could not be so easily accepted without some other form of exceptionality. The other thing that is likely to happen is the co-mingling of race and class (which already happens). In this arrangement poor Blacks will not be able to escape the pernicious impact of race because of their social status.

The work before us falls into what anthropologist Aiwa Ong (1999) calls "flexible citizenship"—the idea that we are no longer limited by fixed notions of identity like race, ethnicity, country of origin but instead we take on multiple shifting and sometimes competing identities. Of course, through various technologies and scientific advances those people who are in the public eye, especially arts and entertainment, are able to alter their physical appearance to move toward an acceptable white aesthetic. In the case of the late entertainer Michael Jackson we see someone who transformed himself from an obviously Black youngster, to a lighter skinned adolescent, to a "White" man. Of course Jackson's is an extreme example.

Sometimes "whitening" is done through marketing, as in the case of Mariah Carey. There was a perceptible difference in her skin tone on the *Ebony* magazine cover and that of *Seventeen* magazine that were issued the same month (April 1994). On the *Seventeen* cover Carey looks White. On the *Ebony* cover it is clear that Carey is mixed race. Additionally, images can be "darkened" to represent a more sinister or evil character as in the case of O.J. Simpson on the June 27, 1994, cover of *Time* versus the same photo on the cover of *Newsweek* that same week.

So if race is such a problematic category, what choices do we have? Lani Guinier and Gerald Torres (2003) suggest we can deploy what they call "political race"—flexible categories of identification that we use to take advantage of political, social, and economic benefits. Political race urges people of color to coalesce and work together to leverage certain benefits rather than accept fixed categories linked to presumed bio-genetic affiliation.

Political race works not just for people of color. Social activists like Morris Dees, Herbert Lehman, and Father Jonathan Daniels have actively worked and/or contributed financially to the civil rights movement. They deployed race strategically realizing their White skin privilege could afford them greater cache or leverage and lend legitimacy to the cause. It is this deployment that we see as an example of the moral activism role of critical race theory.

RACE AND THE WORK OF SOCIAL SCIENTISTS

The challenge for social scientists working with race is that all social science disciplines (to some extent) use the concept "race" as if it were a fact of nature despite the denial of its existence by natural scientists and social scientists. Anthropology is a discipline largely founded on the concept of race and racial hierarchy. Anthropology emerged after the age of western European exploration as "the study of humans" and that study was almost always focused on the people in European colonies (Ladson-Billings, 2013). Thus anthropology was conceived as a study of "the other." Anthropologist Audrey Smedley (1993) points out that race began as a folk classification—"ideologies, distinctions, and selective perceptions that constitute a society's popular imagery and interpretations of the world" (p. 25). But, by the mid- to late 18th century naturalists and other learned men "gave credence and legitimacy [to race] as a supposed product of scientific investigations" (p. 26). Race was regularly on display in World's Fairs and Exhibitions with the classification and ranking of various ethnic and cultural groups. In the past anthropologists regularly provided the so-called science for these classifications and rankings. The major influence of anthropology on our thinking about race was in the formation of race as a worldview.

Late 19th-century students of anthropology were trained in all aspects of the discipline—archaeology, linguistics, ethnology/ethnography, and physical anthropology—that would later be delineated as the four fields of anthropology. The growth of physical anthropology allowed thinking about race as an inherent human category to emerge. In the early 20th century leaders in the sub-field of physical anthropology promoted the idea of race as a taxonomic term that signified differences in human groups based on "biophysical and morphological characteristics" (Smedley, 1993, p. 275). It would take Franz Boas in the early 20th century to change the discipline's thinking about race by pointing out the ways that environment, not heredity, influenced many physical traits (e.g., height, weight).

More recently, the American Anthropological Association (AAA) supported a public education project titled, "Race: Are We So Different?" as a 5,000-square-foot exhibition that explored the science, history, and lived experiences of race and racism in our nation and traveled to 14 museums across the United States. The project also included an interactive website (www.understandingrace.org), a book, and DVD all organized around three central ideas: Race is a recent human invention; race is about culture, not biology; and race and racism are embedded in institutions and everyday life.

Race also plays a prominent role in the discipline of sociology and although there is a clear declaration by sociologists that "race is a social construct" (Omi & Winant, 1994), the American Sociological Association (ASA) has stated that race as a concept is essential to their work—data collection, sorting and stratification, organization and mobilization for explaining the maintenance and challenging of systems, and a basis for examining proximate cases. Perhaps the best statement about the conundrum that race presents for sociologists is Howard Winant's statement that, "the field of sociology is necessarily a part of the problem it is trying to explain" (2007, p. 537). Earlier Winant (2000) pointed out that from the U.S. development of the discipline of sociology race has been a significant theme (as opposed to the emphasis on class in the British development). Evidence of the prominence of race in the field is W. E. B. Du Bois's (1998/1899) study of Black life in Philadelphia and his theoretical construct of "double consciousness" that describes the way race delimits the identity and agency of Blacks.

In *The World Is a Ghetto: Race and Democracy since World War II*, Howard Winant (2001) details the way modernity helped to disperse race throughout the world by a look at its growth and establishment in the United States, South Africa, Brazil, and Europe. While acknowledging the presence of both "colorblind" and "postracial" discourses, Winant (2001) asserts:

> This post-racial view is at odds with the central claims . . . : that racial hierarchy lives on: that it correlates very well with worldwide and national systems of stratification and inequality; that it corresponds to glaring disparities in labor conditions and reflects differential access to democratic and communicative instrumentalities and life chances. . . . [T]he race-concept is anything but obsolete and its significance is not declining. We are not "beyond race." (p. 2)

As we look at the work of psychologists, it is also apparent that race was a pivotal concept for defining intelligence and human capacity. Just as early anthropologists were set on proving White supremacy based on physiology, psychologists seemed determined to use the concept of intelligence as evidence of this supremacy. In Europe, philosophers such as Voltaire, Kant, and Linneaus insisted that there were different mental abilities found in the different races. In 1869, mathematician Francis Galton published *Hereditary Genius*, which set the foundation for the field of eugenics.

In 1912, the Columbia University psychology graduate Frank Bruner reviewed the scientific literature on auditory perception in Black and White subjects in *Psychological Bulletin*, characterizing

> the mental qualities of the Negro as: lacking in filial affection, strong migratory instincts and tendencies; little sense of veneration, integrity or honor; shiftless, indolent, untidy, improvident, extravagant, lazy, lacking in persistence and

initiative and unwilling to work continuously at details. Indeed, experience with
the Negro in classrooms indicates that it is impossible to get the child to do anything with continued accuracy, and similarly in industrial pursuits, the Negro
shows a woeful lack of power of sustained activity and constructive conduct.
(cited in Benjamin, 2006, pp. 188–189)

Stanford University psychologist Lewis Terman developed the Stanford-
Binet Intelligence Test and declared that there was a "higher incidence of
morons" among non-White races. Terman would develop a prolific career
investigating "giftedness" that was based primarily on all White populations. Space constraints do not permit a full detailing of the connections between psychology and race. However, it is significant that such connections
persisted well into the 20th century with University of California, Berkeley
psychologist Arthur Jensen asserting that most of the variation in Black–
White test scores was genetic, no one had proposed a plausible alternative
to the genetic/hereditary thesis, and thus it is more reasonable to assume
that part of the intelligence score differences were genetic (Jencks & Phillips,
1998). The 1994 publication of Hernnstein and Murray's *The Bell Curve*
placed the relationship between race and intelligence back in the public conversation. Interestingly, *The Bell Curve* only devotes two chapters to the
discussion of race, but these two chapters reinscribe the notion of race as
hereditary.

Despite the prominent role of White psychologists in defining race and
intelligence, it was Martinique-born psychiatrist Frantz Fanon (1963) who
would argue that all colonialized subjects were conditioned to experience
themselves as genetically inferior based on the prevailing hegemonic discourses (Wynter, 1995). Fanon's work (1967) challenged Freud's emphasis
on the individual that produced a bias toward ontogeny and suggested the
field of psychology was missing an understanding of group affiliation and
consciousness that produced a "sociogeny."

It is Fanon's perspective that gives primacy to our social selves and
shapes our outlook in this work. A look back at the first iteration of this
chapter (Ladson-Billings, 2000) juxtaposes philosopher Rene Descartes' notion of "I think, therefore I am" with the African notion of "Ubuntu" or "I
am because we are." These fundamental differences in our cultural models
force us to call into question the basis on which each of the Western social
sciences rests. Unfortunately, the Western viewpoint dominates education
scholarship and research and not surprisingly the outcomes of education
perfectly mimic this viewpoint.

Education is a field that pulls heavily on the social science disciplines—
particularly psychology and sociology. Because race is so deeply embedded
in these disciplines, the field of education produces a very similar racial
grammar. The notions of cultural deprivation, cultural disadvantage, and
the more recent notion of "culture of poverty" flow directly from beliefs

about whiteness, White supremacy, and Black inferiority. Even African American social scientists like Kenneth Clark were confined in the paradigmatic use of the social sciences that represented African Americans as inferior. Clark in his famous "doll studies" demonstrated the deleterious effects of segregation but also reinforced the idea that Black culture in and of itself was disadvantaged. Rather than attack race as the destructive concept that crowded out culture, Clark's work contributed to the ideology that made race and culture synonymous.

As a result, the majority of research in education that deals with inequality relies on premises that race is real and objective. Education research on public policies such as school desegregation, compensatory education, expulsion and suspension, academic disparities, tracking, ability grouping, special education, and giftedness all rely on race as a sense-making category. In most instances, research in these areas treats race as a fixed variable. Education researchers rarely entertain notions of hybridity, creolization, and fluidity as a way to consider racial and cultural identity. Such terminology is relegated to "cultural studies" and has little currency in "empirical" studies of inequity and injustice.

Education borrows terms like *normal* from psychology to characterize non-White students as falling below acceptable levels of performance for participating in schooling. It borrows notions of "healthy families" from sociology to determine what kinds of kin relations are legitimate (often discounting fictive kin relations that include "play" cousins, adoptive grandparents, etc.). Education borrows the term *culture* from anthropology when it is actually referencing the result of social arrangements (e.g., poverty, segregation, unemployment) that Black people have little or no control over.

Black children are disproportionately assigned to special education. We want to be clear that we are not talking about obvious disabilities such as hearing, visual, or speech impairments, or other physical disabilities and relatively clear cognitive disabilities. The areas of disproportionality for most African American students are mild cognitive disabilities and behavioral disorders. These are categories of disabilities that are often left to judgment—the judgment of a teacher who is not necessarily trained to identify disabilities. According to Blanchett (2006), "disproportionality exists when students' representation in special education categories exceeds their proportional enrollment in a school's general population" (p. 24). When compared with their White peers, African American children are almost three times more likely to be labeled "mentally retarded." African American students in Connecticut, Mississippi, South Carolina, North Carolina, and Nebraska are more than four times as likely to be identified as "mentally retarded" than White students living in those states. In Florida, Alabama, Delaware, New Jersey, and Colorado, the number of African American students identified as "mentally retarded" was more than three times that of White students. These disparities and disproportion policy practices are often based on the research that emanates from racially derived assumptions about students of color. Thus, as much as we would like to discount the salience of race we continue to be able to document its presence and prevalence in the everyday lives and public policy decisions in the society. In the next section we suggest how critical race theory may be useful in exploring and explaining race both in the society and in qualitative research.

THE PROMISE AND POTENTIAL OF CRITICAL RACE THEORY

Critical race theory (CRT) appeared in legal journals and texts more than 20 years ago (Crenshaw, 2011). Its genealogy is one of both scholarship and activism. When legal scholars determined that the law was a hindrance to justice for marginalized groups they formed a workshop group called, "Critical Legal Studies" (CLS) to explore issues of race, class, and gender in the law. Unfortunately, in the midst of their discussions legal scholars of color felt that issues of race were regularly discounted and/or ignored even though there was a dearth of law professors of color in top-tier law schools, and a lack of access to elite law review by those scholars writing about race and race discrimination. Eventually, legal scholars of color developed their own workshop group and called their work "critical race theory" (CRT) to distinguish themselves from CLS and to place race at the center of their inquiry.

CRT is more accurately a set of theories—not one unified theory. These theories rely on intersectionality (i.e., the nexus of race, gender, class, etc.), a critique of liberalism, the use of critical social science, a combination of structural and post-structural analysis, the denial of neutrality in scholarship, and the incorporation of story-telling, or more precisely, "counternarratives" to speak back against dominant discourses. It is this last tenet—counternarratives—that we choose to deploy as a qualitative research strategy in this era of what we have termed "the postracial imaginary."

One of the common mistakes we see in those who claim to be using CRT is in "telling a story" that fails to engage larger legal and social principles. Rather, many of these stories reflect some personal grievance, which is not placed in a larger and/or systemic pattern of occurrences that may be useful for analysis and further application. CRT scholars often use counternarratives that are fantasy and transcend the boundaries of time and space. Often the point of the story is not to report an agreed-upon truth but rather to illustrate a principle or concept in the way a fable or proverb might. The late Derrick Bell (1992) is often credited as the "father of critical race theory" and was the master of what he called "Chronicles." Richard Delgado (1992) also employed Bell's chronicle approach. Both scholars created alter-egos that were not bounded by human limits of time and space.

For Bell, the character of Geneva Crenshaw could reflect on being present at the Constitutional Convention in the 1700s and at the Supreme Court while *Brown* was being decided. Delgado created Rodrigo as the half-brother of Geneva and allowed the characters to communicate with each other across time and space.

One of Bell's most memorable chronicles shows up in his book *Faces at the Bottom of the Well* (1992)—"The Space Traders." Reminiscent of Ray Bradbury's (2012) *Martian Chronicles*, the Space Traders is a story of aliens bargaining with the powers that be in the United States to provide unlimited gold (to erase the national debt), eradication of air and water pollution, and unlimited energy supplies (oil and gas) in exchange for all Black citizens. The decision is turned over to a national call in referendum that passes easily and before long African Americans are being transported to some alien planet. While the tale is fanciful, Bell tells it to illustrate the nation's willingness to sacrifice Black lives for the benefits of Whites.

In another volume, Bell (1989) creates the "Chronicle of the Sacrificed Black Children" where he describes a group of Black children slated to desegregate a nearby White community who suddenly and mysteriously disappear. Initially, the White community considers the missing Black children a victory that forestalls school desegregation. However, as time goes by and the school district begins losing funding for personnel, buses, and desegregation programs, White parents join in the desperate attempt to locate the Black children. Bell's point in this chronicle underscores his notion that civil rights legislation must always benefit Whites in order to pass. School desegregation is less about Black children receiving quality education than providing ways to enhance the schooling experiences of White children. A careful look at many school desegregation programs reveals the multitude of magnet school programs and other academic inducements that are used to entice White families to continue to participate in public school systems located in racially and ethnically changing communities.

But, it is not merely CRT scholars who have employed storytelling as a research strategy. Scholars like Gloria Anzaldúa (2012) use cuentos and consejos (moral tales like La Llorona) to develop social analysis about inequity and injustice. Of course Native scholars like Warrior (1994) have always used storytelling as a teaching and learning tool. But what is the story or chronicle that we tell regarding the notion of the postracial imaginary? How do we help people see what is happening in the country in the 21st century regarding President Obama as highly predictable and expected rather than racial anomalies?

On one hand people will argue that the opposing party always attacks a sitting president for policies and actions. However, we argue that the particular experiences of President Obama are linked to his racial identity as a Black president and are strategically deployed under the discursive guise of "colorblindness" and "postracial" imaginaries. The racially charged attacks on President Obama are too numerous to delineate in this chapter,[3] but many will recall some of the more high-profile examples. During his first State of the Union address the president was subjected to Southern Congressman Joe Wilson's shout out, "You lie!" So unprecedented and stunning was this outburst that then-Speaker of the House Nancy Pelosi's face registered shock and disbelief. Such a lack of decorum toward the President had never occurred in the Congressional chambers. During the 2008 election campaign (and beyond), the President was accused of not being a citizen (spawning the "birther" controversy) and being a Muslim (not as a faith commitment but as an anti-American, terrorist slur). No sooner than Obama was elected, conservative radio host Rush Limbaugh declared that he hoped the president failed. In the 2012 re-election campaign we saw bumper stickers reading, "Don't re-nig in 2012" as a clear reference to Barack Obama's race. A marquee sign at a bar and grill stated, "Heard the White House smells of collard greens and fried chicken," while a man stood at a Tea Party rally with a t-shirt that read, "Put White back in the White House." At the tragic death of a Florida teenager, President Obama declared, "Trayvon Martin could have been my son." That statement infuriated the right and brought charges of racism on the part of the president. What has been especially interesting from a CRT perspective is the way that the colorblind discourse is deployed to turn all of these egregious actions into the "First Amendment" rights of Whites. Because we are now "colorblind," these statements are framed as mere political opposition, and it is Obama who is seen as making "race" the issue. As a consequence, Barack Obama has been rendered almost fully mute on the topic of race.

CHALLENGES TO CRITICAL RACE THEORY

Radical assessment can encompass illustration, anecdote, allegory, and imagination, as well as analysis of applicable doctrine and authorities.

—Derrick Bell, 1995, *Who's Afraid of Critical Race Theory?*, p. 893

In this section, we discuss the proliferation of critical race theory scholarship in education and the topical concern of conceptual weakness, which include issues regarding rigor or lack thereof, the misappropriation/overuse of key analytical constructs, such as storytelling and voice, and the underutilization of tenets, such as racial realism and the rules of racial standing (Bell, 1995). While we recognize the seduction of CRT as the "latest thing" in academia with respect to understanding race and inequality, a fundamental shortcoming of much of the scholarship in education has been the absence of legal and public policy scholarship to fully contextualize existing inequities and advance meaningful policy solutions. Furthermore, such intellectual fidelity is considered necessary in order for scholarship under the heading of critical race theory to be transformative. That said, before we begin our discussion of what CRT ought to be, we believe it is equally important to more fully articulate what CRT is (Bell, 1995).

Just What Exactly Is Critical Race Theory?

An "intellectual movement" rooted in American jurisprudence scholarship, critical race theory examines and critiques the law's role in constructing and preserving unequal social and political relationships according to race (West, 1995). Treating race as a socially constructed phenomenon, rather than as an immutable biological fact or fixed physical attribute, critical race theory views race as a "fluctuating, decentered complex of social meanings that are formed and transformed under the constant pressures of political struggle" (Lopez, 1996, p. 13) intended to ensure White supremacy.

Situating the American legal system at the nexus of the race-making process, critical race theory explains how professed American ideals and legal principles, such as liberty, freedom, and equality, simultaneously maintain a "regime of white supremacy" (Crenshaw et al., 1995, p. xiii) while subordinating people of color (Crenshaw et al., 1995). A reason for this paradox is law's incongruent and amorphous philosophical underpinnings (Foner, 1988; Freeman, 1988). For example, equality of opportunity according to legal scholar Alan Freeman (1988),

> rests upon a peculiar blend of many philosophical concepts: 'Kantian' individualism (the rights of 'free' and 'autonomous' beings), personality and desert theories of property (you realize yourself through your action upon the external world and deserve to keep what you have fashioned from it), pessimistic behaviorism (people, like laboratory animals, will exert themselves only for rewards, and exert themselves even more for even bigger rewards), and some kind of utilitarian aggregation theory (more is better, and 'we' want more). (p. 377)

For critical race theorists, equality of opportunity "assimilate[s] both the demand and the object against which the demand is made—[meaning] it is to participate in an abstract discourse that carries the moral force of the [civil rights] movement as well as the stability of the institutions that the movement opposed" (Crenshaw, 1995, p. 106). For example, colorblindness, a legal corollary to equality of opportunity and the idealized goal of the Black Civil Rights Movement of the 1950s and 1960s, is currently used by Whites to justify the status quo by asserting that policies intended to improve the educational options of people of color because of a legacy of racism are discriminatory toward White people (M. K. Brown et al., 2003). In other words, to demand equality of opportunity according to CRT is to "demand nothing . . . [because] society's adoption of the ambivalent rhetoric of equality of opportunity law has made it that much more difficult for [non-whites] to name their reality" (Crenshaw, 1995, p. 106). Moreover, historically subordinated groups, (i.e., African Americans, Latina/o Americans, Native Americans, and Asian Americans) are foreclosed from exercising effective legal remedies, because the law actually promotes and entrenches their subordination (Harris, 2001).

Similarly, freedom and liberty as historical and material facts are not only linked to the "power of the national state" (Foner, 1999, p. 98) and the "ability to make crucial individual choices free from outside coercion" (Foner, 1999, p. xviii), both societal axioms serve as the basis of difference, inclusion, exclusion, and oppression. According to Pulitzer Prize–winning historian Eric Foner (1988),

> the universalistic American Creed [freedom and liberty] has been a persistent feature of our history, so too have been efforts to delimit freedom along one or another axis of social existence . . . Non-whites, women, and laborers experienced firsthand the paradox that one person's freedom has frequently been linked to another's servitude. The master's freedom rested on the reality of slavery, the vaunted autonomy of [White] men on the subordinate position of women. By the same token, it has been through battles at the boundaries—the efforts of racial minorities, women, and workers to secure freedom as they understood it—that the meaning (and hence the experience) of freedom has been both deepened and transformed, and the concept extended to realms for which it was not originally intended. (p. xx)

For critical race scholars, law is more than the amalgamation of abstract ideas or concepts. Instead, universal concepts and legal principles, such as freedom, liberty, and equality (and colorblindness), shape and determine one's individual and collective existence. As a human liberation and racial justice project, the goal of critical race theory is to "map the mutually constitutive relationship between race and the law" (Harris, 2002, p. 1217) in the hopes of eliminating all forms of oppression (Bell, 1995; Crenshaw et al., 1995; Harris, 2001; Matsuda et al., 1993). A similar freedom and social justice project has been taken up in the education field.

Critical Race Theory in Education and the Issue of Rigor

Introduced to the field of education by Gloria Ladson-Billings and William F. Tate in 1995 to "theorize race and use it as an analytic tool for understanding school inequity" (p. 48), scholars in education have used CRT to examine a myriad of issues, including segregation and students of color (Rousseau-Anderson, 2011; Chapman, 2005), race and teacher pedagogy (Ladson-Billings, 1999; Lynn, 1999, 2002; Parker & Stovall, 2004), micro-aggressions and campus climate (Solorzano & Yosso, 2000), race, gender, and academic achievement (DeCuir & Dixson, 2004; Howard, 2008), and research methodology (Ladson-Billings, 2000; Ladson-Billings & Donnor, 2005; Parker & Lynn, 2002). While the foregoing topics are by no means exhaustive, a constant criticism of critical race theory scholarship in education has been the lack of or misuse of the legal literature, including case law (Dixson & Rousseau, 2005; Donnor, 2005; Ladson-Billings, 1998, 2013; Tate, 1997).

Beyond referencing the law review articles containing the specific CRT analytical construct one is utilizing to examine race and inequality within his or her particular area of education, a majority of the critical race theory scholarship in the field of education lacks the capacity to connect the contemporary moment to the past or to articulate a "dynamic understanding of the temporal, institutional, and disciplinary emergence CRT provides for engaging today's 'postracialism'" (Crenshaw, 2011, p. 1261). A reason for this shortcoming we argue is the field's continued reliance upon static conceptions of equality, and specific institutional dynamics (see Tate, 1997; Crenshaw, 2011). Indeed, a reason for the doctrinal durability of Derrick Bell's interest convergence principle, we argue, is not simply because of its reliance on legal precedent (i.e., history), but also its understanding of White Supremacy's amorphousness. According to Bell (1980), *true* racial equality requires the surrender of racism's legacy of material and psychological privileges accorded to people of European ancestry historically and contemporaneously. Further, American political history, as Bell points out, suggests that "so great the effort required to bring amelioration of the adverse conditions in education, employment, voting, public accommodations, and housing, that when a barrier is breached, the gain is eagerly accepted with too little question as proof of progress in the long, hard struggle to eliminate racial discrimination" (Bell, 2004, p. 56). Thus, America's dominant social and political institutions according to interest convergence have no choice but to function in a manner that ensures that society operates at a normative level (e.g., how the world *ought* to be), whereby foundational ideals, such as racial equality, do not structurally disrupt how the world actually exists (e.g., the positivistic level) (Bell, 1980).

It is here we contend that the critical race scholarship in education would be better served by the inclusion of a more interdisciplinary and cross-institutional perspective. For instance, the coupling of education policy with other public policies, such as housing, would not only illuminate discipline similarities and dissimilarities, but also enhance both fields' collective understanding of (1) the policy-framing process, including the language and ideas that are evoked (Lakoff, 2004; Brown & Donnor, 2011; Feagin, 2013), (2) how racial advantage and disadvantage are constructed and maintained (Schneider & Ingram, 1993; O'Connor, 2001; Brown & Donnor, 2011), and (3) how government resources are mobilized into service for the first and second points (McDonnell & Elmore, 1987). Indeed, where a family chooses to purchase a home is tied to not only race and socioeconomic status but also perceptions (and expectations) of education quality. As a subdiscipline of political science and history respectively, public policy "is purposeful and attempts to achieve goals by changing people's behavior" (Schneider & Ingram, 1993, p. 335). Furthermore, a focus on social policy provides a more robust understanding of the dynamic interplay between and among government interests, advocacy groups, other political actors, and inequity (Bonastia, 2006).

Because education and public policy are applied fields of study, they are multifarious in their respective aims. Therefore, understanding their specific problems' "institutional home"[4] (Bonastia, 2006, p. 6), including programmatic attempts to ameliorate issues, is paramount. A social problem's policy home, institutionally speaking, not only conveys the symbolic message of a "legitimacy imperative" (Bonastia, 2006, p. 12) but also the metanarrative of "what government is supposed to do, which citizens are deserving (and which are not), and what kinds of attitudes and participatory patterns are appropriate in a democratic society" (Schneider & Ingram, 1993, p. 334). From a critical race theory perspective, coupling a public policy's institutional home with CRT's methodological approaches (i.e., counter-storytelling and voice), not only enhances existing conceptual tools, such as interest-convergence, whiteness as property, and intersectionality, which have been developed over time, this method has the potential for revealing new and insightful ways for speaking back to the postracial and colorblind discourse. Failing to include a more structural understanding of interrelationship between race, public policy, and inequity to critical race theory scholarship in education is to fall prey to the critics that we are just simply telling another story.

CONCLUSION: RACE STILL MATTERS

Despite some of the shortcomings of CRT scholarship in education we recognize that it continues to proliferate and spread across all areas of education research. Scholars are writing about CRT in educational leadership and administration (Lopez, 2003; Parker & Villalpando, 2007), higher education (Hiraldo, 2010; Iverson, 2007), student affairs (Patton, McEwen, Rendon, & Howard-Hamilton, 2007), teaching and learning (Blair, 2009), and special education (Annamma, Connor, & Ferri, 2013) with varying degrees of fidelity to the principles and tenets we outlined in this chapter. We acknowledge that we do not stand as arbiters of what counts as high-quality critical race theory scholarship. Rather, we caution that in the midst of this proliferation liminal perspectives like CRT are always subject to closer scrutiny and critique. Thus we urge our fellow CRT scholars to be scrupulous in their work not only as a way to advance their own scholarship but as a way to protect the integrity of the legacy that scholars like Derrick Bell, Kimberlé Crenshaw, Richard Delgado, Cheryl Harris, Charles Lawrence, Mari Matsuda, Patricia Williams, and many others have sacrificed to develop and preserve.

For us, a more interesting development is the extension of CRT beyond the Black–White binary to include what is now known as LatCrit (Aoki & Johnson, 2008; Trucios-Haynes, 2001; Solorzano & Yosso, 2001) and Tribal Crit (Brayboy, 2005; Writer, 2008) and the internationalization of the work to include scholars in the United Kingdom (Gillborn, 2013; Rollock, Gllborn, Vincent, & Ball, 2014). For a while, critics of CRT argued that the scholarship was too focused on the United States and its ongoing racial problems. However, with the development of work in the United Kingdom we are seeing a more global embrace of CRT and scholarly analyses that make it applicable to contexts beyond the United States.

We argue that despite political "advances" such as a Black man and his family serving as the nation's "first family," the appointment of the first Black Attorney General (who, incidentally, received a contempt of Congress citation), and a team of Black, Latina/o, and Asian American cabinet officers, judges, diplomats, and various other high-level appointments, the nation remains one in which race still matters. Few critics of the Obama Administration reflect on the dire economic state that Barack Obama inherited. The economy was in free fall. Unemployment was at record high levels. There were massive housing foreclosures and job layoffs. The fact that Obama "stopped the bleeding" and pushed through an historic health reform matters little to his critics. To be fair, his critics line up on both sides of the political spectrum. For the right, he has overstepped his role and presided over a "lawless" administration. For those on the left, he has failed to be forceful enough and abandoned the principles of liberalism. Both sides would argue that race is inconsequential in their critique. As critical race theorists, we analyze this era through the lens of CRT.

Unlike other scholars who suggest the ability of Obama to win two national elections reflects both the changing national demographics and the triumph of colorblindness/postracial ideology, we argue that the power relations that are organized around whiteness and white supremacy make it possible to score symbolic wins while continuing to lose in areas of economic security, health, education, governing, and every other quality of life indicator.

The qualitative tools of CRT allow us to construct counter-narratives that underscore the ways that race continues to matter and in true CRT fashion we conclude with a counter-story:

The Attorney General of the United States, Eric Holder, sits upright before a Senate committee that has issued him a contempt of Congress citation.

His interrogators see his straight countenance as a form of defiance and disrespect. He is clearly an "uppity nigger!" "I know this citation means nothing to you, Mr. Holder . . . " and before he can complete his sentence Attorney General Holder interrupts with, "That's where you are wrong, Congressman. I take this citation very seriously, because not only am I sworn to uphold the law, I love the law. More importantly, I love justice. I love justice so much that when the law is unjust I work hard to overturn it in favor of justice. See, you and your colleagues think you know me. You know the biography that says I was born and raised in the Bronx and was educated at Columbia University both as an undergraduate and a law student. You may even know that I participated in a peaceful student demonstration to get the university to rename a lounge in honor of Malcolm X. You know that I have worked for the Justice Department and sat on the District of Columbia Federal bench. But, what you probably don't know or at least you don't understand is that I married into a family that had civil rights credentials greater than my own. I married the sister of Vivian Malone! Do you know who Vivian Malone was?" The stunned Congressman stuttered, "Well . . . no, but what does that have to do with this hearing?" Attorney General Holder does not miss a beat and continues, "My late sister-in-law was one of two young Black students who challenged the unjust segregation customs that kept her and her fellow student, James Hood, from entering the University of Alabama. The two of them confronted then-Governor George Wallace. So when I made that speech where I said we were a nation of 'cowards' when it comes to race, I was speaking from a place of personal experience. It's been more than 50 years since Vivian and James confronted that 'duly elected' segregationist. He had the law on his side but they had justice."

The Congressmen sat in stunned silence. What was he talking about? What did his dead sister-in-law have to do with the fact that we needed to both punish and embarrass this guy and by association embarrass Obama? The Attorney General understood their puzzlement but he pressed on. "The point of invoking my late sister-in-law is to help you understand that I am not the least bit intimidated by your consternation. I tell you this so you can understand my determination and resolve. For me, justice trumps all! And now, I sit here and you actually think you have ME in the hot seat while in truth I have YOU on the horns of a dilemma. You DO know what a dilemma is, right?" At that remark the entire committee raised its collective eyebrows— all except the one African American Congressman on the committee who struggled to stifle a chuckle. "You see," continued the Attorney General, "a problem, no matter how messy does have a solution. A dilemma on the other hand is something that presents you with two or more options, neither of which is fully satisfactory." "Well, what dilemma do you suppose you have us on the horns of, Mr. Holder?" the Congressman asked smugly.

At that question Eric Holder sat back in his chair and appeared the most relaxed he'd been since he entered the chamber. "Congressman, in the next week I will announce my resignation as Attorney General. I am sure it is not secret to you that I have wanted to step down. You probably see this resignation as an answer to a prayer. But, I will promise the President that I will not leave UNTIL my replacement is in place. So, your dilemma is do you hate me so much that you will quickly support the President's nominee or do you hate the President so much that you don't intend to let him have a smooth confirmation over in the Senate? Meanwhile, while you're trying to figure out what to do I will run the Justice Department exactly the way I want to. I will be sending even more officials down to Ferguson, Missouri, to uncover the blatant racism that resulted in Mike Brown, Jr.'s death. I will be investigating Eric Garner's choking death in New York. I will be looking into Oscar Grant's shooting by transit cops in Oakland. Indeed, I will be turning police departments upside down where there are any incidents of police shootings against Black people. I'll be fighting for justice in the ways I've always wanted to and you can't do a thing about it. You can't fire me, because I'm about to announce to the world that I QUIT!" With that the Attorney General got up from his chair and strode out of the chamber. The Congressman, forgetting where he was and that his mic was live, muttered, "Now that IS one uppity nigga!" On the other side of the chamber doors, Attorney General Holder pulled out his cell phone and speed-dialed a familiar number. "Barack, things went exactly as we planned. I always understood that I had to take the hits because they would never cop to their racism. Anyway . . . justice wins!" "Thanks, Bro . . . thanks," came the voice on the other end of the line.

We pose this chronicle as an exemplar of how counter-story telling can work in CRT. The "facts" of the chronicle are true. The construction of the story is fanciful. They reflect the analysis of the "facts" that a CRT scholar would apply. We do recognize that we have been liberal in telling a story that did not and would not happen. We have used the story as an interpretive strategy for understanding the machinations of a governing body that cannot admit to its racism. When we do qualitative research we both document and interpret social phenomenon. We attempt to make sense of "facts" but we rarely fill in the spaces of silence and invisibility. In positivist paradigms we "pretend" that silenced voices imply that there are no other voices and invisible actors mean those actors do not exist. Both assumptions are inaccurate and dangerous.

CRT scholars take observations (of classrooms, of interactions, of communities, etc.) and close readings (of journals, of letters, of official documents, etc.) and provide muted and missing voices that ask questions and propose alternative explanations. What does suspension mean to students who were suspended? How does being an immigrant affect an individual's ability to participate in public life? What narratives do we construct to include and exclude—to construct social cohesion or sow seeds of discord? The use of a CRT lens is not meant to twist or distort reality. Rather, CRT is meant to bring an alternative perspective to racialized subjects so that voices on the social margins are amplified.

Critical race theory is not about special pleadings or race-baiting as some may argue. It is also not the "hot," "new," or "sexy" paradigm that makes a scholar seem more cutting edge or avant-garde. It is about the serious business of permanent and systemic racism that ultimately diminishes the democratic project. It is about dispelling notions of colorblindness and postracial imaginings so that we can better understand and remedy the disparities that are prevalent in our society. It is one of the tools we can use to assert that race still matters.

NOTES

1. This chapter is dedicated to the scholarship and memory of Derrick Bell (1930–2011), a founding father of the critical race theory movement.

2. We will use the terms *African American* and *Black* interchangeably throughout the chapter.

3. See, for example, http://www.alternet.org/story/142747/10_horrifying_racist _attacks_on_obama?page=0%2C1 (retrieved electronically on 10/12/14) and http:// www.bet.com/news/politics/photos/2012/12/the-year-in-racist-attacks-against -obama.html#!120512-politics-the-year-in-racist-attacks-against-obama-dont-re -nig-stickers (retrieved electronically on 10/12/14)

4. According to Bonastia (2006), "the term institutional home refers to the government agency, agencies, or agency division(s) through which relevant policies are interpreted, articulated, and carried out. According to this approach, the structure and mission of an agency have important direct effects on policy outcomes. In addition, the institutional home of a policy has a marked influence on how prior policies and external factors that may influence policy development—such as interest and advocacy groups, other branches of government, and the media—play out in specific cases" (p. 7).

REFERENCES

Acuna, R. (1972). *Occupied America: The Chicano struggle toward liberation.* New York: Canfield Press.

Alarcon, N. (1990). Chicana feminism: In the tracks of "the" native woman. *Cultural Studies, 4,* 248–256.

Annamma, S. A., Connor, D., & Ferri, B. (2013). Dis/ability critical race studies (dis/ crit): Theorizing at the intersections of race and dis/ability. *Race, Ethnicity, & Education, 16,* 1–31.

Anzaldúa, G. (2012). *Borderlands/La Frontera: The new mestiza* (4th ed.). San Francisco: Aunt Lute.

Aoki, K., & Johnson, K. (2008). An assessment of LatCrit theory ten years after. *Indiana Law Journal, 83,* UC Davis Legal Studies Research Paper Series, no 15.

Bai, M. (2008, August 20). Is Obama the end of Black politics? *New York Times Magazine*. Retrieved June 18, 2014, from http://www.nytimes.com/2008/08/10/magazine/10politics-t.html?pagewanted=all

Bell, D. (1980). *Brown v. Board of Education* and the interest-convergence dilemma. *Harvard Law Review, 93*(3), 518–533.

Bell, D. (1989). *And we are not saved: The elusive quest for racial justice.* New York: Basic Books.

Bell, D. (1992). *Faces at the bottom of the well: The permanence of racism.* New York: Basic Books.

Bell, D. (1995). Who's afraid of critical race theory? *University of Illinois Law Review, 1995*(4), 893–910.

Bell, D. (2004). *Silent covenants:* Brown v. Board of Education *and the unfulfilled hopes for racial reform.* New York: Oxford University Press.

Benjamin, L. T. (2006). *Brief history of modern psychology.* New York: Wiley Blackwell.

Blair, C. (2009). *Critical race theory: A framework to study the early reading intervention strategies of primary grade teachers working with African American male students.* Unpublished dissertation, Miami University, Oxford, OH.

Blanchett, W. J. (2006). Disproportionate representation of African Americans in special education: Acknowledging the role of White privilege and racism. *Educational Researcher, 35*(6), 24–28.

Bonastia, C. (2006). *Knocking on the door: The federal government.* Princeton, NJ: Princeton University Press.

Bradbury, R. (2012). *The Martian Chronicles* (reprint ed.). New York: Simon & Schuster.

Brayboy, B. M. J. (2005). Toward a tribal critical race theory in education. *Urban Review, 37*, 425–446.

Brown, A. L., & Donnor, J. K. (2011). Toward a new narrative on Black males, education, and public policy. *Race, Ethnicity and Education, 14*(1), 17–32.

Brown, M. K., Carnoy, M., Currie, E., Duster, T., Oppenheimer, D. B., Shultz, M. M., & Wellman, D. (2003). *Whitewashing race: The myth of color-blind society.* Berkeley, CA. University of California Press.

Center for American Progress. (2014). *Looking at the best teachers and who they are.* Retrieved from http://www.americanprogress.org/wpcontent/uploads/2014/04/TeacherDistributionBrief1.pdf

Chapman, T. K. (2005). Peddling backwards: Reflections of *Plessy* and *Brown* in the Rockford public schools *de jure* desegregation efforts. *Race, Ethnicity and Education, 8*(1), 29–44.

Crenshaw, K., Gotanda, N., Peller, G., & Thomas, K. (1995). Introduction. In K. Crenshaw, N. Gotanda, G. Peller, & K. Thomas (Eds.), *Critical race theory: The key writings that formed the movement* (pp. xiii–xxxii). New York: The New Press.

Crenshaw, K. W. (1997). Color-blind dreams and racial nightmares: Reconfiguring racism in the post–Civil Rights era. In T. Morrison & C. B. Lacour (Eds.), *Birth of a nation'hood: Gaze, script, and spectacle in the O.J. Simpson case* (pp. 97–168). New York: Pantheon.

Crenshaw, K. W. (2011). Twenty years of critical race theory: Looking back to move forward. *Connecticut Law Review, 43*(5), 1253–1352.

Davis, P. C. (1989). Law as microaggression. *Yale Law Journal, 98*(8), 1559–1577.

DeCuir, J., & Dixson, A. D. (2004). "So when it comes out, they aren't that surprised that it is there": Using critical race theory as a tool of analysis of race and racism in education. *Educational Researcher, 33*(5), 26–31.

Delgado, R. (1992). Rodrigo's chronicle. *Yale Law Review, 101*, 1357–1383.

Denzin, N. K., & Lincoln, Y. S. (Eds.). (2005). *The SAGE handbook of qualitative research* (3rd ed.). Thousand Oaks, CA: Sage.

Dixson, A. D., & Rousseau, C. K. (2005). And we are still not saved: Critical race theory in education ten years later. *Race Ethnicity and Education, 8*(1), 7–27.

Donnor, J. K. (2005). Towards an interest-convergence in the education of African American football student athletes in major college sports. *Race, Ethnicity and Education, 8*(1), 45–68.

Donnor, J. K. (2011a). Moving beyond *Brown*: Race in education after *Parents v. Seattle School District No. 1*. *Teachers College Record, 113*(4), 735–754.

Donnor, J. K. (2011b). Whose compelling interest? The ending of desegregation and the affirming of racial inequality in education. *Education and Urban Society, 20*(1), 1–18.

Du Bois, W. E. B. (1998). *The Philadelphia Negro: A social study*. Philadelphia: University of Pennsylvania Press. (Original work published 1899)

Espiritu, Y. L. (1992). *Asian American panethnicity: Bridging institutions and identities*. Philadelphia: Temple University Press.

Fanon, F. (1963). *The wretched of the Earth*. New York: Grove.

Fanon, F. (1967). *Black skin, White masks*. New York: Grove Press.

Feagin, J. R. (2013). *The white racial frame: Centuries of racial framing and counter-framing*. New York: Routledge.

Foner, E. (1999). *The story of American freedom*. New York: W.W. Norton & Company.

Freeman, A. D. (1978). Legitimizing racial discrimination through antidiscrimination law: A critical review of Supreme Court doctrine. *Minnesota Law Review, 62*, 1049–1119.

Freeman, A. D. (1988). Racism, rights, and the quest for equality of opportunity. *Harvard Civil Rights–Civil Liberties Law Review, 23*(2), 295–392.

Friedman, T. (2007). *The world is Flat, 3.0: A brief history of the twenty-first century* (3rd ed.). New York: Picador Press.

Gillborn, D. (2013). Interest-convergence and the colour of cutbacks: Race, recession and the undeclared war on Black children. *Discourse: Studies in the cultural politics of education, 34*(4), 477–491.

Guinier, L., & Torres, G. (2003). *The miner's canary: Enlisting race, resisting power, transforming democracy*. Cambridge, MA: Harvard University Press.

Harris, C. I. (2001). Equal treatment and the reproduction of inequality. *Fordham Law Review, 69*(3), 1753–1783.

Harris, C. I. (2002). Critical race studies: An introduction. *UCLA Law Review, 49*(5), 1215–1239.

Hernnstein, R., & Murray, C. (1994). *The bell curve: Intelligence and class structure in American life*. New York: The Free Press.

Hiraldo, P. (2010). The role of critical race theory in higher education. *The Vermont Connection, 31*, 53–59.

Howard, T. C. (2008). Who really cares? The disenfranchisement of African American males in preK-12 schools: A critical race theory perspective. *Teachers College Record, 110*(5), 954–985.

Hsu, H. (2009, January 1). The end of White America? *The Atlantic.* Retrieved electronically from http://www.theatlantic.com/magazine/archive/2009/01/the-end-of-white-america/307208/ on 06/18/14

Ikemoto, L. (1995). Traces of the master narrative in the story of African American/Korean American conflict: How we constructed "Los Angeles." In R. Delgado (Ed.), *Critical race theory: The cutting edge* (pp. 305–315). Philadelphia: Temple University Press.

Iverson, S. V. (2007). Camouflaging power and privilege: A critical race analysis of university policies. *Educational Administration Quarterly, 43,* 586–611.

Jencks, C., & Phillips. M. (1998). *The black-white test score gap.* New York: The Brookings Institution.

Ladson-Billings, G. (1998). Just what is critical race theory and what's it doing in a *nice* field like education? *International Journal for Qualitative Studies in Education* 11(1), 7–24.

Ladson-Billings, G. (2000). Racialized discourses and ethnic epistemologies. In N. Denzin & Y. Lincoln (Eds.), *Handbook of qualitative research* (2nd ed., pp. 257–277). Thousand Oaks, CA: Sage.

Ladson-Billings, G. (2013). Critical race theory—What it is not! In M. Lynn & A. D. Dixson (Eds.), *Handbook of critical race theory in education* (pp. 34–47). New York: Routledge.

Ladson-Billings, G. J., & Donnor, J. K. (2005). Waiting for the call: The moral activist role of critical race theory scholarship. In N. K. Denzin & Y. S. Lincoln (Eds.), *Handbook of qualitative research* (3rd ed., pp. 279–301). Thousand Oaks, CA: Sage.

Ladson-Billings, G., & Tate, W. F. (1995). Toward a critical race theory of education. *Teachers College Record, 97*(1) 47–68.

Lakoff, G. (2004). *Don't think of an elephant! Know your values and frame the debate.* White River Junction, VT: Chelsea Green.

Lawrence, C. (1976). When the defendants are foxes too: The need for intervention by minorities in reverse discrimination suits like *Bakke. The Guild Practitioner, 34,* 1–20. Retrieved December 15, 2005, from the HeinOnline database.

Lind, M. (1996). *The next American nation.* New York: Free Press Paperbacks.

Lopez, G. R. (2003). The (racially neutral) politics of education: A critical race theory perspective. *Educational Administration Quarterly, 39,* 68–94.

Lopez, I. H. (1996). *White by law: The legal construction of race.* New York: New York University Press.

Lopez, I. H. (2014). *Dog whistle politics: How coded racial appeals have reinvented racism and wrecked the middle class.* New York: Oxford University Press.

Lowe, L. (1996). *Immigrant acts: On Asian-American cultural politics.* Durham, NC: Duke University Press.

Lynn, M. (1999). Toward a critical race pedagogy: A research note. *Urban Education, 33*(5), 606–626.

Lynn, M. (2002). Critical race theory and the perspectives of Black men teachers in the Los Angeles public schools. *Equity & Excellence in Education, 35*(2), 119–130.

Matsuda, M. J., Lawrence, C. R., Delgado, R., & Crenshaw, K. W. (1993). *Words that wound: Critical race theory, assaultive speech, and the first Amendment.* Boulder, CO: Westview Press.

McCristal Culp, J. (1994). Colorblind remedies and the intersectionality of oppression: Policy arguments masquerading as moral claims. *New York University Law Review, 69,* 162–196.

McDonnell, L. M., & Elmore, R. F. (1987). Getting the job done: Alternative policy instruments. *Educational Evaluation and Policy Analysis, 9*(2), 133–152.

Minh-ha, T. (1989). *Woman, narrative, other: Writing postcoloniality and feminism.* Bloomington: Indiana University Press.

O'Connor, A. (2001). *Poverty knowledge: Social science, social policy, and the poor in twentieth-century U.S. history.* Princeton, NJ: Princeton University Press.

Omi, M., & Winant, H. (1994). *Racial formation in the United States* (2nd ed.). New York: Routledge.

Ong, A. (1999). *Flexible citizenship: The cultural logic of transnationality.* Durham, NC: Duke University Press.

Parker, L., & Lynn, M. (2002). What's race got to do with it? Critical race theory's conflicts with and connections to qualitative research methodology and epistemology. *Qualitative Inquiry, 8*(1), 7–22.

Parker, L., & Stovall, D. O. (2004). Actions following words: Critical race theory connects to critical pedagogy. *Educational Philosophy and Theory, 36*(2), 167–182.

Parker, L., & Villalpando, O. (2007). A race(cialized) perspective on educational leadership: Critical race theory in educational leadership. *Educational Administration Quarterly, 43,* 519–524.

Patton, L., McEwen, M., Rendon, L., & Howard-Hamilton, M. (2007). Critical race perspectives on theory in student affairs. *New Directions for Student Services, 120,* 39–53.

Rollock, N., Gillborn, D., Vincent, C., & Ball, S. (2014). *The colour of class: The education struggles of the Black middle class.* London: Routledge.

Rousseau-Anderson, C. (2011). What do you see? The Supreme Court decision in PICS and the resegregation of two Southern school districts. *Teachers College Record, 113*(4), 755–786.

Schneider, A., & Ingram, H. (1993). Social construction of target populations: Implications for politics and policy. *American Political Science Review, 87*(2), 334–347.

Smedley, A. (1993). *Race in North America: Origin and evolution of a worldview.* Boulder, CO: Westview Press.

Solorzano, D., & Yosso, T. (2001). Critical race and LatCrit theory and method: Counter-storytelling. *International Journal of Qualitative Studies in Education, 14,* 471–495.

Tate, W. F. (1997). Critical race theory and education: History, theory, and implications. *Review of Research in Education, 22,* 195–247.

Tolson, J. (2008, February 15). Does Obama's winning streak prove that race doesn't matter? *U.S. News & World Report.* Retrieved electronically from http://www.usnews.com/news/campaign-2008/articles/2008/02/15/-does-obamas-winning-streak-prove-that-race-doesnt-matter on 06/18/14.

Trucios-Haynes, E. (2001). Why "race matters:" LatCrit theory and Latina/o racial identity. *La Raza Law Journal, 12*, 1–42.

U.S. vs. Bhagat Singh Thind, 261 U.S. 204 (1923).

U.S. Department of Justice, Office of Justice Programs. (2007). *Black victims of violent crime*. Retrieved from http://www.bjs.gov/content/pub/pdf/bvvc.pdf

Warrior, R. A. (1994). *Tribal secrets: Recovering American Indian intellectual traditions*. Minneapolis: University of Minnesota Press.

Wellman, D. (2002). *Portraits of White racism* (2nd ed.). New York: Cambridge University Press.

West, C. (1995). Foreword. In K. Crenshaw, N. Gotanda, G. Peller, & K. Thomas (Eds.), *Critical race theory: The key writings that formed the movement* (pp. xi–xii). New York: The New Press.

Winant. H. (2000). Race and race theory. *Annual Review of Sociology, 26*, 169–185.

Winant, H. (2001). *The world is a ghetto: Race and democracy since World War II*. New York: Basic Books.

Winant, H. (2007). The dark side of the force: One hundred years of the sociology of race. In C. Calhoun (Ed.), *Sociology in America: A History* (pp. 535–571). Chicago: University of Chicago Press.

Writer, J. H. (2008). Unmasking, exposing and confronting: Critical race theory, tribal crit, and multicultural education. *International Journal of Multicultural Education, 10*(2), 1–15.

Wynter, S. (1992). *Do not call us "negros": How "multicultural" textbooks perpetuate racism*. San Francisco: Aspire Books.

Wynter, S. (1995). 1492: A new world view, in Hyatt & Nettleford, *Race, discourse, and the origins of the Americas* (pp. 5–57). Washington, DC: Smithsonian Institution Press.

The Social Funding of Race
The Role of Schooling

In 1948 U.S. Senator Strom Thurmond from South Carolina ran for the office of president of the United States as a third-party, Dixiecrat candidate. The focus of Senator Thurmond's campaign was to uphold racial segregation and to prohibit black people from participating fully in the society. "All the bayonets in the Army cannot force the Negro into our homes, our schools, our churches, and our places of recreation," Thurmond reportedly said in one of his campaign speeches (Bass & Thompson, 2003). However, at the same time that Thurmond was defending white segregationists' practices, he was financially supporting and maintaining a relationship with a daughter who was the product of his secret liaison with a black woman who had worked for his family. His actions force me to ask, "What is this race thing that could so drive the ideology of a society and at the same moment slip from the consciousness of individual actions?"

During most of my scholarly life, I have been preoccupied with the concept of race. It turns out that I am not alone in that preoccupation. Winant (2000) identifies it as a central and controversial theme of the discipline of sociology. Volumes of scholarly literature exist to make sense of race as a scientific and/or social construct. Although scientists generally agree that no biological basis for race exists and social scientists concede that it is a social construct, it continues to be one of our most baffling notions. This paper probably will do little to clarify race as a concept. Instead, I want to use this analysis as a way to think through how we "fund" race as a society and how that funding contributes to continued inequitable, unjust, and undemocratic practices in schooling and education in the United States. To build my argument, I will talk briefly about race as a concept and move to a discussion of the notion of "funding" and how funding race creates inequitable schooling. I conclude the analysis with a discussion of the work teacher educators must do to "defund" the concept if our teachers are going to be better prepared to create more equitable and just classrooms.

I CAN'T TELL YOU WHAT IT IS,
BUT I KNOW IT WHEN I SEE IT

In 1806 a jurist by the name of St. George Tucker imposed a racial determination test on three generations of women—a daughter, grandmother, and mother. These women could not prove that they were descendants from a free maternal ancestor, which at that time was the determiner as to who was white, and their owner, a Mr. Hudgins, could not prove that they were descendants from a female enslaved African (Lopez, 1995). To determine whether the Wrights were black (and thus slaves) or Indian (and allegedly free), Judge Tucker of the Virginia courts insisted that in addition to skin color, there were two markers of blackness that endured over many generations. Those markers were the flatness of the nose and the coarse texture of the hair:

> Nature has stampt upon the African and his descendants two characteristic marks, besides the difference of complexion, which often remain visible long after the characteristic distinction of colour either disappears or becomes doubtful; a flat nose and woolly head of hair. The latter of these disappears the last of all; and so strong an ingredient in the African constitution is this latter characteristic, that it predominates uniformly where the party is in equal degree descended from parents of different complexions, whether white or Indians. (*Hudgins v. Wright*, 11 Va 134, Sup. Ct. App. 1806, cited in Lopez, 1995, p. 191)

By this standard, Judge Tucker looked at the long, straight hair of Hannah Wright and judged the women not to be of African descent and, therefore, free. The full ruling includes an operationalized definition of race declaring that one single African descendant, a "flat nose," or a "woolly head of hair" made one black. Almost 200 years later this perception remains.

The concept of race, although prefigured in early history by polar notions of civilization and barbarity (Snowden, 1983) or citizen and slave (Hannaford, 1996), is a modern one, according to Winant (2000). Along with his colleague Omi, Winant points out that there is no biological basis for race, and even the socio-historical categories we use to differentiate among groups are both imprecise and arbitrary (Omi & Winant, 2014). Winant (2000) asserts that the concept of race as we now know it began to form "with the rise of a world political economy" (p. 172). As nation-states began to participate in a worldwide economy—seaborne empires, conquest of the Americas, and the rise of the Atlantic slave trade—the development of race became a practical project to create an "Other" whose threat and necessity could be integrated and deployed into every aspect of society. Such an "Other" justified not only the conquering of militarily defenseless nations, but its existence was also mapped onto an entire set of symbol systems and rationalities that made labeling a person as "other" seem natural and normal.

Thus, while European rulers saw the "Other" standing in the way of empire building, aristocrats and planters in the Americas saw a cheap source of labor, and the church saw the "Other" as both potential adherents and symbols of depravity and evil. Wynter (1990) points out that there exist prescriptive rules and canons for regulating thought and action in every society. After the 15th century, the prescriptive rules of Western societies began to embrace a notion of race that placed "European-ness" (whatever that might be) in a superior social space. I offer this truncated description of the concept to remind us that although we act as if biologically based human characteristics define race, race's meaning only began to take shape at the end of the Middle Ages. If this notion of race is not biologically based and its social construction is arbitrary and unstable, how is it that we in the United States use it so regularly and effortlessly?

When I was a graduate student, one of my professors was recruiting students to serve as coders for a project that looked at teacher interactions with Latino students. The job of the coder was simply to tabulate the number of times classroom teachers called upon Latino students over the course of a specified class period. Among the coders the professor hired were a number of international students. Quickly it became clear that the international students had difficulty determining who was Mexican American and who was "white." The professor reassigned the international students to another aspect of the project and replaced them with U.S.-born students who had no difficulty making the distinctions. The fairest Mexican American with the lightest eyes and hair is still recognized as other than white to students of the United States. How this happens and the implications for education are the focus of this portion of the paper.

I would be remiss if I did not acknowledge the work of a number of scholars who have attempted to creatively rearticulate race. In their volume, Guinier and Torres (2002) offer the concept of political race that represents a way of recruiting and mobilizing it to fight against oppressive, anti-democratic structures. Rather than rely on spurious notions of biology and genetic heritability, their work recognizes the political power that might be harnessed by oppressed people throughout the society. Rather than consider the biology of race, Guinier and Torres ask questions about how the concept can be deployed strategically in order to garner social benefits. It is a new way of thinking about something that most of the society believes it already understands. However, their work is indicative of cutting-edge thinking that has not yet gained traction in our current racial miasma. In this paper I work hard to make sense of what we already have while contemplating what might be possible.

UNDERSTANDING SOCIAL FUNDING

In her outstanding work on literacy, Brandt (1998) argues for a concept of "sponsors of literacy" in which "sponsors . . . are any agents, local or distant, concrete or abstract, who enable, support, teach, model, as well as recruit, regulate, suppress, or withhold literacy—and gain advantage by it in some way" (p. 166). Brandt (1998) further argues, "Sponsors are delivery systems for the economies of literacy, the means by which these forces present themselves to—and through—individual learners" (p. 167).

As elegant as Brandt's argument is, it is not a seamless fit for the argument I am attempting to make concerning race. For that I turn to the work of Philip Fisher (2004) who, in his description of how we as a society lack a syntax for aesthetic appreciation, suggests that we do have such a syntax of literate appreciation because literacy is "fully funded." Fisher (2004) uses this phrase—fully funded—not to describe the financial commitment the society makes to literacy but rather to describe the *total* investment of the society in literacy. His conceptualization refers to the way, as a society, we embed literacy and literate activity in every aspect of our culture such that children come to school (and preschool) with a fully formed notion of the book as a sacred artifact, that writing conveys meaning, and that words are powerful conveyers of thought.

School becomes a site where literacy is further funded through explicit and implicit instruction as well as the public recognition of its value. Students learn that it is important to become "good readers" because praise and admiration flow to good readers. They also learn that reading and literate activities integrally link with other learning activities. But it is not merely the formal curriculum that aids in the continual funding of literacy. Literacy is funded by the myriad informal activities that surround school. A student who is absent or tardy from a school activity often is admonished to "bring a note." A student who misbehaves may receive a "written referral" to the disciplinary office. "Passing notes" or texting during class may be seen as a serious rule infraction. Brandt (1998) helps us to see the "trucks and trains," or traffic, between sponsorship and literacy—how the relationships between the macro social spaces such as the economy move back and forth to the micro social spaces such as individuals as literacy learners. Fisher's (2004) notion represents a more diffuse yet comprehensive "loading" of value onto the concept even when one may believe that she is participating in a counter-social activity (e.g., the note or text in class, the holdup note in the bank, the ransom letter in a kidnapping). In the counter-social activities, we see that the concept of literacy is so fully funded that it is impossible to withdraw it from use even when it does not work to a mainstream advantage.

My argument is that, like literacy, race is also fully funded by the society. Various psychologists (Cross, 1978; Helms, 1990; Parham, 1989) originally argued that children learn to identify race through various developmental stages, and others later argued that children acquire the skill as a part of a more holistic, ecological process (Johnson, 1992; Miller, 1992; Ramirez, 1998; Trimble, 2000; Wijeyesinghe, 2001). Both groups, however, do not acknowledge the emphasis culture places or attention it "invests" in prioritizing racial identification. I want to move away from the development of the individual to suggest that the extant "regime of truth" (Foucault, 1972) determines what is possible to think and imagine about race because the present cultural model relies so heavily on race as a sense-making category.

In the United States, even before individuals start to think about their racial identification, culture sends both explicit and implicit messages about race. Novelist Toni Morrison (1989) states that "race has become metaphorical—a way of referring to and disguising forces, events, classes, and expressions of social decay and economic division far more threatening to the body politic than biological race ever was" (p. 63). So even as our natural scientists refute its biological existence and social scientists discount its material reality, we continue to fully fund it in our economic, political, social, and cultural realms.

For example, many years ago when my daughter was a preschool student, I served as a participating parent at her school. One of the children in her class was a 4-year-old whose parents had recently emigrated from Northern Italy. On one particular day, "Mario"[1] and I were working on a puzzle together. He happened to notice that my daughter and the one other African American child in the school were playing together at a table across the room. "Which one is yours?" he asked me. Before I could respond to what I saw as his honest query, there was a collective gasp uttered by both white teachers. From my vantage point Mario was asking a logical question based on the color perception that all children have. Just as we would expect him to recognize the distinction between a blue ball and a yellow ball (and have a preference if he so chose), he should be able to recognize that it was likely that one (or both) of the brown-complexioned children was associated with me. But, the not-so-subtle response of both authority figures signaled to him that there was either something wrong with him or something wrong with his question.

Later, in another interaction with Mario, I commented on a lovely handmade sweater he was wearing. He told me proudly that his grandmother in Italy made the sweater and, in fact, made sweaters for everyone in his family—his mom, dad, and sister. "Oh," I exclaimed in jest, "I'd better go live at your house so I can get one of those nice sweaters." "You can't live at my house," laughed Mario. "There are no brown people living in my house!" At that response, the same teachers this time not so subtly exclaimed in unison, "Mario! That's not nice!" If Mario was not certain about the problem in the question he asked in the first incident, he was now unmistakably sure that he had transgressed in the second interaction and his transgression was around race.[2] Mario's lack of U.S. concepts of race demonstrates how, unlike Brandt's (1998) notion of sponsorship, the funding of race can actually occur when the ostensible action is to work against racial categorization or identification. Mario, because he lived in a household with parents who came from a culture that did not fund race in the same way as we do in the United States, was unaware of the racial coding in the same way his classmates were. He did not know that although race would be fully funded for him in this society, he had to disguise or camouflage that knowledge. But, despite the delay in the development of this funding, by the time Mario entered the middle grades in school, race would have been fully funded for him.[3] By that time, making a social faux pas about race would have become a thing of the past because he would have all of the racial coding in place to either continue this social practice or consciously begin to challenge it.

A third example regarding young children also supports this argument. My daughter's best friend in kindergarten immigrated to the United States from China shortly before she began school. Her family were our neighbors, and the two girls played together every day at school, after school, and on the weekends. When we moved to the Midwest from the Bay Area at the end of the school year, they were visibly upset. In addition to the close relationship our daughters had developed, we were instrumental in helping the Chinese parents negotiate the business of living in the United States. We helped them with major purchases such as an automobile and local, state, and federal bureaucracies (e.g., Department of Motor Vehicles, utility companies, and tax authorities). After some tearful goodbyes, we were certain that we would only see them during return visits to the Bay Area. However, within a year, the father landed a faculty position at an institution in the Midwest. As a result, during the Christmas holiday vacation the year they moved to the area, we were able to get the girls together for a brief ski trip and a sleepover at our home.

As the two girls were playing, I overheard my child's playmate Zhang[4] tell my daughter that she was one of two "yellow" kids in her class in her new school. My daughter quickly reminded her, "When we were in Palo Alto you said you were white." Zhang responded in an almost embarrassed way, "Yeah, I didn't know." I could only wonder what had happened to this child in the past few years to let her know that she was ineligible for membership in this category called "white." Somewhere between kindergarten and second grade the society had begun funding race for her. Even though her best friend and her best friend's parents who were fundamental to her family's survival in their initial year in the United States had demonstrated that black people could prove to be important culture brokers with more than enough cultural capital (Bourdieu & Passeron, 1977) to assist them, she was beginning to understand that there was something special about being white. Zhang was having the concept of race funded for her beyond the confines of her household.

In his book on whiteness and the labor movement, historian Roediger (1991) states, "Even in an all-White town, race was never absent" (p. 3). Roediger goes on to describe the more pervasive and overt racism that was a part of growing up in the civil rights era. At that historical moment no one would refute the notion that we were fully funding race and racism. Today, however, one might likely argue that we are more sensitive and responsive to race and racism, and we want our children to learn to get along with everybody. Generational change in the conceptualization of race is similar to change occurring in the retirement system.

A generation ago people in the United States who were planning for retirement relied on their payroll deductions and the company contributions that comprised their pensions. They knew what they contributed, what the company contributed, and what the formulae were that governed their annuity. The retirement was both funded and public (i.e., individuals knew what to expect from their pensions). Today, with the economic restructuring and the counseling workers receive advising them to diversify their portfolio of retirement savings options (e.g., tax shelters, IRAs, mutual funds, stocks, bonds along with some company-supported savings), people continue to fund their retirements, but the process is much more private (i.e., working class and lower middle class individuals are less aware of the sources and return possibilities of their retirement savings). In the case of race, historically it has been appropriate to speak, talk, write, and act openly about race in the United States. By the 1960s, this discourse started to move into more private sectors, but it still existed. Today, we are fully funding race in myriad ways that make it difficult for teachers and other educators to defund or bankrupt the concept.

More than a decade ago, when I began thinking about this concept of the social funding of race, I had just watched then-U.S. National Security Advisor Condoleezza Rice testify before the president's 9/11 commission. Whether or not one endorsed Rice and the administration's policies, it was clear that she performed well—she was well prepared, she was cordial and noncombative, she answered the questions on her own terms, and she was careful to not go "off message." Although presented with several openings to trash the previous witness, terror specialist Richard Clarke, who called her leadership and judgment into question, Dr. Rice never took the bait. Instead, she insisted on putting his advice in a larger context and tried to construct an evidence-based trail to support her testimony. In the back of my mind I wondered whether the social funding of race would arise. At the end of her testimony, the television station I was watching started with its commentaries and the very first comment from the broadcaster was, "National Security Adviser Condoleezza Rice was articulate." What a strange first statement. She is the National Security Advisor of the United States of America! The word *articulate* means, "able to speak; expressing oneself readily, clearly, or effectively" (Mish, 2014). Shouldn't articulateness be a minimum requirement for such a position (Alim & Smitherman, 2012)? For those who consider this observation hypersensitive or polemic, I point it out not to make the case but to illustrate it. Such a pronouncement by a seasoned national journalist illustrates how fully funded our notion of race is. The sotto voce message of "Dr. Rice is articulate" is "we didn't expect that out of her." I cannot think of any public examples where the adjective "articulate" is used to describe a white person in a position of high regard or power. However, both Colin Powell (in his testimony before the United Nations as a part of the case for the war in Iraq) and Condoleezza Rice were repeatedly referred to as "able to speak" and "expressing themselves readily, clearly, or effectively"—that is, "articulate." It is a descriptor that characterized President Barack Obama throughout his administration as well. This is the pernicious effect of having fully funded race. We are at a moment where there is almost no place in the culture or the language where there is not a racial overlay.

Our tendency is to think about all things racial in dichotomous terms. Things are black or white, right or wrong, good or bad. When the subject is race and racism, we quickly default to the racists versus the nonracists. I am suggesting that because society so completely and consistently funds race it is difficult to see where one (racists) leaves off and the other (nonracists) begins. An analogy that might help my explanation here is an experience I had in Sweden. In a lovely northern city my graduate students and I decided to travel what was called the "Art Trail." People were invited to drive a number of kilometers to see a series of public art pieces. One piece can best be described as a wood-fired heated stone bench. Some sections of the bench were comfortable and the heat was evenly distributed. Other sections were too hot and some sections were cool. What was unique about the bench was the public was both invited to sit on it and encouraged to open the lid at the end of the bench and place another fire log in before leaving. As visitors we benefited from the previous visitors' efforts to keep the bench warm, and we maintained that warmth by throwing another log on the fire.

The way the social funding of race operates reminds me of that bench. It is already "warm" when we enter the society. We are invited to sit upon it and share its benefits, and we are encouraged to add fuel as we move on. We did not construct the bench, but we take responsibility for maintaining it. Some of us sit on a section of the bench that is cold. We are excluded from the benefits. Others sit on a section that is too hot. We are victimized by the very thing that brings others pleasure. Although the analogy may be crude, I think it helps illustrate the way we may unwittingly participate in a process that we believe benefits us without being aware of the way it regularly and systematically disadvantages others.

WHAT FUNDING RACE MEANS IN SCHOOLS

Given that race is fully funded in our society, what does such funding mean in schools and classrooms? Since the late 1920s, schools have been grappling with the issue of bringing unequal status groups of learners together in a classroom as a part of a larger project of social improvement and to improve individual and group achievement. Banks (2004) documents the work of community and school-based groups to incorporate immigrants (particularly European immigrants) and later non-white communities, particularly African Americans, into the mainstream. As important as this inter-group movement was and as benevolent as its founders and activists may have been, it is important to understand that their major purpose was to assimilate the "Other" into what they firmly believed was the superior culture—white, Anglo-Saxon American culture.

In addition, the school has been a site of citizenship and human rights contestation for centuries in U.S. society. Meyer (1977) argued that societies use schools as legitimating institutions that confer theories of knowledge and theories of personnel (i.e., what is worth knowing and who the knowers should be). Early in the history of the United States, schooling was reserved for the social elites—white, male, wealthy children. Over time, more groups and categories of people were deemed eligible for schooling. African Americans were among the last groups able to avail themselves of universal, K–12 public schooling. Historian James Anderson (2002) points out that secondary high school education did not become universally available in the South for African Americans until the 1960s.

At the highest level of U.S. society the inclusion and exclusion of particular groups of students from school (a key access point to social mobility) has been a major site of conflict. The landmark Supreme Court decision, *Brown v. The Topeka Board of Education* (1954), while ostensibly motivated by efforts to defund race to create equal education, was actually driven by foreign relations and the problem of selling democracy to other nations during the Cold War in the midst of apartheid-like school and social arrangements (Dudziak, 1988/1995).

Today, although African American children have access to K–12 public schooling, there are aspects of schooling that fund race in ways that further solidify race and the social responses to it. Although it is difficult to give full attention to the myriad ways in which race is funded in schools, the concept works and is foundational to our understanding of us as Americans. In the rest of this essay, I offer broad categories of aspects of schooling that display the concept of the social funding of race.

Access to Equal Education

More than 60 years have transpired since the Supreme Court of the United States ruled that separate schooling was inherently unequal (*Brown v. Topeka Board of Education*, 1954). Over that 60-year period, we have seen the growth of white resistance, the displacement of black teachers and administrators, and resegregation that compounds race and poverty. It is important to note that for a brief period, southern schools actually were more desegregated than their northern counterparts. This brief period of southern school desegregation was the result of favorable court decisions and somewhat supportive presidential administrations (i.e., Kennedy and Johnson). However, by the time Richard Nixon came into office, he made it clear that the school desegregation decisions had to be reversed. According to Orfield and Eaton (1996), "Following Nixon's election, H. R. Haldeman, Nixon's chief of staff, recorded in his diary the [p]resident's directives to staff to do as little as possible to enforce desegregation" (p. 9). This work to block and reverse school desegregation was a part of what became the Republican Party's "southern strategy." By cultivating an antigovernment discourse (i.e., a modern version of states' rights) and appointing conservative justices to the courts, Nixon created a template that would serve subsequent conservative candidates and office-holders well. Richard Nixon appointed four justices to the Supreme Court, and among his appointments was William H. Rehnquist who had served as a clerk for Justice Jackson during the *Brown v. Board of Education* case. Although he tried to distance himself from this opinion,[5] as a clerk, Rehnquist wrote a memo that stated, "I realize that it is an unpopular and unhumanitarian position, for which I have been excoriated by 'liberal' colleagues, but I think *Plessy v. Ferguson* was right and should be reaffirmed" (Senate Hearing on the Judiciary, 1986).

The ability of the Republican Party to create a "solid South" reflects a social funding of race where the language that is recruited never has to include the word "race" or related vocabulary yet clearly signals that race is the central issue. The terms "school desegregation," "forced busing," "neighborhood schools," "social engineering," "school choice," and "vouchers" have been used to mask the deeper malady that race and racism represent in the society. The race language has been removed, but because race is so well funded in our consciousness, one can talk about it without having to do so explicitly.

What is brilliant about this strategy is that the language and discourse, which can be presented in ways that seem to be sanitized of any racialized meanings, have been employed with families of color to persuade them to support schooling that is against their own self-interests. For example, families of color are encouraged to advocate for neighborhood schools or choice even though their choices are likely to comprise poor schools and substandard alternatives (Fitzpatrick, Gartner, & LaForgia, 2015). Although the words are cleverly disguised not to denote race-based concepts at first, once one is familiar with these types of conversations, it becomes obvious what these words connote.

Today, the 12 largest urban school districts in the United States can be described as "hyper-segregated." School districts such as Detroit, Dallas, Memphis, Baltimore, Houston, Los Angeles, and Chicago have few white students with whom to diversify the student populations. The very notion of an "urban school" or an "inner-city school" conjures up visions of black and brown schoolchildren. For example, in Riverside County, California, in 1998, a school district needed to name a new school, and the debate surrounding the selection of the name illustrates how certain terms tend to connote "blackness," and therefore something "Other." Just before the Martin Luther King, Jr. holiday, the school board decided to name the new high school after the "American" hero and civil rights leader. The school would serve a primarily white, upper-middle-income community. At the school board meeting, a number of parents protested. A Mr. Dale Dunn stated, "Martin Luther King was a great man but naming the school after him would be a mistake. Everybody will think we have a Black school out there" (Terry, 1998). What did Mr. Dunn mean by the term "black" school and what disadvantage did he imagine his children might suffer from such a designation? How had the naming of a school after a national hero become a source of racial fear?

Curriculum

The school's advertised curriculum is another site for the social funding of race. What intellectual information and experiences students have access to, what they are denied access to, and what distortions of information they encounter can serve as powerful funders of our racial ideology. Many scholars have done content analyses of curriculum texts to determine the degree to which various groups and perspectives are represented in the information and materials schoolchildren receive. Textbook examination work offers quantitative analyses of how many instances of various people and groups of color and/or women appear in standard textbooks, particularly in history/social science and language arts/literature texts. Although these methods contribute greatly to scholarship, here I choose to consider the qualitative issues about that representation and how more specific narratives can contribute to the social funding of race, that is, when we put the data in the context of particular life stories we better understand how racial aggressions and microaggressions harm individual citizens as well as the body politic.

King (2004) proposes a typology of knowledge moving from hegemony to autonomy that identifies concepts that she calls invisibilizing knowledge, marginalizing knowledge, expanding knowledge, and deciphering knowledge. Invisibilizing knowledge focuses on a monocultural depiction of the society that uses the term "we" and "our" to signal a notion of common interests, while simultaneously silencing the interests of the socially and culturally excluded. This type of curriculum elevates the achievement of the West over all others and tacitly regards only the contribution of Europeans and European Americans as notable. Morrison (1989) suggests that there are "structured absences" and silences on certain topics that writers use to construct an imagined white self (King, 2004).

Marginalizing knowledge in the curriculum can include "selected 'multicultural' curriculum content that simultaneously distorts the historical and social reality that people actually experienced" (King, p. 361). For example, a textbook may refer to "our common culture" and characterizes each ethnic group's arrival in the United States as an "immigrant experience." Such a textbook would describe the European Americans' experience as immigrants at Ellis Island, Asian Americans' experience as immigrants at Angel Island, Native Americans as "first immigrants" across the land bridge, and African Americans as "forced immigrants" on slave trade ships. In this model, various groups are represented, but the nature of their representation distorts the specificity (and harsh realities) of their real experiences.

Expanding knowledge reflects what James Banks (2004) calls an additive approach to the curriculum. Here curriculum developers create additional canons (e.g., black canons, Latino canons, Native American canons, Asian canons) without disturbing or interrogating the legitimacy of a hegemonic European canon. Thus, students can take a variety of courses and read a variety of literature that add to the size of the curriculum without raising fundamental questions about how such additional studies come to be "in addition to" what represents the official curriculum (Apple, 1993).

Finally, King (2004) addresses what she terms deciphering knowledge that is designed to "expose the belief structure of race in literature, school texts, and other discursive practices" (p. 363). This work pulls on Foucault's (1972) notion of the archaeology of knowledge and is evident in Morrison's (1992) literary criticism that beseeches us to decipher the racial presence and ideology that exist in ostensibly "white" texts. Rather than be consumed with trying to add to the extant canon, this is work that requires us to look at what images, ideas, perspectives, values, and ideologies are made available and instantiated by reading certain texts. According to those who advocate for deciphering knowledge, the problem with *Huckleberry Finn* is not simply Huck's use of the "N-word." Rather the reader needs to struggle with why an adult black male is made serviceable and childlike vis-à-vis an adolescent, indigent white boy. Or, in reading the *Tempest* or *Heart of Darkness*, we have to help students understand the way race (or specifically, blackness) is prefigured as degradation and savagery and grasp the effect this perception has on the depiction of the characters and setting of the novels.

Although this discussion references contemporary understandings of the role of the curriculum, this issue of the role of the curriculum reflects a long-standing debate. Carter G. Woodson (1933) argued that the same curriculum that told white children that they and their ancestors were responsible for building and contributing everything good to civilization tells black children that they and their ancestors have done nothing and contributed nothing to civilization. More pointedly, Woodson (1933) asserts that lynching, as a racist practice, would not have been possible had it not already occurred in the classroom. These strong words speak to the power of the curriculum and the way it can inspire much more than the dissemination of biased information.

Instruction

Curriculum alone cannot explain the way schools participate in the social funding of race. The instruction that students receive also contributes to this project. The degree to which teachers are willing to reinforce or interrupt the racial discourse represents a constant source of social funding of race as a concept. In an earlier work (Ladson-Billings, 2003), I argued that although more children's and young adult literature authors had been more deliberate and persistent in taking up racial themes in their books, few teachers were willing to engage the full range of questions and issues such books present. Books that use historical events (e.g., slavery, school desegregation, the civil rights movement) are presented as long-ago, far-away problems that the society has solved, while books that take up social issues (e.g. racism, prejudice, discrimination) are taught as examples of individual character flaws. Rarely do teachers engage students in questions about their current-day experiences with race and racism. Thus, it is possible for a teacher to be teaching a text that deals with the resistance to school desegregation and keep the discussion solely contained within the text while children are sitting in classrooms (and schools) that are segregated.

Instruction is also implicated in the social funding of race by the way teachers arrange their classrooms and the way schools group students. Ability groups very often map onto students' race (and class)[6] positions, with the "high-ability" group filled with high-status (i.e., white and or upper income) students and the "low-ability" groups filled with low-status students. At the secondary level, this racial differentiation is made starker by the creation of tracks and/or special programs for students. Some schools brag about their student diversity, but inside the programs and classrooms there exists a resegregation. Honors programs and Advanced Placement Programs are almost exclusively white and upper middle class while basic courses (see data from Quinton, 2014), remedial courses, and courses that fail to lead to admission into colleges or universities are filled with black and brown faces. In addition to the actual segregation of the students, the data suggest that students in the low-status programs are more likely to be taught by teachers who have less experience and are less well qualified (Darling-Hammond, 2000). This particular social arrangement serves to reinforce notions of racial inferiority without ever having to overtly express such thoughts. Students quickly learn that to be taught by certain teachers, in certain courses, in certain schools, confers either an elite or a deprived status, and that status very conveniently coincides with race.

Discipline and Classroom Management

Schools have to be places where children and adults are safe. They have to be places where there is some form of order and regularity. They do not have to be places of punishment. Unfortunately, that is exactly what they represent for some children. In a visit to a working-class elementary school that had gained a reputation for having unruly students, the principal took me to see the "Restitution Room." This innovation was her answer to misbehavior. She seemed quite proud and asked me what I thought. I was horrified to see a room, devoid of any decorations, books, or other learning material, filled with rows of desks and little black boys (the school is about 50% black) ages 6 to 11 seated silently with their hands folded. An adult paraprofessional was in the room to ensure they did not speak or get up from their desks. "Well," I replied, "I guess this is just great if what you are preparing the students for is prison!"

Public records of suspensions and expulsions indicate that black and brown students are much more likely to experience such sanctions. Although some might argue that standards of behavior should apply to all students, we see that the meaning attributed to behaviors and the implementation of discipline standards vary greatly depending on students' race and class positions. African American male students, according to Majors and Billson (1993), are more likely to be suspended for "non-contact" violations (e.g., wearing a hat in the building, donning banned attire, being in the "wrong" place) than any other group of students.

While observing a student teacher I noted that she had reprimanded an Asian American child nine times for leaving his seat. "Sit down, Stanley." "Go back to your seat, Stanley." "I'm warning you, Stanley." After a while, a little black boy got up from his seat and the student teacher angrily responded, "Larry, you're out of here!" and dispatched him to the principal's office. During our post-observation conference, I showed her my log with the times and instances of Stanley's infractions and Larry's one misbehavior and her reaction to it. This young woman was one of my better student teachers. She expressed commitments to social justice and equity in her university coursework and desired to teach in a multiracial, multilingual school. When she saw my observation log, she was shocked by her own behavior.

Race was so fully funded for her that she had come to see the black child as the problem even when his behavior was no different from the Asian student. Of course, she may have been nervous to have her supervisor watching her every move. She may also have just had it with little boys leaving their seats uninvited. She alone is not to blame—the culture that engendered this behavior in her is as well.

In a more extreme example, I was in a high school (not as a professor but as a parent), and a white male student was in a heated altercation with a white male teacher. At one point in the argument, the student called the teacher a "sorry M—F—!" At that point all of the people within earshot (which included a black janitor, another white student, and me) sucked in their collective breaths. The teacher then said to the student, "Why are you talking to me like that? You're not black!" Both the janitor and I were rendered speechless. There was no talk of detention, suspension, or expulsion. Blackness had just become equivalent to rudeness, disrespect, obscenity, and license. And what meaning did the white students, both the offender and the bystander, take from this outburst and subsequent reaction—that black people alone are capable of bad behavior? This scenario serves as another example of the social funding of race.

Assessment

In the current climate of accountability it is important not to overlook the way testing and assessment have been instrumental in the social funding of race. At its crudest level, intelligence testing and the interpretation of such tests have long been a mechanism for the social funding of race. Authors Herrnstein and Murray (1999) created quite a stir in the late 1990s when they revived the genetic difference theories of the 18th century by citing group IQ test scores as if there was not debate about the validity of such measures. Interestingly, the debate about their volume quickly devolved into a discussion about race. Most of the data in their book is about class, which is a part of the volume's subtitle. But race is the flashpoint term. In a society committed to the quantification and ranking of almost everything, the ability to affix numbers to individuals and aggregate those numbers to particular groups is an interesting and curious phenomenon.

In addition, as much as most people decry Herrnstein and Murray's (1999) interpretations, we continue to use a variety of measures to quantify student learning and to determine who is most worthy for a variety of society's benefits. The current testing frenzy occurring in most urban (and rural) classrooms has almost stripped such classrooms of anything approaching real teaching and learning (McNeil, 2000; Rothstein, 2004). Testing has become a proxy for student learning without any consideration for the differential challenges with which many students live. Because testing serves as the proxy for student achievement, much of the discourse about the "achievement gap" fails to address the ecological racism that characterizes the society. However, some advocacy groups take on racism directly. ERASE (Expose Racism & Advance School Excellence) is an initiative of the Applied Research Center (ARC) that published a report on the relationship between testing and race. According to Gordon and Piana (1999):

> Almost all standardized tests, including IQ tests and the SATs, have what is called a statistical "outcome bias" against African American and other people of color. That is, African Americans consistently score measurably lower on these tests than do white test-takers. (The fact that a test has an outcome bias does not mean that the people who designed the test were consciously, or even unconsciously, biased. It simply means that there is more than an accidental difference among the scores of different groups of test-takers.)

Even if we could devise a fair test, we have to acknowledge the conditions under which students who are victimized by the social funding of race come to the test. Steele (1999) has done work suggesting that if we can manipulate the setting to minimize the import of race, African American students do as well as their white peers. In an experiment he conducted in 1999, Steele studied the performance of Stanford University sophomore students on a graduate admissions test, using a control and intervention group to measure the differences in performance when students enter the test with different expectations. When the control group took the test, the students in this group were told that the test was one that measures intellectual ability. In the control group, the African American subjects performed much poorer than their white counterparts. When the intervention group took the test, they were told that the test is not a measure of intellect. There is no measurable difference in the performance of African American and white students in this group. Steele refers to the phenomenon of "stereotype threat" as "the threat of being viewed through the lens of a negative stereotype, or the fear of doing something that would inadvertently confirm that stereotype" (Steele, 1999, p. 45). Steele (2003) asserts that all are susceptible to stereotype threat regarding stereotypes that are associated with groups with which individuals affiliate (e.g., women drivers, midwestern naïveté, Arab terrorists). However, individuals of marginalized races likely face a greater stereotype threat because of the way society funds race. When society funds race, the damage it does compounds since there are an exponentially greater number of instances where that stereotype threat can be activated, particularly when so many things have come to stand for race (e.g., crime, poverty, school failure).

So, how do we prepare teachers in a context that is suffused with race and racism?

WHAT'S A TEACHER EDUCATOR TO DO?

I make the assumption that most teacher educators want to do good work—not only in their classrooms, but also in the society. They want to prepare teachers who are competent as pedagogues, subject matter experts, and engaged citizens in a democratic society. One of our challenges is structural. The typical teacher education program has access to prospective teachers for two years or less. Most teacher educators have access to prospective students for one or two semesters in specific courses, field experiences, and/or seminars. In addition, only one or two teacher educators in a program take on issues of race and racism directly, despite the great impact it has on schooling and its presence in society. Teacher educators have written in a compelling fashion about the difficulty of helping prospective teachers confront race and racism in themselves and in their teaching practices (Anderson, 2017; Cochran-Smith, 2000; Irvine, 2001; Kailin, 1999; King, 1991; Obidah, 2000). Their stories are telling both because of how prospective (and in-service) teachers respond and how their institutions fail to support their work. The teacher educators who want to do this work represent some of the members of the academy most committed to dismantling racism. However, if we think about the work race and racism does for the society, we may begin to see why this is such a difficult task.

Tim Wise, a well-known antiracist who writes for *Z-Magazine* and *Alter-Net*, discusses the power of this race-driven ideology (1999). Wise's elderly grandmother spent most of her life fighting against racism and injustice. She was so passionate about her commitments that she challenged her own father—a southerner and member of the Ku Klux Klan—to choose between her and the Klan. All of Wise's grandmother's civic work was aimed at eradicating racism and probably had a major impact on the kind of person Tim would become. However, as her mind began to deteriorate and the family placed her in convalescent care, Wise was shocked to experience the depths of what he calls the "racist socialization" that his grandmother (and everyone) receives. His grandmother could no longer remember the names of her children and her grandchildren. She could not do the simple everyday tasks of feeding herself and carrying on a coherent conversation. However, there was one thing that remained present for her. She looked upon her convalescent home attendants, almost all of whom were African American, and regularly called to them using the society's most despised pejorative—"Nigger."

Wise points out that our thoughts and feelings about race are deeply embedded in our psyches, and that appeals to reason regarding racism are unlikely to undo the tremendous amount of work the culture has done to establish and maintain race and racism as foundational categories for understanding ourselves and others. What he calls racial socialization I think of as funding. As previously argued, I see funding as a more global construct that speaks to the direct and indirect benefits that accrue (or fail to accrue) to members of the society. If a society decides to fund its military and not fund social welfare, that funding decision has implications for everyone in the society. It is not as if people who disagree with that funding priority are somehow not affected by this decision.

I am cognizant that throughout much of this essay I have focused on the symbolic, social, and psychological components of race. This focus is deliberate in that I am attempting to show that even when structural barriers are removed, the social funding of race maintains the belief systems and actions of members of the society. However, it is important not to minimize the structural components. Indeed, one of the ways we fund race is through structures. The quality of schools, neighborhoods, and goods and services, as well as the response of institutions, differ greatly along racial lines. In many ways the question of structural versus symbolic is a chicken-and-egg one. Did preexisting structures create symbolic language and beliefs about race, or did symbolic language and beliefs precipitate structures that maintained racial inequality? In perhaps a coward's way out, I argue that the two—the structural and the symbolic—are intertwined. In the United States, the society was both building a nation (that included economic, political, social, and cultural components) and building an ideology. Race was an important part of both projects and came to have salience in both arenas.

To speak of schooling is to speak of both structures and symbols. We consider not only bricks and mortar, or even organizational structures; we also consider the language and symbols that make school a recognizable construct across cities and municipalities, states and national boundaries, and generations. To "go to school" is not merely about going to a place. It is also about imagining a place. Similarly, we have a set of structural and symbolic notions that undergird our conception of the teacher. Although teaching as an occupation has changed over the history of the United States—going from a more male-dominated to a female-dominated profession and from a somewhat prestigious career to one whose status is regularly called into question—it too has both structural and symbolic components. Structurally, we understand teaching to be a profession that requires a particular set of skills and knowledge. Minimally, teachers must complete a four-year college education. However, increasingly, beginning teachers are expected to do work beyond their undergraduate degree. Much of this work takes place in professional schools and colleges of education. Although we decry the poor quality of teachers in the United States, these structural parameters do limit who can enter the profession.

But our understanding of teachers does not begin (or end) with the structural components. Regularly, I ask my students the question, "Who is the teacher in the popular imagination?" We explore this question by viewing a variety of commercial film depictions of teachers. Because most of my graduate students have already worked as teachers, they are keenly aware of the sharp contrast between the actual work of teaching and the Hollywood screen depictions of teaching. These screen depictions contribute to our symbolic notions of teachers and their work. In some cases they serve as a recruitment tool for those who might enter the profession (and perhaps as a deterrent for others).

The typical teacher education program requires students to complete about 40 semester credits of liberal studies requirements, another 30 of upper-level concentration in a disciplinary major, another 20 upper-level concentration in a disciplinary minor, and at least 30 semester credits in professional education coursework. The professional education coursework sequence most likely includes courses in educational foundations (i.e. sociology, philosophy, history), child or adolescent development, and methods of teaching, as well as field experiences. If we look carefully at this organizational structure of teacher preparation, we can see that our task is like the work of Tantalus. When students enter the teacher preparation program, there is hope that their efforts might provide relief to schools and students challenged by racial biases. Unfortunately, teacher education that attempts to defund race cannot satiate these schools yearning for change. Prospective teachers come to us with notions about race so well-funded that it seems we merely get closer to, but can never quite reach, the waters of educational equity.

Ultimately, we must reach prospective teachers earlier in their educations. Our access to and influence on prospective teachers needs to begin much earlier than their junior year of college (or after their senior year as is true in many postbaccalaureate programs). We have to have ways to engage them through the general liberal arts courses and concentrated majors and minors that they pursue on their way to professional education coursework. The educational foundations, developmental psychology, teaching methods, and field experiences courses have to serve as correctives to the structural and symbolic systems that have worked so efficiently and effectively to suture notions of race to common sense in our society. Instead of only presenting students with data about racial differences (that often invokes guilt and anger but little action), we need ways to interrogate the work that race does in the society. Even among our most well-meaning prospective teachers we find a degree of helplessness and hopelessness around the notion of race. Our students have come to accept race as a given and racial inequity as a project too big for them to challenge. They almost never consider the spurious nature of the concept and how it has been used to shape their consciousness about human beings.

Of course, the major danger of this work is that teachers and teacher educators will default to the notion of "color blindness." This is a romantic notion taken up by social conservatives in an effort to increase the likelihood that disenfranchised people of color will suffer further social marginalization and alienation from the society. The movement in California under Proposition 209 is a primary example of this thinking. By declaring that admissions to state universities and colleges should be "race neutral," the state virtually guaranteed that large numbers of black and brown students would be excluded from these institutions. This is an important example of how it is impossible to disentangle the symbolic from the structural. Color-blind rhetoric can only work in color-blind structures, which we do not have in U.S. society (see Bowen & Bok, 1998). Where a society has worked hard to create structures that uphold racial inequity it is difficult, indeed disingenuous, to leverage a language and symbols that destroy and/or counteract it. Thus, color-blind rhetoric is actually a new tool in the social funding of race. By pretending that the structural and symbolic instruments are not in place (or that they are inconsequential), color-blind rhetoric can claim the high moral ground while instantiating the status quo and rolling back any progressive movement toward racial justice.

The other difficult aspect of this work for teacher educators is that they have to try to defund the concept of race while simultaneously using it. When poet-activist Lourde (1983) insisted that you cannot destroy the master's house with the master's tools, Henry Louis Gates, Jr. (2012, p. 15) rejoined that the *only* way to destroy the master's house is with the master's tools. Although my political and ideological perspectives align more closely with Lourde's than with Gates's, I must confess that in this particular instance I am forced to agree with Gates. I must use the concept of race to bankrupt it as a concept. How do we get teachers to bankrupt race as a concept without having them talk about and engage it more fully? We can't. What are missing from most teacher education programs are deep intellectual interrogations of race and the work of race in the society. We must provide prospective students with data that either reinscribes students' long-standing notions of race or evokes emotional responses that trouble the students (and change their ways) without employing race in their teaching practice.

At least a decade ago in a course on social foundations, a colleague and I gave students some data on the differences in life chances between African American and white children (Edelman, 1987). These data were stark and, in some cases, shocking in the degree to which so many black children have little or no chance of leading successful lives. My colleague and I asked the students to describe how this was possible in the United States of America. We used what we understood as the students' devotion to the nation as a place of fairness and justice to provoke them to make sense of the contradiction of black life in the society. More than half of the responses indicated that the reason for these disparities was the institution of slavery.[7] Another portion of the responses indicated that blacks had not received an "equal opportunity" to succeed in the society. Only one student in three cohorts of prospective teachers (over a three-year period) identified the structure of U.S. society as the cause of racial inequality. Of course, more than 10 years ago, none of our students would identify race as a construct as a part of the problem. Even more disturbing for us as teacher educators were the students' expressions that "this was just the way things are" and that "this was the only way things could be." They could not imagine any other alternatives to the current racial hierarchy.

I detail this experience with our students—all white, generally all socio-economically privileged—to demonstrate how we must begin to question their thinking about race early in their preparation. We assume that what they know and understand about race is consistent with what we are teaching about race. In other classroom activities, I have asked students to write a racial autobiography in which they describe the first time they noticed race in their lives and what role race has played in who they are. These essays tend to evoke strong emotions and sometimes anger. One student responded when asked to think about her white racial identity, "Why do I have to be white? Why can't we just be Americans?" I replied, "What's wrong with being white? Is there any shame in that designation?" Another student rushed to her defense by stating, "No, white people have lots to be proud of. They discovered America and made it great. White people can be proud that they are the only ones to be presidents of the United States and if it weren't for white people the slaves wouldn't be free!"[8] In just these few sentences, one can see how difficult the work of defunding the concept will be. Not talking about race would not dispel the first student's notion that a color-blind approach would solve our racial difficulties or the second student's obvious ignorance about the structural and symbolic inequities that place us in our current dilemma. We have to talk about race in order to redefine it.

Perhaps the only way out of race as a sense-making concept is through the use of metaphors. Our work must resemble the work of liberation fighters. Liberation fighters use the currency of their oppressors because that is the only money worth anything. They use the language of their oppressors because that is the only way they can be made understandable. They use the available weapons of the oppressors because they work. The differences lie in the purpose to which they put that currency, those words, and those weapons. Teacher educators have to talk about race not to re-inscribe it and give it even more power, but rather to take control of it and expose it for the lie it is. We have to find ways to render it useless.

Although this work sounds impossible and impractical, it is exactly the kind of work African Americans have been participating in since their arrival in the Americas. Theirs has been a project not only of survival, but also of subversion and revolutionary freedom. The work of African American survival necessitates the creation of new language and forms of human expression. Increasingly, it is black cultural forms that energize and attract majority-culture white students but the dominant culture works hard to snuff out or appropriate and stereotype such forms. Our best examples of democracy may not come in the form of distant patriots of the 18th century. They come in the yearnings of people such as Fannie Lou Hamer and Martin Luther King, Jr. They may come in the long-suffering of Nelson Mandela and the compassion of Desmond Tutu. They may come in the poignant vocals of Marvin Gaye who asks, "What's going on?" and in the insistence of Grand Master Flash and KRS-1 who know we really do have a "fear of a Black Planet."

Finally, teacher educators must work to defund race, however impossible the task. Bell (1991) argues that we must fight against racism despite its permanence in U.S. society and culture. Fighting for justice is never just about winning. It is about the hope of winning, but more important, it is about fighting for the right cause regardless of the odds. Our responsibility to democracy and democratic education extends much further than the current occupants of the White House and the state houses. It extends much further than offering the current students we hope to shape into democratic educators who will live and work in a multicultural society. It extends into spaces and places we can only imagine, but extend it must. We are obligated to retrieve a vision of democracy that, although never intended to extend to non-whites, women, or poor people, belongs to them just the same. This vision can never be realized as long as its foremost enemy—the construct of race—serves the current shape of democracy so well.

NOTES

1. This name is also a pseudonym.
2. This is a retelling of this story from a previous article (Ladson-Billings, 1992).
3. Although Mario thinks of himself as "Italian," he will learn that Italians were included in the category of whiteness sometime in the 20th century (Roediger, 2006).
4. This name is also a pseudonym.
5. Later Rehnquist would assert that the memo did not reflect his views, but rather the early views of Justice Jackson (Davis, 1984).
6. Although the focus of this essay is on race, I am cognizant of the way race and class co-vary and the tremendous overlap between the two subject positions.
7. What I find curious about "slavery" as the most cited reason is that discussions of reparations fall on deaf ears. People believe slavery is the cause of the inequity but do not believe attempts to remediate it are warranted.
8. This was obviously prior to the election of Barack Obama.

REFERENCES

Alim, H. S., & Smitherman, G. (2012). *Articulate while Black: Barack Obama, language and race in the US.* New York, NY: Oxford University Press.
Anderson, J. D. (2002, February 28). *Historical perspectives on Black academic achievement.* Paper presented at the Visiting Minority Scholars Series, Wisconsin Center for Educational Research, Madison, WI.

Anderson, M. D. (2017, January 9). How teachers learn to discuss racism. *The Atlantic*. Retrieved from https://www.theatlantic.com/education/archive/2017/01/how-teachers-learn-to-discuss-racism/512474/

Apple, M. W. (1993). *Official knowledge: Democratic education in a conservative age*. New York, NY: Routledge.

Banks, C. M. (2004). Intercultural and intergroup education, 1929–1959. In J. A. Banks & C. M. Banks (Eds.), *Handbook of research in multicultural education* (2nd ed., pp. 753–769). San Francisco, CA: Jossey Bass.

Banks, J. A. (2004). Multicultural education: History, characteristics, and goals. In J. A. Banks & C. M. Banks (Eds.), *Handbook of research in multicultural education* (2nd ed., pp. 3–29). San Francisco, CA: Jossey Bass.

Bass, J., & Thompson, M. W. (2003). *Ol' Strom: An unauthorized biography of Strom Thurmond*. New York, NY: Longstreet Press.

Bell, D. (1991). *Faces at the bottom of the well: The permanence of racism*. New York, NY: Basic Books.

Bourdieu, P., & Passeron, J. (1977). *Reproduction in education, society, and culture*. London, England: Sage.

Bowen, W. G., & Bok, D. (1998). *The shape of the river: Long-term consequences of considering race in college and university admissions*. Princeton, NJ: Princeton University Press.

Brandt, D. (1998). Sponsors of literacy. *College Composition and Communication*, 49(2), 165–185. doi:10.2307/358929.

Brown v. Topeka Board of Education, 347 U.S. 483 (1954).

Cochran-Smith, M. (2000). Blind vision: Unlearning racism in teacher education. *Harvard Educational Review*, 70(2), 157–190. doi:10.17763/haer.70.2.e77x215054558564.

Cross, W. E. (1978). The Thomas and Cross models of psychological Nigrescence: A review. *Journal of Black Psychology*, 5, 12–31. doi:10.1177/009579847800500102

Darling-Hammond, L. (2000). Teacher quality and student achievement. *Education Policy Analysis Archives*, 8(1). Retrieved from http://epaa.asu.edu/epaa/v8n1/

Davis, S. (1984). Justice Rehnquist's equal protection clause: An interim analysis. *University of Nebraska Law Review*, 63(2), 288, 308.

Dudziak, M. L. (1995). Desegregation as a Cold War imperative. In R. Delgado (Ed.), *Critical race theory: The cutting edge* (pp. 110–121). Philadelphia, PA: Temple University Press. (Original work published 1988)

Edelman, M. W. (1987). *Families in peril: An agenda for social change*. Cambridge, MA: Harvard University Press.

Fisher, P. (2004, March 3). *Aesthetic attention*. Lecture presented at the Center for Advanced Study in the Behavioral Sciences, Stanford, CA.

Fitzpatrick, C., Gartner, L., & LaForgia, M. (2015, August 14). Failure factories. *Tampa Bay Times*, p. A1, A3.

Foucault, M. (1972). *The archaeology of knowledge* (A. M. Sheridan-Smith, trans.). London, England: Tavistock.

Gates, H. L., Jr. (2012). *The Henry Louis Gates, Jr. Reader*. New York, NY: Basic Civitas Books.

Gordon, R., & Piana, L. D. (1999). *No exit? Testing, tracking and students of color in U.S. public schools*. Retrieved from http://www.arc.org/Pages/Estudy.html

Guinier, L., & Torres, G. (2002). *The miner's canary: Enlisting race, resisting power, transforming democracy.* Cambridge, MA: Harvard University Press.

Hannaford, I. (1996). *Race. The history of an idea in the West.* Washington, DC: Woodrow Wilson Center Press.

Helms, J. E. (1990). *Black and white racial identity: Theory, research and practice.* New York, NY: Greenwood Press.

Herrnstein, R., & Murray, C. (1999). *The bell curve: Intelligence and class structure in America.* New York, NY: Free Press.

Irvine, J. J. (2001). *Caring, competent teachers in complex classrooms.* Paper presented at the Charles W. Hunt Memorial Lecture for the American Association of Colleges for Teacher Education, Dallas, TX.

Johnson, D. J. (1992). Developmental pathways: Toward an ecological theoretical formulation of race identity in Black–White children. In M. P. P. Root (Ed.), *Racially mixed people in America* (pp. 37–49). Thousand Oaks, CA: Sage.

Kailin, J. (1999). How white teachers perceive the problem of racism in their schools: A case study in "liberal" Lakeview. *Teachers College Record, 100,* 724–750. doi:10.1111/0161-4681.00014.

King, J. E. (1991). Dysconscious racism: Ideology, identity, and the miseducation of teachers. *Journal of Negro Education, 60,* 133–146. doi:10.2307/2295605.

King, J. E. (2004). Culture-centered knowledge: Black studies, curriculum transformation, and social action. In J. A. Banks & C. M. Banks (Eds.). *Handbook of research in multicultural education* (pp. 349–378). San Francisco, CA: Jossey Bass.

Ladson-Billings, G. (1992, November). I don't see color, I just see children: Dealing with stereotyping and prejudice in young children. *Social Studies and the Young Learner, 5,* 9–12.

Ladson-Billings, G. (2003, February). *Still playing in the dark: Whiteness in the literary imagination of children's and young adult literature.* Paper presented at the NCTEAR Mid-Winter Conference, Minneapolis, MN.

Lopez, I. H. (1995). The social construction of race. In R. Delgado (Ed.), *Critical race theory: The cutting edge* (pp. 191–203). Philadelphia, PA: Temple University Press.

Lourde, A. (1983). The master's tools will never dismantle the master's house. In C. Moraga & G. Anzaldúa (Eds.) *This bridge called my back: Writings by radical women of color* (pp. 94–101). New York, NY: Kitchen Table Press.

Majors, R., & Billson, J. (1993). *Cool pose: The dilemma of Black manhood in America.* New York, NY: Touchstone Books.

McNeil, L. M. (2000). *Contradictions of school reform.* New York, NY: Routledge.

Meyer, J. (1977). Institutionalized organizations: Formal structures as myth and ceremony. *American Journal of Sociology, 83*(2), 340–363. doi:10.1086/226550.

Miller, R. L. (1992). The human ecology of multiracial identity. In M. P. P. Root (Ed.), *Racially mixed people in America* (pp. 24–36). Thousand Oaks, CA: Sage.

Mish, F. C. (2014). *Merriam Webster's Collegiate Dictionary,* 11th edition. Springfield, MA: Merriam Webster, Inc.

Morrison, T. (1989). Unspeakable things unspoken: The Afro-American presence in American literature. *Michigan Quarterly Review, 28*(1), 1–34.

Morrison, T. (1992). *Playing in the dark: Whiteness and the literary imagination.* Cambridge, MA: Harvard University Press.

Obidah, J. (2000). Mediating boundaries of race, class, and professional authority as a critical multiculturalist. *Teachers College Record, 102*(6), 1035–1060. doi:10.1111/0161-4681.00091.

Omi, M., & Winant, H. (2014). *Racial formation in the United States: From the 1960s to the 1990s* (3rd ed.). New York, NY: Routledge.

Orfield, G., & Eaton, S. (1996). *Dismantling desegregation: The quiet reversal of Brown v. Board of Education.* New York, NY: The New Press.

Parham, T. A. (1989). Cycles of psychological Nigrescence. *Counseling Psychologist, 17*(2), 187–226. doi:10.1177/0011000089172001.

Quinton, S. (2014, December 11). The race gap in high school honors classes. *The Atlantic.* Retrieved from https://www.theatlantic.com/politics/archive/2014/12/the-race-gap-in-high-school-honors-classes/431751/

Ramirez, M., III. (1998). *Multicultural/multiracial psychology: Mestizo perspectives on personality and mental health.* Elmsford, NY: Pergamon Press.

Roediger, D. J. (1991). *The wages of whiteness.* New York, NY: Verso.

Roediger, D. J. (2006). *Working toward whiteness: How America's immigrants became white.* New York, NY: Basic Books.

Rothstein, R. (2004, February 1). Testing our patience. *The American Prospect.* http://www.prospect.org/web/page.ww?sectionroot&nameViewPrint&articleId7000

Senate Hearing on the Judiciary (1986). *Hearings on the nomination of Justice William Hobbs Rehnquist,* 99th Congress, 2nd Session, 325.

Snowden, F. M. (1983). *Before color prejudice: The ancient views of Blacks.* Cambridge, MA: Harvard University Press.

Steele, C. (1999, August). Thin ice: "Stereotype threat" and Black college students. *The Atlantic Monthly, 284*(2), 44–47, 50–54.

Steele, C. (2003). A threat in the air: How stereotypes shape intellectual identity and performance. In J. A. Banks & C. M. Banks (Eds.), *Handbook of research in multicultural education* (pp. 682–698). San Francisco, CA: Jossey Bass.

Terry, D. (1998, January 7). Mostly White city honors Dr. King, amid dissent. *New York Times,* p. A12.

Trimble, J. E. (2000). Social psychological perspectives on changing self-identification among American Indians and Alaska Natives. In R. H. Dana (Ed.), *Handbook of cross-cultural/multicultural personality assessment* (pp. 197–222). Mahwah, NJ: Erlbaum.

Wijeyesinghe, C. L. (2001). Racial identity in multiracial people: An alternative paradigm. In C. L. Wijeyesinghe & B. W. Jackson, III (Eds.), *New perspectives on racial identity and development: A theoretical and practical anthology* (pp. 153–181). New York: New York University Press.

Winant, H. (2000). Race and race theory. *Annual Review of Sociology, 26,* 169–185. doi:10.1146/annurev.soc.26.1.169.

Wise, T. (1999). Exploring the depths of racist socialization. Retrieved from http://www.Zmag.org/zmag/articles/july99wise.htm

Woodson, C. G. (1933). *The mis-education of the Negro.* Washington, DC: Association Press.

Wynter, S. (1990). *Do not call us "negros": How "multicultural" textbooks perpetuate racism.* San Francisco, CA: Aspire Books.

Index

The letter *t* or *n* after a page number refers to a table or a note, respectively.

Murray, C., 191, 223
Muting, 111
Myrdal, G., 43

"Naming one's reality." *See* Voice
Narayan, K., 166
National Academy of Education, 1
National Assessment of Education
  Progress, 60, 86–87
National Center for Education Statistics,
  61
National Council for Accreditation of
  Teacher Education, 117
National Council of Education Standards
  and Testing, 24n46
National debt and deficit definitions,
  62–63, 74
National Governors' Association, 60
National interests, 128–129
National Public Radio Staff, 1
National Voting Rights Act of 1965, 68
Native languages, 116
Nazi ideology, 129
Nettles, M., 175
New Orleans and post-Katrina rebuilding,
  51
"New racism," 184
"New studies," 115, 168
New York City public schools, 67
Niemi, R. G., 68–69
Nixon, R. M., 132, 218
"Non-market effects of schooling," 64
Normal term, 192
Norms, 156
Notes on the State of Virginia (Jefferson),
  156
Nussbaum, M., 105

Oakes, J., 21n22, 21n23, 30n82
Obama, B., 8–9, 45, 186, 194–195,
  195n3, 200
Obeler, S., 158
Ogbu, J., 28n72
Okin, S., 105
Olivas, M., 110
Olneck, M., 31n93, 106
Omi, M., 8, 18n6, 19n13, 20n14, 155,
  190, 210
Ong, A., 188
Oppenheimer, D. B., 196
Orfield, G., 25n50, 74, 132, 134, 137,
  218

Othering, 160–161, 211. *See also* Double
  consciousness; Liminal perspective
Outlaw, L., 176–177
Owens, J., 129

Palumbo-Liu, D., 105
Pandian, J., 160
Pan-Indianism, 159
Parham, T. A., 212
Parker, L., 41, 111, 198
Particularism versus universalism, 26–27,
  26n58, 110
Passeron, J., 214
"Patriotic education," 1
Patterson, J. T., 139
"Pedagogy of poverty," 112
Peller, G., 164, 196, 197
Perna, L., 175
Phillips, M., 191
Piana, L. D., 224
Pilgrim metaphor, 143
Plessy, H., 127
Plessy v. Ferguson, 67, 74–75, 127, 128
Podair, J., 70
Police violence, 1–2, 202
Political race, 188, 211
Popkewitz, T., 5
Postcolonial theory, 115
Postmoderism, 115–116
Postracial perspective, 183, 186, 187
Postsecondary education, 65, 87–88
Postwar period, 128–129
Powell, J., 141
Prendergast, C., 130
Private schooling, 134–135
"Project" of race, 10
Property rights, 7, 22–23, 28–30, 31, 164
Proposition 209 (CA), 228
Protests of police violence, 1–2
Psychological Bulletin, 190–191
Psychology field, 190–191
Public policy field, 198–199
Public versus private race funding, 215

Qualitative research, 174–175
Quality control, 8
Quality of education, 70, 136–137, 142
Quinton, S., 221

Race. *See also* Race funding; Social (race)
  funding
  assumptions about, 220

About the Author

Gloria Ladson-Billings is professor emerita at the University of Wisconsin–Madison and president of the National Academy of Education (2018–2021). Her books include _Culturally Relevant Pedagogy: Asking a Different Question_ and _Teacher Educators as Critical Storytellers: Effective Teachers as Windows and Mirrors._